The Burgee

Premier Marina Guidebook

By David Kutz

Second Edition

Pierside Publishing
23911 Newell Ln. N.E.
Kingston, WA 98346
(360) 297-2935

The Burgee

Premier Marina Guidebook

By David Kutz

Published by:

Pierside Publishing
23911 Newell Ln. N.E.
Kingston, WA 98346 USA
Telephone: (360) 297-2935
Fax: (360) 297-3505

SEE PAGE 150 FOR ORDERING INFORMATION

First Edition First Printing 1994
Second Edition First Printing 1996

Printed in the United States of America

Cover and illustrations by David Kutz

Editing assistance by Janice Kutz, and numerous marina facility personnel.

Library of Congress Cataloging of Publication Data
Kutz, David J.
The Burgee: Premier Marina Guidebook / by David Kutz.— 2nd Edition
Includes index.
CIP 95-092841
ISBN 0-9641934-1-8: **US $22.95 Softcover**

HOW TO USE THIS GUIDEBOOK

"The Burgee Book" lists marinas and marine parks that provide overnight moorage available to the general boating public. To have a listing, the facility must have actual docking facilities.

•**Yacht Club Reciprocals.** 'The Burgee Book" also offers Yacht Club Reciprocal Moorage information offered by many clubs in the Northwest and Vancouver Island. *If you utilize yacht club reciprocal moorage, you must hold a current membership with the reciprocating club.* Your yacht club should have a list of clubs you are reciprocal with.

•**Map and Locations.** Marinas are listed by town or city alphabetically in each regional chapter as depicted in the area map on Page 4.

•**Accuracy.** The information listed in this book is intended to be as accurate as possible, but please remember things change frequently, especially rates and available services.

•**Chartlets.** The chartlets depicting the marina facilities are not to scale and only intended to be a general guide to give you an idea where the guest facilities are located.

•**Lat./Lons.** The latitudes and longitudes are not exact and only intended to be used as a general guide.

•**Compasses.** The compasses shown in the chartlets are in the general direction of **Magnetic North.** They are not exact and only intended to be used for general direction.

DISCLAIMER

"The Burgee Book" is designed to provide only general information for the marine facilities listed. It is sold with the understanding that the publisher and author are not engaged in rendering legal navigational or informational services. The chartlets (illustrations) contained in this book are not to scale and not intended for use in navigation. Selected laws require all ships to have on board, maintain, and use appropriate navigational charts. Our chartlets (illustrations) of the marina facilities do not meet that requirement. Every effort has been made to make this guidebook as accurate as possible but the book contains current information only up to the printing date. There may be mistakes both typographical and in content. Therefore, this text should be used only as a general guide and not as the ultimate source of acquiring details about marina facilities. The author and Pierside Publishing shall have neither liability nor responsibility to any person or entity with respect to any loss or damage caused, or alleged to be caused, directly or indirectly by the information contained in this book.

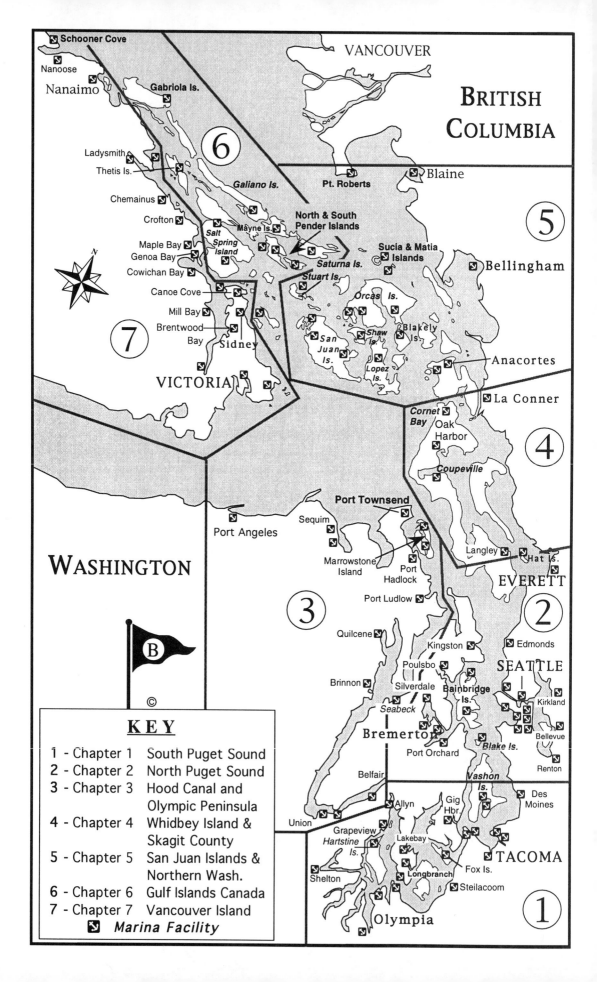

VANCOUVER

BRITISH COLUMBIA

Schooner Cove

Nanoose

Nanaimo

Gabriola Is.

⑥

⑤

Blaine

Ladysmith

Thetis Is.

Galiano Is.

Pt. Roberts

Chemainus

Bellingham

Crofton

North & South
Pender Islands

Maple Bay

Salt
Spring
Island

Mayne Is.

Sucia & Matia
Islands

Genoa Bay

Saturna Is.

Cowichan Bay

Stuart Is.

Canoe Cove

Orcas Is.

Anacortes

N

Mill Bay

Shaw
Is.

Blakely
Is.

Brentwood
Bay

⑦

San
Juan
Is.

La Conner

Sidney

Lopez
Is.

Cornet
Bay

VICTORIA

Oak
Harbor

④

Coupeville

Port Townsend

WASHINGTON

Sequim

Port Angeles

Marrowstone
Island

Langley

Hat Is.

Port
Hadlock

EVERETT

Port Ludlow

②

③

Quilcene

Kingston

Edmonds

Poulsbo

SEATTLE

B

Brinnon

Silverdale

Bainbridge
Is.

Kirkland

Seabeck

Bellevue

KEY

Bremerton

Blake Is.

Port Orchard

Renton

1 - Chapter 1   South Puget Sound

Belfair

Vashon
Is.

Des
Moines

2 - Chapter 2   North Puget Sound

Allyn

Gig
Hbr.

3 - Chapter 3   Hood Canal and
                Olympic Peninsula

Union

Grapeview

Lakebay

4 - Chapter 4   Whidbey Island &
                Skagit County

Hartstine
Is.

Fox Is.

TACOMA

5 - Chapter 5   San Juan Islands &
                Northern Wash.

Longbranch

Steilacoom

6 - Chapter 6   Gulf Islands Canada

Shelton

7 - Chapter 7   Vancouver Island

①

⬛ *Marina Facility*

Olympia

Table of Contents

A WORD FROM THE AUTHOR

For those new to the world of boating, a *Burgee* is a small pennant representing the logo of a Yacht and/or Boating Club. It is generally triangular in shape, sometimes with a swallow tail. A Burgee is flown from the bow staff of power vessels or from the mast of a sailing vessel. Since one of the unique features of this book is yacht club reciprocal facilities, the title *"Burgee"* was chosen.

The two Burgee Book editions (this the Second Edition) were created over the course of six years of extensive research and computer work. The chartlets and data were designed with Macintosh formats. Thank goodness it is still allowable to have fun while one works. We have many days of enjoyment compiling and updating this book's data on our 35' single engine trawler, *Shine*.

To find this book useful, it is not necessary to belong to a specific yacht or boating club. There are dozens of public boating facilities included in the Burgee Book. We are sure will find the information contained in this book helpful to promote your enjoyment of the great sport of recreational boating. Thank you and good cruising! *-David Kutz*

ABOUT THE AUTHOR

David Kutz and his wife Janice have been avid recreational boaters in Washington and Canadian waters for many years. Kutz is an active member and Past Commodore of the Kingston Cove Yacht Club, active member of the International Order of the Blue Gavel (IOBG), and currently serving as a Trustee of the Recreational Boating Association of Washington.

In 1990, Kutz saw a niche to fill in the boating book market and endeavored to start a small publishing company and complete the First Edition of the Burgee Book in 1994. The Second Edition followed in 1996 and future editions are planned with updates as needed. In addition to Pierside Publishing, Kutz and his wife own and operate Northstar Sportswear Corporation located in downtown Kingston, Washington.

BOATING SERVICE ORGANIZATIONS

In addition to the many yacht clubs shown in this book, attention should be given to the increasing importance of two boating organizations that look after the interests of not only Northwest boaters but all recreational boaters who enjoy this great sport across the country.

The Burgee Book encourages all active Northwest boaters to participate as individual members and join these organizations. Membership fees are nominal and your support will go a long way to preserve and enhance recreational boating.

RECREATIONAL BOATING ASSOCIATION OF WASHINGTON

For more than thirty years, the Recreational Boating Association of Washington (RBAW) has been a forum to bring together in a common voice ideas, goals and objectives of Northwest Boaters. As a unified group, the Recreational Boating Association conveys positions of sound reasoning to the Washington State Legislature. These important communications are implemented much more effectively by this group than could be done by an individual. The Recreation Boating Association's goal is to represent the interests Northwest boaters effectively. The Association has a professional lobbyist who makes sure the collective voice is heard by Washington State lawmakers, especially on issues concerning taxation. The Association also works to enhance Washington State Marine Parks, boating safety and educational programs, environmental issues, and works on Federal issues that affect recreational boating. RBAW has about 85 boating and yacht club memberships along with individual members to constitute a membership of over 30,000 boaters. Membership is economical and encouraged for everyone who enjoys boating in the Northwest. For membership information, please call (206) 441-6020 or write Recreational Boating Ass'n of Washington, 2033 6th Ave., Suite 804, Seattle, WA 98121.

NATIONAL BOATING FEDERATION

The National Boating Federation (NBF) consists of nineteen Boating Associations (including RBAW) from across the country. Founded in 1966, NBF is the largest nationwide alliance of recreational boaters and works exclusively on Federal issues that concern boating. Effectively the NBF works on subjects to enhance and protect boating like boating safety, fuel taxes, licensing, Coast Guard, NOAA, and the FCC on VHF radio matters. The NBF is counseled by a professional lobbyist who represents boating interests from several organizations. NBF Officers, Directors, and Delegates are dedicated volunteers and represent no commercial interests. They speak for 2 million boaters nationwide. For membership information please contact National Boating Federation, 3217 Fiji Lane, Alameda, CA 94502.

CHAPTER

1

SOUTH
PUGET SOUND

Allyn

NAME OF MARINA: *PORT OF ALLYN* RADIO: None

ADDRESS: P.O. Box 686, Belfair, WA 98528

TELEPHONE: 360-275-8714 MGR: Marjann Read

SHORT DESCRIPTION & LOCATION:

47°23.90' - 122°49.60' Small guest/service float on waterfront in town of Allyn. Dock is open to southerly winds and moorage recommended in fair weather only and low water hazards exists at extreme low tides.

GUEST BOAT CAPACITY: ....Appx. 6-8 boats

SEASON: ....All year

RESERVATION POLICY:..................................None

AMT W/ELECTRICITY: ....None

FUEL DOCK: ....None

MARINE REPAIRS: ....None

TOILETS: ....Yes

HOT SHOWERS: ....None

RESTAURANT: ....Close by

PICNIC AREA: ....Yes

PLAY AREA: ....Yes

BASIC STORE: ....Close by

ELECTRICITY: ....None

DAILY RATE: ....Appx. .25¢ per foot

GUEST DOCK:.................Appx. 50'

GUEST SLIPS:........5 large spaces

WATER: ....At head of pier

AMPS: ....None

PUMP OUT STATION ....None

HAUL OUT: ....None

BOAT RAMP:............................Yes

LAUNDRY: ....None

LOUNGE: ....Close by

POOL:......................................None

BBQ: ....None

GOLF: ....Close by

OTHER: Convenient location close to town, shops, and restaurant.

CAUTION! This chartlet not intended for use in navigation.

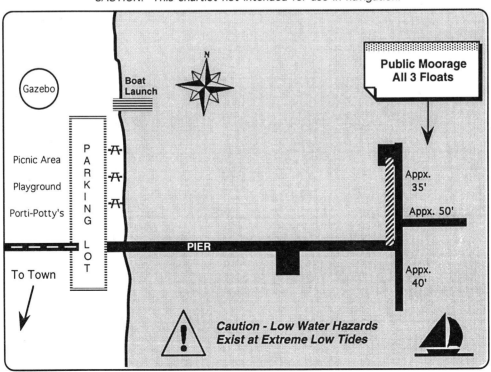

Des Moines

NAME OF MARINA: **DES MOINES MARINA** RADIO: VHF Ch. 16

ADDRESS: 22307 Dock Ave. Des Moines WA 98198

TELEPHONE: 206-824-5700 MGR: Joe Dusenbury

SHORT DESCRIPTION & LOCATION:

47°24.10' - 122°19.80' Located on the E. shore of East Passage about 4 miles SE of Three Tree Pt. between Seattle & Tacoma. The modern & large marina offers sheltered moorage behind a 2200 ft. rock breakwater close to shopping ctr. and public services.

GUEST BOAT CAPACITY: ....Appx. 50-60 boats	GUEST DOCK: ....175' plus slips
SEASON: ....All year	GUEST SLIPS: 40
RESERVATION POLICY: ....None	WATER: ....Yes
AMT W/ELECTRICITY: ....All	AMPS: ....20-30 A
FUEL DOCK: ....Gas, Dsl, & LP	PUMP OUT STATION ....Yes
MARINE REPAIRS: ....On premises	HAUL OUT: ....Travel-Lift
TOILETS: ....Yes	BOAT RAMP: ....Sling
HOT SHOWERS: ....Yes	LAUNDRY: ....Close by
RESTAURANT: ....Yes	LOUNGE: ....Yes
PICNIC AREA: ....Yes	POOL: ....Close by
PLAY AREA: ....Yes	BBQ: ....Yes
BASIC STORE: ....Close by	GOLF: ....Close by
ELECTRICITY: ....$3.00 per day	OTHER: Fishing pier, antique
DAILY RATE: DEPENDING ON LENGTH:	shops, museum,
....................$6-$15/Night for 7 days	Waterland Festival
.................$9-$23/Night over 7 days	during last week of July.

NAME OF YACHT CLUB: **DES MOINES YACHT CLUB**

CLUB ADDRESS: P.O. Box 98362, Des Moines, WA 98198-0362

CLUB TELEPHONE: 206-878-7220 PERSON IN CHARGE: .....Club Stewards

LOCATION & SPECIAL NOTES

DMYC extends privileges of club facilities to members of reciprocal boating clubs. All visitors must register with club stewards upon arrival. Dock space is available all year on the DMYC dock & also the S. side of "A" dock during the summer. Max. boat size is 50'.

RECIPROCAL BOAT CAPACITY:.... 10-20 boats	RECIPROCAL DOCK: Appx. 230'
RECIPROCAL SEASON:................................All year	RECIPROCAL SLIPS: Docks only
RESERVATION POLICY: ....Groups only	WATER: ....Yes
TOILETS: ....Yes	AMT W/ELECTRICITY: ....All
HOT SHOWERS: ....Yes	AMPS: ....30 A
RESTAURANT: ....Close by	LOUNGE: ....Close by
DAILY RATE: ....$3.00/Night for power ....FORTY-EIGHT HOUR LIMIT	OTHER: ....Same as marina listing

NOTE: THIS IS PRIVATE MOORAGE _ONLY_ AVAILABLE TO MEMBERS OF RECIPROCAL YACHT CLUBS! YOUR CLUB _MUST_ HAVE RECIPROCAL PRIVILEGES AND YOU MUST FLY YOUR BURGEE!

CAUTION! This chartlet not intended for use in navigation.

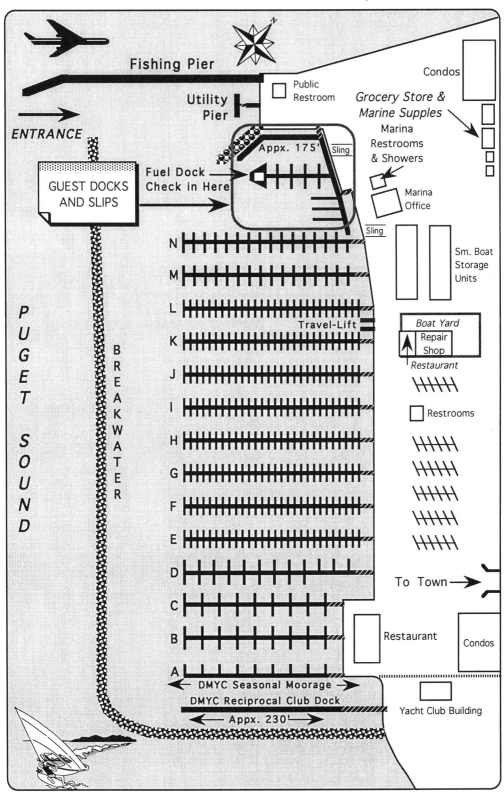

Fishing Pier

Public Restroom

Utility Pier

ENTRANCE

Condos

Grocery Store & Marine Supples

Marina Restrooms & Showers

Appx. 175'

Sling

Fuel Dock Check in Here

GUEST DOCKS AND SLIPS

Marina Office

Sling

N

M

L

K

J

I

H

G

F

E

D

C

B

A

Travel-Lift

Sm. Boat Storage Units

Boat Yard

Repair Shop

Restaurant

Restrooms

P U G E T   S O U N D

B R E A K W A T E R

To Town →

Restaurant

Condos

DMYC Seasonal Moorage

DMYC Reciprocal Club Dock

Appx. 230'

Yacht Club Building

Des Moines

NAME OF YACHT CLUB: *SOUTH SOUND ELKS YACHT CLUB*

ADDRESS: Auburn Elks, 1317 Harvey Rd   Auburn,   WA   98002

TELEPHONE: PERSON IN CHARGE: Commodore

SHORT DESCRIPTION & LOCATION:

The South Sound Elks Yacht club offers reciprocal moorage located at the **Des Moines Marina** Guest Dock when available. The reciprocal member must pay the moorage charges to the Marina, then send the bill to South Sound Elks Y.C. for reimbursement.

RECIPROCAL BOAT CAPACITY..................Varies

SEASON: ....All year

RESERVATION POLICY:....................None

TOILETS: ....At Des Moines Marina

HOT SHOWERS: ....At Des Moines Marina

RESTAURANT: ....Close by

DAILY RATE: ....No Charge
                LIMIT: One day in 30 day period

RECIPROCAL DOCK: ....At marina

RECIPROCAL SLIPS: ...At marina

WATER: ....Yes

AMT W/ELECTRICITY: ....All

AMPS: ....20-30 A

LOUNGE: ....Close by

OTHER: Services same as Des Moines Marina listing on Page 10 & 11

NOTE: THIS IS PRIVATE MOORAGE AND ONLY AVAILABLE TO MEMBERS OF RECIPROCAL YACHT CLUBS. YOUR CLUB MUST HAVE RECIPROCAL PRIVILEGES AND YOU MUST FLY YOUR BURGEE.

SEE DATA & CHARTLET ON PAGE: 10 & 11

NOTES

Des Moines

NAME OF YACHT CLUB: *THREE TREE POINT YACHT CLUB*

ADDRESS: P.O. Box 98700   Des Moines,   WA   98198

TELEPHONE: PERSON IN CHARGE: .....Recip. Chairman

SHORT DESCRIPTION & LOCATION:

Three Tree Point Y.C. offers 2 nights reciprocal moorage at the **Des Moines Marina** general guest dock. Upon arrival check in at the fuel dock & show your current Y.C. membership card to be assigned moorage. Moorage is limited to 2 boats per night.

RECIPROCAL BOAT CAPACITY.............2 boats

SEASON: ....All year

RESERVATION POLICY:...................None

TOILETS: ....At Des Moines Marina

HOT SHOWERS: ....At Des Moines Marina

RESTAURANT:..................................Close by

DAILY RATE: ...Electricity charge - $3.00/ day
              Moorage - No charge/2 nights.

RECIPROCAL DOCK: ....At marina

RECIPROCAL SLIPS: ...At marina

WATER: ....Yes

AMT W/ELECTRICITY: ....All

AMPS: ....20-30 A

LOUNGE: ....Close by

OTHER: Services same as
              Des Moines Marina listing
                 on Pages 10 & 11

NOTE: THIS IS PRIVATE MOORAGE AND ONLY AVAILABLE TO MEMBERS OF RECIPROCAL YACHT CLUBS. YOUR CLUB **MUST** HAVE RECIPROCAL PRIVILEGES AND YOU MUST FLY YOUR BURGEE.

SEE DATA & CHARTLET ON PAGE: 10 & 11

NOTES

Fox Island

NAME OF YACHT CLUB: *FOX ISLAND YACHT CLUB*

ADDRESS: P.O. Box 1   Fox Island   WA   98333

TELEPHONE: 206-549-2603   PERSON IN CHARGE: Commodore

SHORT DESCRIPTION & LOCATION:

47°14.50' - 122°36.00' (Entrance) Located in pristine Cedrona Cove on NE side of Fox Is. about 3 mi. SW of Narrows Bridge. Modern clubhouse & grounds offer a pleasant atmosphere. Caution is necessary upon entering Cove & a large scale chart advised. In addition to recip. dock, FIYC has 4 mooring buoys inside harbor & 1 buoy outside harbor.

RECIPROCAL BOAT CAPACITY...........Appx 6-10	RECIPROCAL DOCK: ....180 ft.
SEASON: ....All year	RECIPROCAL SLIPS: Dock only
RESERVATION POLICY:....................None	WATER: ....Yes
TOILETS: ....In clubhouse when open	AMT W/ELECTRICITY: ....All
HOT SHOWERS: ....In clubhouse when open	AMPS: ....30 A
RESTAURANT: ....None	LOUNGE: ....None
DAILY RATE: ....$2.00 Electricity charge Moorage fee:...........................None Length of Stay:.........2 days max	OTHER: 5 Reciprocal mooring buoys, playground, BBQ, & boat launch ramp.

<u>NOTE:</u> THIS IS PRIVATE MOORAGE AND ONLY AVAILABLE TO MEMBERS OF RECIPROCAL YACHT CLUBS. YOUR CLUB <u>MUST</u> HAVE RECIPROCAL PRIVILEGES AND YOU MUST FLY YOUR BURGEE.

CAUTION! This chartlet not intended for use in navigation.

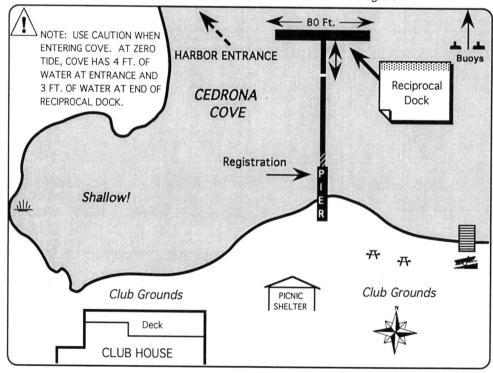

Gig Harbor

NAME OF MARINA: **ARABELLA'S LANDING MARINA**   RADIO: VHF Ch. 68
ADDRESS: 3323 Harborview Dr.   Gig Harbor,   WA 98332
TELEPHONE: 206-851-1793   MGR: Judy Stearns

SHORT DESCRIPTION & LOCATION:

47°19.85' - 122°34.90' Gig Harbor's newest marina is located near the center of historic Gig Harbor. This modern facility is close to many shops and restaurants and offers full facilities for boaters. Additional slips are rented to overnighters if open.

GUEST BOAT CAPACITY: ....Appx. 10-30 boats	GUEST DOCK: ....Appx. 250 ft.
SEASON: ....All year	GUEST SLIPS: ....2 Lg. 60' slips
RESERVATION POLICY: ....Accepts	WATER: ....Yes
AMT W/ELECTRICITY: ....All	AMPS: ....30-50 A
FUEL DOCK: ....Close by	PUMP OUT STATION ....Yes
MARINE REPAIRS: ....Close by	HAUL OUT: ....Close by
TOILETS: ....Yes	BOAT RAMP: ....Close by
HOT SHOWERS: ....Yes	LAUNDRY: ....Yes
RESTAURANT: ....Close by	LOUNGE: ....Close by
PICNIC AREA: ....Yes	POOL: ....None
PLAY AREA: ....None	BBQ: ....None
BASIC STORE: ....Close by	GOLF: ....Close by
ELECTRICITY: ....Included in moorage	OTHER: Meeting & function
DAILY RATE: ....Appx. .50¢ per foot	room rental for groups.

Outside 60' slips are rented at a
flat rate of $30.00 per night.

CAUTION! This chartlet not intended for use in navigation.

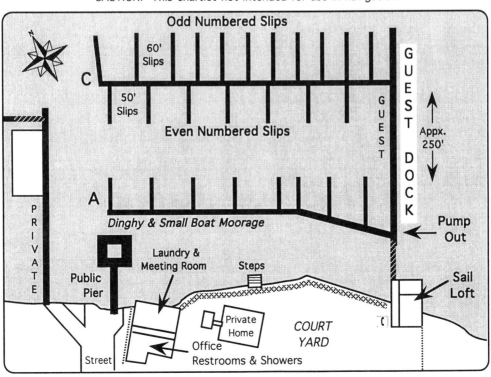

Gig Harbor

NAME OF MARINA: *GIG HARBOR PUBLIC DOCK*   RADIO: None

ADDRESS: P.O. Box 145   Gig Harbor   WA   98332

TELEPHONE: 206-851-8145   MGR: Public Works Supervisor

SHORT DESCRIPTION & LOCATION:

47°19.75' - 122°34.70' Located in heart of historic Gig Harbor at base of giant American flag in Jerisich Park. Nice park setting and close to many shops and restaurants.

GUEST BOAT CAPACITY: ....Appx. 15-20 boats	GUEST DOCK: ....Appx. 340 ft.
SEASON: ....All year	GUEST SLIPS: ....None
RESERVATION POLICY: ....None	WATER: ....None
AMT W/ELECTRICITY: ....None	AMPS: ....None
FUEL DOCK: ....Close by	PUMP OUT STATION ....None
MARINE REPAIRS: ....Close by	HAUL OUT: ....Close by
TOILETS: ....Yes	BOAT RAMP: ....Close by
HOT SHOWERS: ....None	LAUNDRY: ....Close by
RESTAURANT: ....Close by	LOUNGE: ....Close by
PICNIC AREA: ....Yes	POOL: ....None
PLAY AREA: ....None	BBQ: ....None
BASIC STORE: ....Close by	GOLF: ....Close by
ELECTRICITY: ....None	OTHER: Rafting prohibited, no
DAILY RATE: ....Appx. .25¢ per foot	barbecues allowed on
24 Hour Maximum Stay	dock, nice picnic area on
	pier at head of dock.

CAUTION! This chartlet not intended for use in navigation.

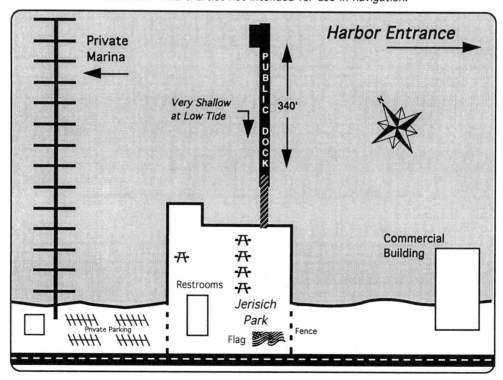

Gig Harbor

NAME OF MARINA: **MURPHY'S LANDING MARINA**   RADIO: None

ADDRESS: 3901 Harborview Drive   Gig Harbor   WA 98332

TELEPHONE: 206-851-3539   MGR: Bruce Rogers

SHORT DESCRIPTION & LOCATION:

47°20.20' - 122°35.40' Modern and well kept condominium moorage located at the head of the harbor with small guest dock. About one-half mile from downtown Gig Harbor and walking distance to many shops and restaurants.

GUEST BOAT CAPACITY: ....Appx. 1 boat	GUEST DOCK: ....Appx 45 ft.
SEASON: ....All year	GUEST SLIPS: ....None
RESERVATION POLICY: ....None	WATER: ....Yes
AMT W/ELECTRICITY: ....All	AMPS: ....30 A
FUEL DOCK: ....Close by	PUMP OUT STATION ....Yes
MARINE REPAIRS: ....Close by	HAUL OUT: ....Close by
TOILETS: ....Yes	BOAT RAMP: ....Close by
HOT SHOWERS: ....Yes	LAUNDRY: ....Yes
RESTAURANT: ....Close by	LOUNGE: ....Close by
PICNIC AREA: ....None	POOL: ....None
PLAY AREA: ....None	BBQ: ....None
BASIC STORE: ....Close by	GOLF: ....Close by
ELECTRICITY: ....Included in moorage	OTHER: No rafting, no bbq on dock, bicycle areas, dinghy area.
DAILY RATE: ....Appx. .30¢ per foot	

CAUTION! This chartlet not intended for use in navigation.

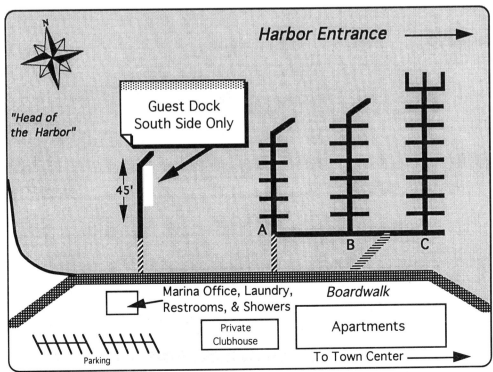

Gig Harbor

NAME OF MARINA: *SHORELINE RESTAURANT MOORAGE* **RADIO:** None

ADDRESS: 8827 N. Harborview   Gig Harbor,   WA   98335

TELEPHONE: 206-851-9822   **MGR:** Kathy Roader

SHORT DESCRIPTION & LOCATION:

47°20.30' - 122°35.22' Nice restaurant and lounge with complimentary moorage for restaurant patrons; located at head of Gig Harbor. Caution: Guest docks go partially dry at low water.

GUEST BOAT CAPACITY: ....Appx. 10 boats	**GUEST DOCK:** ....Appx. 100 ft.
SEASON: ....All year	**GUEST SLIPS:** 2 lg. guest docks
RESERVATION POLICY:.........................None	**WATER:** ....Yes
AMT W/ELECTRICITY: ....Appx. 4 outlets	**AMPS:** ....110 Only
FUEL DOCK: ....Close by	**PUMP OUT STATION** ....None
MARINE REPAIRS: ....Close by	**HAUL OUT:** ....None
TOILETS: ....None	**BOAT RAMP:** ....Close by
HOT SHOWERS: ....Close by	**LAUNDRY:** ....Close by
RESTAURANT: ....Yes	**LOUNGE:** ....Yes
PICNIC AREA: ....Yes	**POOL:**...................................None
PLAY AREA: ....None	**BBQ:** ....None
BASIC STORE: ....Close by	**GOLF:** ....Close by
ELECTRICITY: ....No charge	**OTHER:** Appx. 3/4 miles from
DAILY RATE: ....No charge for overnight	heart of town of Gig
moorage if dining at restaurant.	Harbor. Walking distance
	to shops and marine
	services.

CAUTION! This chartlet not intended for use in navigation.

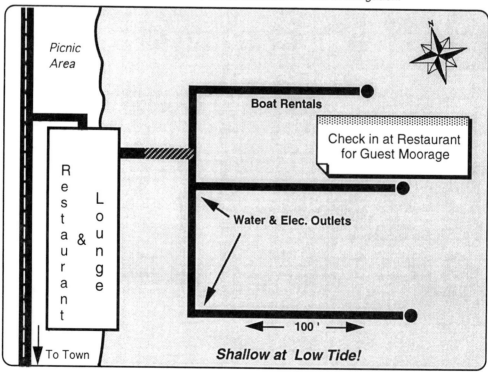

Gig Harbor

NAME OF MARINA: **TIDES TAVERN**   RADIO: None

ADDRESS: 2925 Harborview Drive   Gig Harbor   WA   98335

TELEPHONE: 206-858-3982   MGR: Greg Stalker

SHORT DESCRIPTION & LOCATION:

47°19.68' - 122°34.50' The Tide's guest float is just inside the entrance of Gig Harbor and is one of the first few docks on the south side upon entering. Overnight moorage is complimentary to restaurant patrons and rafting is mandatory upon request.

GUEST BOAT CAPACITY: ....Appx. 10-20 boats	GUEST DOCK: ....120 ft.
SEASON: ....All year	GUEST SLIPS: ....None
RESERVATION POLICY:..................................None	WATER: ....None
AMT W/ELECTRICITY: ....None	AMPS: ....None
FUEL DOCK: ....Close by	PUMP OUT STATION ....None
MARINE REPAIRS: ....Close by	HAUL OUT: ....Close by
TOILETS: ....Yes - In tavern	BOAT RAMP: ....Close by
HOT SHOWERS: ....None	LAUNDRY: ....Close by
RESTAURANT: ....Yes	LOUNGE: ....Beer & wine only
PICNIC AREA: ....None	POOL:...None
PLAY AREA: ....None	BBQ: ....None
BASIC STORE: ....Close by	GOLF: ....Close by
ELECTRICITY: ....None	OTHER: Central town location is
DAILY RATE: ....No charge to restaurant and	close to many shops and
tavern customers - 24 hour limit.	attractions. **Dock goes partially dry at very low tide.**

CAUTION! This chartlet not intended for use in navigation.

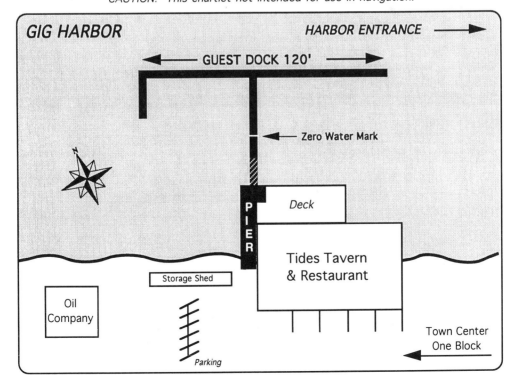

Gig Harbor

NAME OF MARINA: *PENINSULA YACHT BASIN*   **RADIO:** None

ADDRESS: 8913 N. Harborview Dr.   Gig Harbor   WA   98335

TELEPHONE: 206-851-2250   **MGR:** Steve Luengren

SHORT DESCRIPTION & LOCATION:

47°20.32' - 122°35.22' Marina is located at the head of beautiful and protected Gig Harbor within walking distance to the heart of the historic boating town. Although no designated guest dock, open slips are rented out to overnighters.

GUEST BOAT CAPACITY: ....Appx. 10 boats	GUEST DOCK: ....Slips only
SEASON: ....All year	GUEST SLIPS: ....Varies
RESERVATION POLICY: ....None	WATER: ....Yes
AMT W/ELECTRICITY: ....All	AMPS: ....30 A
FUEL DOCK: ....Close by	PUMP OUT STATION ....None
MARINE REPAIRS: ....Close by	HAUL OUT: ....Close by
TOILETS: ....Yes	BOAT RAMP: ....Close by
HOT SHOWERS: ....Yes	LAUNDRY: ....Close by
RESTAURANT: ....Close by	LOUNGE: ....Close by
PICNIC AREA: ....Yes	POOL: ....None
PLAY AREA: ....None	BBQ: ....None
BASIC STORE: ....Close by	GOLF: ....Close by
ELECTRICITY: ....$ 1.00 per day	OTHER: Security gate, many
DAILY RATE: ....Appx. .40¢ per foot	nice shops and restaurants close by.

NOTE CORRECTED PHONE # 206-858-2250

NAME OF YACHT CLUB: *GIG HARBOR YACHT CLUB*   **B**

CLUB ADDRESS: P.O. Box 22, Gig Harbor, WA 98335

CLUB TELEPHONE: **PERSON IN CHARGE:**   Commodore

LOCATION & SPECIAL NOTES

GHYC has an 80 ft. guest dock for reciprocal use at Peninsula Yacht Basin located on the shore side of the end of "A" dock. Rafting is permitted. Security gate instructions can be found in annual letter sent to your Yacht Club by GHYC.

RECIPROCAL BOAT CAPACITY:...........2-4 Boats	RECIPROCAL DOCK: ....Appx. 80'
RECIPROCAL SEASON:...............................All year	RECIPROCAL SLIPS: See above
RESERVATION POLICY: ....Groups only	WATER: ....Yes
TOILETS: ....At Marina	AMT W/ELECTRICITY: 2
HOT SHOWERS: ....At Marina	AMPS: ....30 A
RESTAURANT: ....Close by	LOUNGE: ....Close by
DAILY RATE: ....Up to 48 hours free moorage. ....Nominal charge for electricity.	OTHER: ....Same as marina listing

NOTE: *THIS IS PRIVATE MOORAGE ONLY AVAILABLE TO MEMBERS OF RECIPROCAL YACHT CLUBS! YOUR CLUB MUST HAVE RECIPROCAL PRIVILEGES AND YOU MUST FLY YOUR BURGEE!*

Gig Harbor

CAUTION! This chartlet not intended for use in navigation.

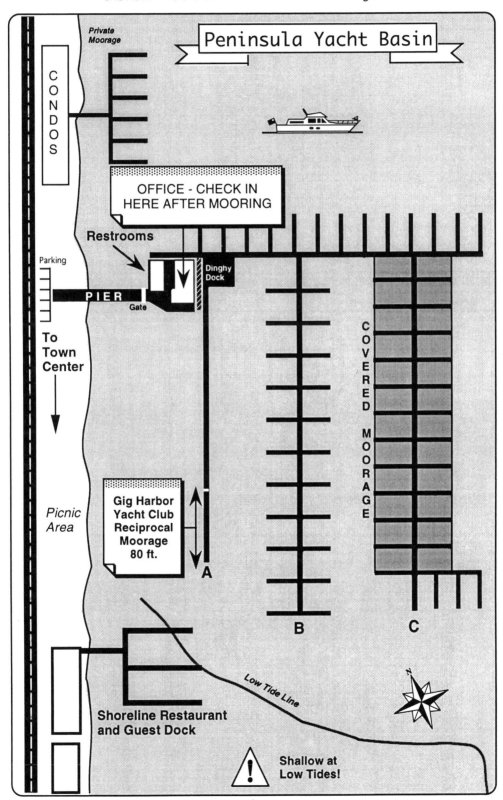

Grapeview

NAME OF MARINA: *FAIR HARBOR MARINA*   RADIO: None
ADDRESS: P.O. Box 160   Grapeview   WA 98546
TELEPHONE: 360-426-4028   MGR: Vern & Susan Nelson

SHORT DESCRIPTION & LOCATION:

47°20.40' - 122°49.80' Located on the N.W. side of Case Inlet just N. of Stretch Island behind Reach Island. The full service marina in Fair Harbor offers ample moorage in a sheltered harbor. The area has golfing and sightseeing attractions for boaters.

GUEST BOAT CAPACITY:.......Appx. 40-45 boats	GUEST DOCK:....350' of moorage
SEASON: ....All year	GUEST SLIPS: ....Ends of docks
RESERVATION POLICY:............................Accepts	WATER: ....No
AMT W/ELECTRICITY: ....All	AMPS: ....30 A
FUEL DOCK: ....Gas only	PUMP OUT STATION ....None
MARINE REPAIRS: ....On premises	HAUL OUT: ....None
TOILETS: ....Yes	BOAT RAMP: ....Yes
HOT SHOWERS: ....Yes	LAUNDRY: ....None
RESTAURANT: ....None	LOUNGE: ....None
PICNIC AREA: ....Yes	POOL: ....None
PLAY AREA: ....Yes	BBQ: ....Yes
BASIC STORE: ....Yes	GOLF: ....Close by
ELECTRICITY: ....$2.50 per day	OTHER: Country store on dock,
DAILY RATE: ....Appx. .40¢ per foot	gifts, bait & marine
	hardware, transp. to golf
	course, maritime
	museum close by.

CAUTION! This chartlet not intended for use in navigation.

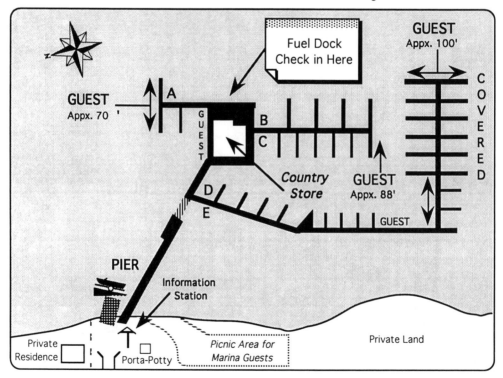

Hartstine Island

NAME OF MARINA: *JARRELL'S COVE MARINA*   RADIO: None

ADDRESS: E. 220 Wilson Rd.   Shelton,   WA   98584

TELEPHONE: 360-426-8823   MGR: Lorna & Gary Hink

SHORT DESCRIPTION & LOCATION:

47°17.00' - 122°53.40' Located on N.W. corner of Hartstine Island in picturesque Jarrell Cove. One of South Sound's finest marina resorts with many amenities.

GUEST BOAT CAPACITY: ....Appx, 5-7 boats	GUEST DOCK: ....Appx. 200 ft.
SEASON: ....All year	GUEST SLIPS: Guest docks only
RESERVATION POLICY:...........................Accepts	WATER: ....Yes
AMT W/ELECTRICITY: ....All	AMPS: ....30 A
FUEL DOCK: ....Gas, Dsl, & LP	PUMP OUT STATION ....Yes
MARINE REPAIRS: ....None	HAUL OUT: ....None
TOILETS: ....Yes	BOAT RAMP:..........................None
HOT SHOWERS: ....Yes	LAUNDRY: ....Yes
RESTAURANT: ....None	LOUNGE: ....None
PICNIC AREA: ....Yes	POOL:......................................None
PLAY AREA: ....Yes	BBQ: ....Yes
BASIC STORE: ....Yes	GOLF: ....Appx. 10-15 miles
ELECTRICITY: ....$3.00 per day	OTHER: Shore side camping,
DAILY RATE: ....Appx. .50¢ per foot	picnic & game areas,
	horseshoes, clams,
	fishing, dinghy to park.

CAUTION! This chartlet not intended for use in navigation.

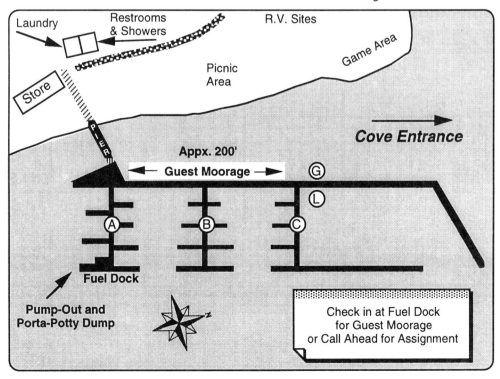

Hartstine Island

NAME OF PARK: *JARRELL COVE STATE PARK*
ADDRESS: E. 391 Wingert Rd.   Shelton, WA   98584
TELEPHONE: 360-426-9226   MGR: Tom Snyder

SHORT DESCRIPTION & LOCATION:

47°17.00'-122°53.10' Located on east side of Jarrell Cove on northwest corner of Hartstine Is. The park size is 42 acres with 3056 feet of shoreline. The park is busy in the summer and has two floats and mooring buoys to serve boaters as well as campsites.

GUEST BOAT CAPACITY: ....Appx. 45 boats

SEASON: ....All year

AMT W/ELECTRICITY: ....None

TOILETS: ....Yes

HOT SHOWERS: ....Yes

PICNIC AREA: ....Yes

PLAY AREA: ....Yes

BASIC STORE: ....Close by

DAILY RATE: Mooring Buoys.................$5.00/night
            Boats under 26 ft..........$8.00/night
            Boats 26 ft. & Over.....$11.00/night
            Subject to Change in 1997

GUEST DOCK: 2 Floats = 275 ft.

MOORING BUOYS: 13

WATER: ....Ashore

PAY PHONES: ....At marina

BOAT RAMP: ....None

PICNIC SHELTER: ....Yes

BBQ: ....Yes

PUMP OUT STATION: ....Yes

OTHER: Campsites, trails, picnic tables, fishing, hiking, bird watching, canoeing, kayaking, and clamming.

CAUTION! This chartlet not intended for use in navigation.

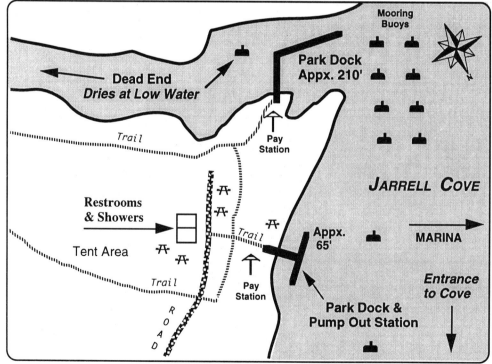

Lakebay

NAME OF MARINA: *LAKEBAY MARINA* RADIO: None
ADDRESS: 15 Lorenz Rd. K.P.S. Lakebay WA 98349
TELEPHONE: 206-884-3350 MGR: Dewey Hostetler

SHORT DESCRIPTION & LOCATION:

47°15.40' - 122°45.20' Older marina located at the head of Mayo Cove on the SW shore of Carr Inlet in a village with a store and several small private piers. The channel to the marina is difficult to navigate at low tide & caution and local knowledge are advised.

GUEST BOAT CAPACITY: ....Appx. 6-10 boats	GUEST DOCK: ....Appx. 124 ft.
SEASON: ....All year	GUEST SLIPS: ....Varies
RESERVATION POLICY: ....Accepts	WATER: ....Yes
AMT W/ELECTRICITY: ....Limited	AMPS: ....15 A
FUEL DOCK: ....Gas only	PUMP OUT STATION ....None
MARINE REPAIRS: ....None	HAUL OUT: ....None
TOILETS: ....Yes	BOAT RAMP: ....Close by
HOT SHOWERS: ....None	LAUNDRY: ....Close by
RESTAURANT: ....Close by-1.5 mi	LOUNGE: ....Close by
PICNIC AREA: ....Yes	POOL: ....None
PLAY AREA: ....None	BBQ: ....None
BASIC STORE: ....Yes	GOLF: ....Close by
ELECTRICITY: ....Included in moorage	OTHER: Caters to fishermen bait
DAILY RATE: ....Appx. .30¢ per foot	& tackle sold in store,
	close to Park, great
	dinghy area., taxi service.

CAUTION! This chartlet not intended for use in navigation.

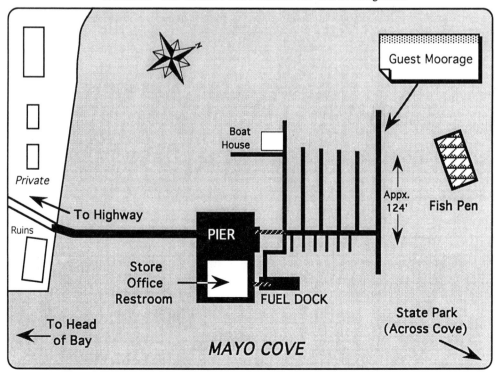

Lakebay

NAME OF PARK: *PENROSE POINT STATE PARK*
ADDRESS: 321 158th Ave. KPS   Lakebay, WA   98349
TELEPHONE: 206-884-2514   MGR: Dave Roe

SHORT DESCRIPTION & LOCATION:

47°15.50' - 122°45.10'   Located on the E. shore of Mayo Cove on W. side of Carr Inlet 3 miles N. of Long Branch. The park has a large shoreline in a beautiful setting. The floats go dry at extreme low tides.

GUEST BOAT CAPACITY: ....Appx 9-12 boats

SEASON: ....Closed winter

AMT W/ELECTRICITY: ....None

TOILETS: ....Yes

HOT SHOWERS: ....Yes

PICNIC AREA: ....Yes

PLAY AREA: ....None

BASIC STORE: ....None

DAILY RATE: Mooring Buoys.................$5.00/night
             Boats under 26 ft...........$8.00/night
             Boats 26 ft. & Over.....$11.00/night
             Subject to Change in 1997

GUEST DOCK: ....Appx. 135 ft.

MOORING BUOYS: 8

WATER: ....Yes

PAY PHONES: ....Yes

BOAT RAMP: ....Close by

PICNIC SHELTER: ....Yes

BBQ: ....Yes

PUMP OUT STATION: ....Yes

OTHER: Nature & hiking trails with interpretative signs, 2 miles of clamming & beachcombing.

CAUTION! This chartlet not intended for use in navigation.

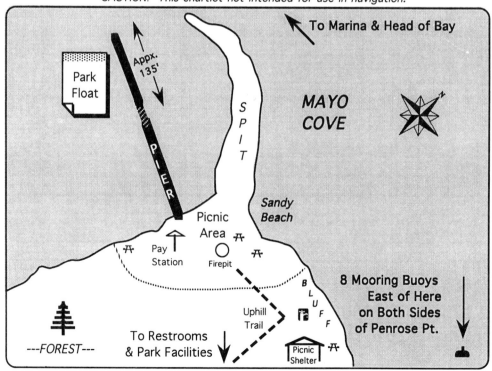

Longbranch

NAME OF PARK: **JOEMMA BEACH STATE PARK** (Formerly R.F.K. Park)

ADDRESS: 321 158th Ave K.P.S.   Lakebay, WA   98349

TELEPHONE: 206-884-2514   MGR: Allan Jacobson

SHORT DESCRIPTION & LOCATION:

47°13.60' - 122°48.70'   Located on S.E. end of Case Inlet just W. of Whiteman Cove. The new "E" shaped floats offer good depth with ample moorage. A long pier with an observation deck provides access to floats from the 22 acre upland park.

GUEST BOAT CAPACITY: ....Appx. 20 boats	GUEST DOCK: Appx. 128' + Slips
SEASON: ....Closed winter	MOORING BUOYS: 5
AMT W/ELECTRICITY: ....None	WATER: ....Yes
TOILETS: ....Yes	PAY PHONES: ....Yes
HOT SHOWERS: ....None	BOAT RAMP: ....Yes
PICNIC AREA: ....Yes	PICNIC SHELTER: ....Yes
PLAY AREA: ....None	BBQ: ....Yes
BASIC STORE: ....None	PUMP OUT STATION: ......None
DAILY RATE: Mooring Buoys................$5.00/night Boats under 26 ft..........$8.00/night Boats 26 ft. & Over.....$11.00/night ***Subject to Change in 1997***	OTHER: .....Fishing, bicycling, shell fishing, camping.

CAUTION! This chartlet not intended for use in navigation.

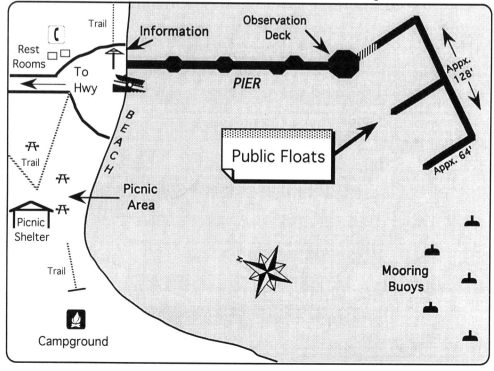

Longbranch

NAME OF MARINA: *LONGBRANCH MARINA*   RADIO: VHF Ch. 16
ADDRESS: P.O. Box 111,   Lakebay,   WA 98349
TELEPHONE: 206-884-5137   MGR: Glen Miller

SHORT DESCRIPTION & LOCATION:

47°12.60' - 122°45.00' Well maintained friendly marina in lovely Filucy Bay located on east side of Key Peninsula. Sheltered cove provides very comfortable moorage. This is a popular location for South Sound club cruises.

GUEST BOAT CAPACITY: ....Appx. 40 boats	GUEST DOCK: ...Longest =202 ft.
SEASON: ....All year	GUEST SLIPS: ....3 Large docks
RESERVATION POLICY: ....None	WATER: ....Yes
AMT W/ELECTRICITY: ....All	AMPS: ....20-30 A
FUEL DOCK: ....None	PUMP OUT STATION ....None
MARINE REPAIRS: ....None	HAUL OUT: ....None
TOILETS: ....Porta-Potty	BOAT RAMP: ....None
HOT SHOWERS: ....None	LAUNDRY: ....None
RESTAURANT: ....Planned for 1996	LOUNGE: ....None
PICNIC AREA: ....Potluck Cover	POOL: ....None
PLAY AREA: ....Yes	BBQ: ....None
BASIC STORE: ....Yes	GOLF: ....None
ELECTRICITY: ....$3.00 per day	OTHER: Fishing, good dinghy
DAILY RATE: ....Appx. .35¢ per foot	area, bicycling, and rock
	crabbing, taxi service to
	Key Center.

CAUTION! This chartlet not intended for use in navigation.

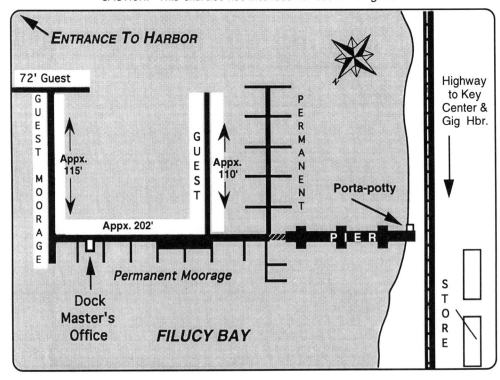

Olympia

NAME OF MARINA: **BOSTON HARBOR MARINA**   RADIO: None

ADDRESS: 312 73rd Ave. N.E.   Olympia,   WA 98506

TELEPHONE: 360-357-5670   MGR: Gary Jessen

SHORT DESCRIPTION & LOCATION:

47°08.60' - 122°45.10' Small quiet & friendly marina in neighborhood location in crescent shaped cove at Dofflemeyer Point at entrance to Budd Inlet. Actually located about 8 miles north of downtown Olympia. Fresh clams & oysters, salmon in season.

GUEST BOAT CAPACITY: ....Appx. 15 boats	GUEST DOCK: ....200' plus slips
SEASON: ....All year	GUEST SLIPS: ....6 small slips
RESERVATION POLICY: ....Accepts	WATER: ....Yes
AMT W/ELECTRICITY: ....All	AMPS: ....20 A
FUEL DOCK: ....Gas & Diesel	PUMP OUT STATION ....None
MARINE REPAIRS: ....Close by	HAUL OUT: ....None
TOILETS: ....Yes	BOAT RAMP: ....Yes
HOT SHOWERS: ....None	LAUNDRY: ....None
RESTAURANT: ....None	LOUNGE: ....None
PICNIC AREA: ....Yes	POOL: ....None
PLAY AREA: ....None	BBQ: ....Yes
BASIC STORE: ....Yes	GOLF: ....Close by
ELECTRICITY: ....$2.00 per day	OTHER: Pay phones, dinghy area,
DAILY RATE: ....Appx. .30¢ per foot	fishing, beach combing,
	bicycling, bus service to
	downtown Olympia.

CAUTION! This chartlet not intended for use in navigation.

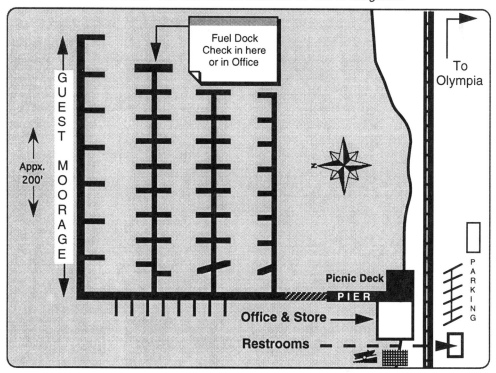

Olympia

NAME OF MARINA: **EAST BAY MARINA**   RADIO: VHF Ch. 65
ADDRESS: 1022 Marine View   Olympia   WA 98501
TELEPHONE: 360-786-1400   MGR: Bill McGregor

SHORT DESCRIPTION & LOCATION:

47°03.50' - 122°36.65' Modern and spacious well kept marina located on east side of Budd Inlet approximately one mile north of downtown Olympia.

GUEST BOAT CAPACITY: ....Appx. 85 boats
SEASON: ....All year
RESERVATION POLICY:....................Holidays only
AMT W/ELECTRICITY: ....All
FUEL DOCK: ....Close by
MARINE REPAIRS: ....Close by
TOILETS: ....Yes
HOT SHOWERS: ....Yes
RESTAURANT: ....Close by
PICNIC AREA: ....Yes
PLAY AREA: ....Yes
BASIC STORE: ....None
ELECTRICITY: ....Included in moorage
DAILY RATE: .....Boats up to 20' = $7.00 per day.
                      Add .30¢ per ft.after 20 ft.

GUEST DOCK: ....700' plus slips
GUEST SLIPS: ....Appx. 50
WATER: ....Yes
AMPS: ....30-50 A
PUMP OUT STATION ....Yes
HAUL OUT: ....Close by
BOAT RAMP: ....Yes
LAUNDRY: ....Yes
LOUNGE: ....Close by
POOL: ....None
BBQ: ....None
GOLF: ....Close by
OTHER: Security personnel,
     bicycle trails close by,
     State Capitol building
     and related attractions

CAUTION! This chartlet not intended for use in navigation.

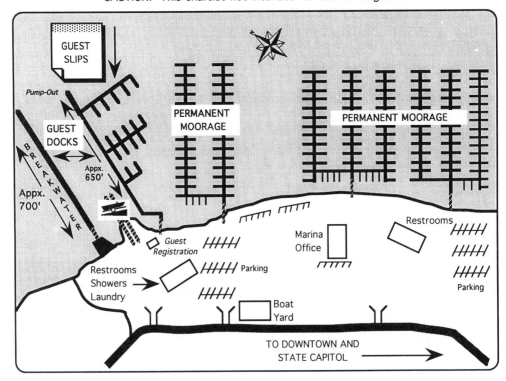

Olympia

NAME OF MARINA: *ZITTEL'S JOHNSON POINT MARINA* RADIO: None

ADDRESS: 9144 Gallea St. N.E. Olympia WA 98506

TELEPHONE: 360-459-1950 MGR: Mike Zittel

SHORT DESCRIPTION & LOCATION:

47°09.90' - 122°45.10' Located appx. 1 mile SSE of Johnson Point at foot of Case Inlet. Local use marina catering to sport fishermen. Guest Dock is exposed to northerly winds. Rural location about 10 driving miles from Olympia..

GUEST BOAT CAPACITY: ....Appx. 10-15 boats

SEASON: ....All year

RESERVATION POLICY:...........................Accepts

AMT W/ELECTRICITY: ....Some

FUEL DOCK: ....Gas & Diesel

MARINE REPAIRS: ....On premises

TOILETS: ....Yes

HOT SHOWERS: ....None

RESTAURANT: ....None

PICNIC AREA: ....None

PLAY AREA: ....None

BASIC STORE: ....Yes

ELECTRICITY:

DAILY RATE: ....Appx. .35¢ per foot

GUEST DOCK: ....Appx. 300 ft.

GUEST SLIPS: ....None

WATER: ....Yes

AMPS: ....None

PUMP OUT STATION ....None

HAUL OUT: ....45-50 Ton

BOAT RAMP:...............................Yes

LAUNDRY: ....None

LOUNGE: ....None

POOL:...None

BBQ: ....None

GOLF: ....Close by

OTHER: Snack Bar, fishing supplies, storage, boat rentals, marine supplies, boat and motor sales.

CAUTION! This chartlet not intended for use in navigation.

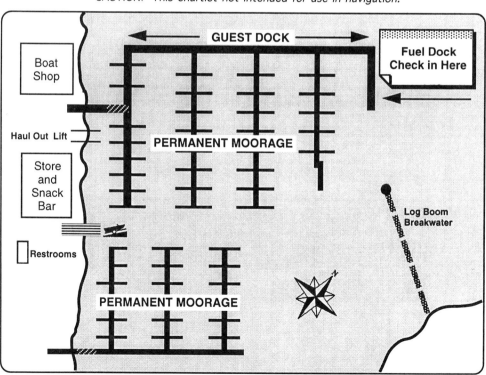

Olympia

NAME OF MARINA: *PERCIVAL LANDING PARK*   RADIO: None
ADDRESS: 222 N. Columbia   Olympia,   WA 98501
TELEPHONE: 360-753-8382   MGR: Terry Meyer

SHORT DESCRIPTION & LOCATION:

47°02.8'-122°54.3' The 3 moorage floats offer one of the most interesting boating stops in the Northwest. Located at the head of Budd Inlet adjacent to downtown Olympia, this well kept facility is convenient to many shops, restaurants, & sights.

GUEST BOAT CAPACITY: ......Appx. 45-60 boats	GUEST DOCK: 940 ft. combined
SEASON: ....All year	GUEST SLIPS: ..Guest docks only
RESERVATION POLICY: ....None	WATER: ....Yes
AMT W/ELECTRICITY: ....Appx. 60%	AMPS: ....30 A
FUEL DOCK: ....None	PUMP OUT STATION ....Yes
MARINE REPAIRS: ....Close by	HAUL OUT: ....Close by
TOILETS: ....Yes	BOAT RAMP: ....None
HOT SHOWERS: ....Yes	LAUNDRY: ....Close by
RESTAURANT: ....Close by	LOUNGE: ....Close by
PICNIC AREA: ....Yes	POOL: ....None
PLAY AREA: ....Close by	BBQ: ....None
BASIC STORE: ....Close by	GOLF: ....None
ELECTRICITY: ....$ 3.00 per day	OTHER: State Capitol Bldg. &
DAILY RATE: ....29' and under = $6.00	related tourist activities,
30'-39' = $7.00..........40'-49' = $8.00	boating and fishing
...................50' & over = $9.00	supplies close by.
<u>Max stay, 7 days in a 30 day period</u>	

NAME OF YACHT CLUB: *OLYMPIA YACHT CLUB*

CLUB ADDRESS: 201 North Simmons St, Olympia, WA 98501

CLUB TELEPHONE: 360-357-6767   PERSON IN CHARGE: Caretaker

LOCATION & SPECIAL NOTES

Located adjacent to Percival Landing directly in front of Yacht Club Building. Sign in and acquire key card from Caretakers (deposit required). Closed Sunday & Monday - no key cards available. Occasional vacated member slips available if needed. Check w/Caretakers.

RECIPROCAL BOAT CAPACITY:......15-30 boats	RECIPROCAL DOCK: ....350 ft.
RECIPROCAL SEASON:...................All year	RECIPROCAL SLIPS: If Available
RESERVATION POLICY: ....None	WATER: ....Yes
TOILETS: ....Yes	AMT W/ELECTRICITY: ....All
HOT SHOWERS: ....Yes	AMPS: ....20-30 A
RESTAURANT: ....Close by	LOUNGE: ....Close by
DAILY RATE: $2 per day for power. Free for 2 Days - 30¢ per foot after 2nd day.	OTHER: ....*5 DAY LIMIT*

<u>NOTE:</u> THIS IS PRIVATE MOORAGE <u>ONLY</u> AVAILABLE TO MEMBERS OF RECIPROCAL YACHT CLUBS! YOUR CLUB <u>MUST</u> HAVE RECIPROCAL PRIVILEGES AND YOU MUST FLY YOUR BURGEE!

Olympia

CAUTION! This chartlet not intended for use in navigation.

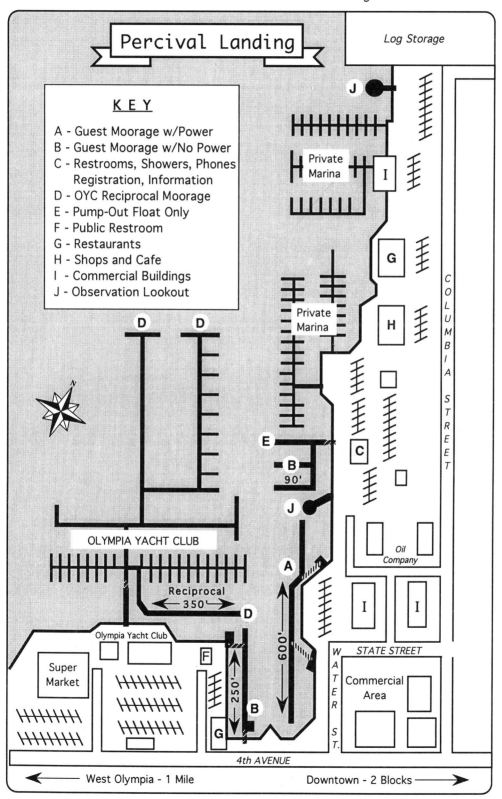

Percival Landing

Log Storage

KEY

A - Guest Moorage w/Power
B - Guest Moorage w/No Power
C - Restrooms, Showers, Phones
Registration, Information
D - OYC Reciprocal Moorage
E - Pump-Out Float Only
F - Public Restroom
G - Restaurants
H - Shops and Cafe
I - Commercial Buildings
J - Observation Lookout

Private Marina

Private Marina

OLYMPIA YACHT CLUB

Reciprocal 350'

Olympia Yacht Club

Super Market

COLUMBIA STREET

Oil Company

STATE STREET

WATER ST.

Commercial Area

4th AVENUE

← West Olympia - 1 Mile

Downtown - 2 Blocks →

33

Olympia

NAME OF MARINA: *WEST BAY MARINA*   RADIO: None

ADDRESS: 2100 West Bay Drive   Olympia,   WA 98502

TELEPHONE: 360-943-2022   MGR: Neil Falkenburg

SHORT DESCRIPTION & LOCATION:

47°03.90'-122°54.80' This modern marina is located on the S.W. side of Budd Inlet about 1.5 mi. from downtown Olympia in a semi-industrial location. Although marina has no designated guest moorage, it generally has a few slips available for guest moorage.

GUEST BOAT CAPACITY: ....Appx. 5-10 boats	GUEST DOCK: ....None
SEASON: ....All year	GUEST SLIPS: ....Varies
RESERVATION POLICY: ....None	WATER:...Yes
AMT W/ELECTRICITY: ....All	AMPS: ....20-30 A
FUEL DOCK: ....Gas, Dsl, & LP	PUMP OUT STATION ....Yes
MARINE REPAIRS: ....On premises	HAUL OUT: ....Travel-Lift
TOILETS: ....Yes	BOAT RAMP:...........................None
HOT SHOWERS: ....Yes	LAUNDRY: ....Yes
RESTAURANT: ....Yes	LOUNGE: ....Yes
PICNIC AREA: ....None	POOL:...None
PLAY AREA: ....None	BBQ: ....None
BASIC STORE: ....Yes	GOLF: ....Close by
ELECTRICITY: ....Included in moorage	OTHER: Full service boat yard,
DAILY RATE: ....$10.00 per night up to 30'	convenient to Olympia's
............$15.00 per night 30' & over	west side area and
	South Sound.

NAME OF YACHT CLUB: *WEST BAY YACHT CLUB*   **B**

CLUB ADDRESS: P.O. Box 7711, Olympia, WA 98507

CLUB TELEPHONE: 360-754-1639   PERSON IN CHARGE: Vice Commo.

LOCATION & SPECIAL NOTES

WBYC offers a 75' reciprocal dock at the West Bay Marina. The dock has a great view of the Inlet & downtown Olympia. If the reciprocal dock is full contact the marina office for a list of member slips available for reciprocal use. A gate key is available in the lock box.

RECIPROCAL BOAT CAPACITY:............Appx.4-6	RECIPROCAL DOCK: ....75 ft.
RECIPROCAL SEASON:................................All year	RECIPROCAL SLIPS: ....Varies
RESERVATION POLICY: ....None	WATER: ....Yes
TOILETS: ....Yes	AMT W/ELECTRICITY: ....All
HOT SHOWERS: ....Yes	AMPS: ....30 A
RESTAURANT: ....None	LOUNGE: ....None
DAILY RATE: ....No Charge	OTHER: ....Same as marina listing
..................................72 HOUR LIMIT	

<u>NOTE:</u> *THIS IS PRIVATE MOORAGE <u>ONLY</u> AVAILABLE TO MEMBERS OF RECIPROCAL YACHT CLUBS! YOUR CLUB <u>MUST</u> HAVE RECIPROCAL PRIVILEGES AND YOU MUST FLY YOUR BURGEE!*

Olympia

CAUTION! This chartlet not intended for use in navigation.

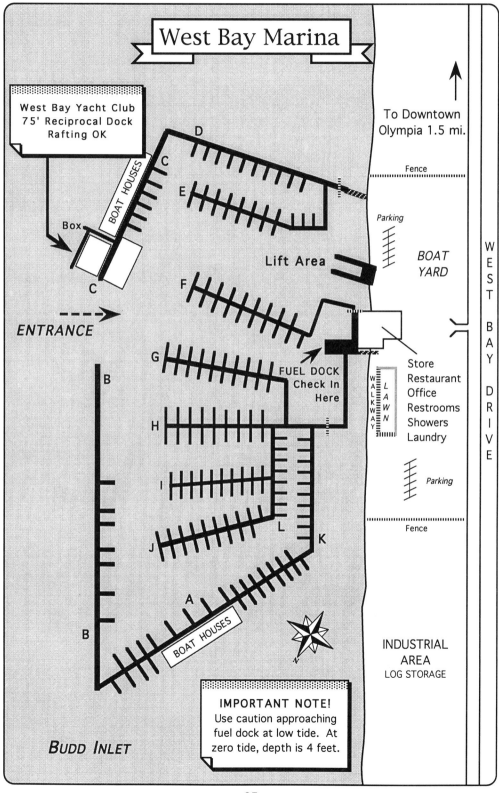

West Bay Marina

West Bay Yacht Club
75' Reciprocal Dock
Rafting OK

BOAT HOUSES

D

C

E

Box

C

ENTRANCE

Lift Area

F

G

B

FUEL DOCK
Check In
Here

H

I

L

J

K

A

B

BOAT HOUSES

BUDD INLET

To Downtown
Olympia 1.5 mi.

Fence

Parking

BOAT YARD

WEST BAY DRIVE

WALKWAY LAWN

Store
Restaurant
Office
Restrooms
Showers
Laundry

Parking

Fence

INDUSTRIAL
AREA
LOG STORAGE

IMPORTANT NOTE!
Use caution approaching
fuel dock at low tide. At
zero tide, depth is 4 feet.

Shelton

NAME OF MARINA: *PORT OF SHELTON - Shelton Yacht Club* RADIO: None
ADDRESS: P.O. Box 2270 Shelton, WA 98584
TELEPHONE: 360-426-9476 MGR: Mike Byrne

SHORT DESCRIPTION & LOCATION:

47°12.85' - 123°05.10' The Shelton Marina is located at the head of Hammersly Inlet 5 blocks from downtown Shelton with shopping, restaurants, and marine services. The Marina is owned by the Port but managed & maintained by Shelton Yacht Club

GUEST BOAT CAPACITY: ....Appx. 8 boats
SEASON: ....All year
RESERVATION POLICY:.............................None
AMT W/ELECTRICITY: ....All
FUEL DOCK: ....None - closest fuel 14 miles
MARINE REPAIRS: ....Close by
TOILETS: ....Porta-Potty
HOT SHOWERS: ....None
RESTAURANT: ....Close by
PICNIC AREA: ....None
PLAY AREA: ....None
BASIC STORE: ....Close by
ELECTRICITY: ....$2.00 per day
DAILY RATE: ....Appx. .25¢ per foot

GUEST DOCK:.............Appx. 90 ft.
GUEST SLIPS: ....Dock only
WATER: ....Yes
AMPS: ....30 A
PUMP OUT STATION ....Yes
HAUL OUT: ....None
BOAT RAMP:..............................None
LAUNDRY: ....Close by
LOUNGE: ....Close by
POOL:...None
BBQ: ....None
GOLF: ....Close by
OTHER: Shelton Yacht Club offers reciprocal moorage free for first 48 hrs. not including power.

CAUTION! This chartlet not intended for use in navigation.

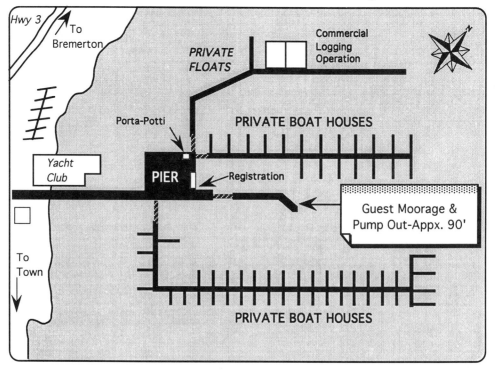

Steilacoom

NAME OF MARINA:	*STEILACOOM MARINA* **RADIO:** None
ADDRESS:	402 First St. Steilacoom, WA 98388
TELEPHONE:	206-582-2600 **MGR:** Shirley Lin Wang

SHORT DESCRIPTION & LOCATION:

47°10.50'-122°35.90' Steilacoom is on the mainland just N. of Ketron Isl. in Nisqually Reach about 9 mi. SSW of Tacoma's Point Defiance. The small size marina is about 1 mi. S. of the ferry landing. Moorage could be subject to adverse weather in the winter.

GUEST BOAT CAPACITY:	Appx. 5-10 boats	**GUEST DOCK:**	Appx. 70 ft.
SEASON:	All year	**GUEST SLIPS:**	Appx. 8
RESERVATION POLICY:	Accepts	**WATER:**	Yes
AMT W/ELECTRICITY:	All	**AMPS:**	20 A
FUEL DOCK:	None	**PUMP OUT STATION**	None
MARINE REPAIRS:	On premises	**HAUL OUT:**	Sm. boat sling
TOILETS:	Yes	**BOAT RAMP:**	None
HOT SHOWERS:	Yes	**LAUNDRY:**	Yes
RESTAURANT:	Close by	**LOUNGE:**	Close by
PICNIC AREA:	Yes	**POOL:**	None
PLAY AREA:	Yes	**BBQ:**	Yes
BASIC STORE:	Yes	**GOLF:**	Close by
ELECTRICITY:	$2.00 per day	**OTHER:**	Fishing pier, wonderful beach park, historic Ft. Steilacoom, several museums, tackle, bait, boat rentals.
DAILY RATE:	Appx. .40¢ per foot		

CAUTION! This chartlet not intended for use in navigation.

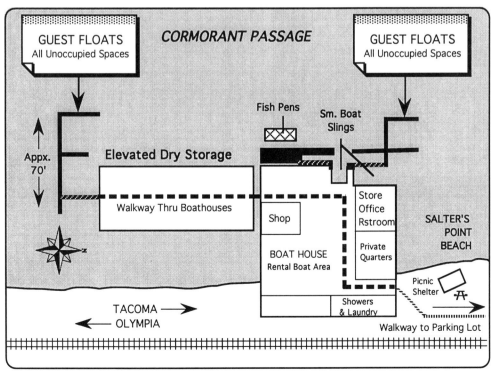

Tacoma

NAME OF MARINA: *BREAKWATER MARINA*   RADIO: None

ADDRESS: 5603 Waterfront Drive   Tacoma,   WA   98407

TELEPHONE: 206-752-6663   MGR: Michael Marchetti

SHORT DESCRIPTION & LOCATION:

47°18.50' - 122°30.80' Located on E. side of ferry terminal at Pt. Defiance in the Tacoma Yacht Club Boat Basin about 4 mi. NW of downtown Tacoma.. The marina has no designated guest moorage but it generally has 10-15 slips available for overnighters.

GUEST BOAT CAPACITY: ....Appx. 10-15 boats	GUEST DOCK: ....None
SEASON: ....All year	GUEST SLIPS: ....Varies
RESERVATION POLICY: ....Accepts	WATER: ....Yes
AMT W/ELECTRICITY: ....All	AMPS: ....20-30 A
FUEL DOCK: ....Gas, Dsl, & LP	PUMP OUT STATION ....None
MARINE REPAIRS: ....On premises	HAUL OUT: ....None
TOILETS: ....Yes	BOAT RAMP: ....Close by
HOT SHOWERS: ....Yes	LAUNDRY: ....None
RESTAURANT: ....Close by	LOUNGE: ....Close by
PICNIC AREA: ....Close by	POOL: ....None
PLAY AREA: ....Close by	BBQ: ....Close by
BASIC STORE: ....Yes	GOLF: ....Close by
ELECTRICITY: ....$ 2.00 per day	OTHER: Tackle & bait,
DAILY RATE: ....Appx. .50¢ per foot	Pt. Defiance park, & zoo
	nearby, pump-out on
	city float close by, bus
	service to city.

NAME OF YACHT CLUB: *TACOMA YACHT CLUB*   **B**

CLUB ADDRESS: 5401 N. Waterfront Dr., Tacoma, WA 98404

CLUB TELEPHONE: 206-752-3555   PERSON IN CHARGE: Fred Swift

LOCATION & SPECIAL NOTES

47°18.50' - 122°30.80' The TYC boat basin is situated at the NW entrance to Commencement Bay at Pt. Defiance about 4 mi NW of downtown Tacoma.. Reciprocal moorage is near the clubhouse and guests must register upon arrival at the clubhouse.

RECIPROCAL BOAT CAPACITY:...Appx 4 boats	RECIPROCAL DOCK: ..Appx. 130'
RECIPROCAL SEASON:..................All year	RECIPROCAL SLIPS: ...Dock only
RESERVATION POLICY: ....None	WATER: ....Yes
TOILETS: ....Yes	AMT W/ELECTRICITY: ....All
HOT SHOWERS:................................Yes	AMPS: ....30 A
RESTAURANT: ....Yes	LOUNGE: ....Yes
DAILY RATE: Electrical service - $2.00 per night ....Moorage - N/C for first 48 hrs.	OTHER: Modern clubhouse with nice restaurant.

NOTE: THIS IS PRIVATE MOORAGE _ONLY_ AVAILABLE TO MEMBERS OF RECIPROCAL YACHT CLUBS! YOUR CLUB _MUST_ HAVE RECIPROCAL PRIVILEGES AND YOU MUST FLY YOUR BURGEE!

Tacoma

CAUTION! This chartlet not intended for use in navigation.

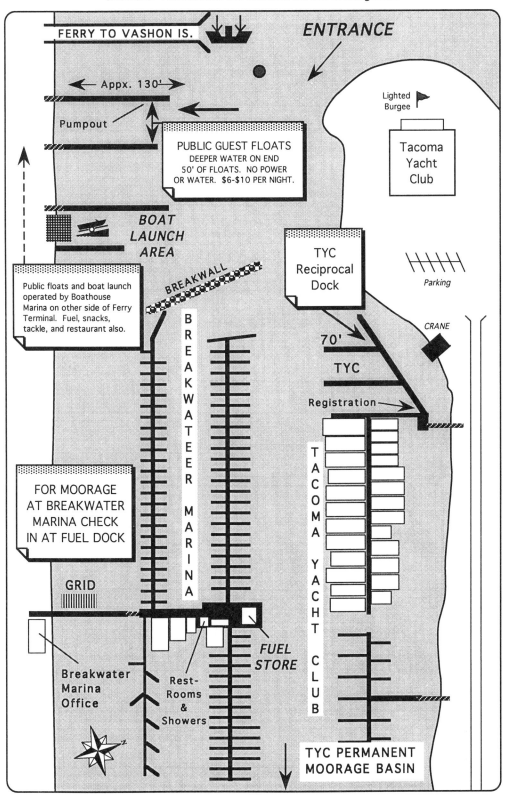

FERRY TO VASHON IS.

ENTRANCE

← Appx. 130' →

Pumpout

Lighted
Burgee

Tacoma
Yacht
Club

PUBLIC GUEST FLOATS
DEEPER WATER ON END
50' OF FLOATS. NO POWER
OR WATER. $6-$10 PER NIGHT.

*BOAT
LAUNCH
AREA*

Public floats and boat launch
operated by Boathouse
Marina on other side of Ferry
Terminal. Fuel, snacks,
tackle, and restaurant also.

BREAKWALL

TYC
Reciprocal
Dock

Parking

70'

CRANE

TYC

Registration →

B R E A K W A T E E R   M A R I N A

FOR MOORAGE
AT BREAKWATER
MARINA CHECK
IN AT FUEL DOCK

T A C O M A   Y A C H T   C L U B

GRID

*FUEL
STORE*

Breakwater
Marina
Office

Rest-
Rooms
&
Showers

**TYC PERMANENT
MOORAGE BASIN**

Tacoma

NAME OF MARINA: *CHINOOK LANDING MARINA*   RADIO: VHF Ch. 79

ADDRESS: 3702 Marine View   Tacoma,   WA 98422

TELEPHONE: 206-627-7676   MGR: Dennis LaPointe

SHORT DESCRIPTION & LOCATION:

47°16.90' - 122°24.20' This new & modern marina is located just inside the entrance of Hylebos Waterway about 2 miles SE of Browns Pt. The lg. guest dock has no power but the slips have full services & non leased or vacant slips are available for overnighters.

GUEST BOAT CAPACITY: ....Appx. 25-30 boats	GUEST DOCK: ....430 ft. plus slips
SEASON: ....All year	GUEST SLIPS: ....Varies
RESERVATION POLICY:...........................Accepts	WATER: ....Yes
AMT W/ELECTRICITY: ....Slips only	AMPS: ....30 A
FUEL DOCK: ....None	PUMP OUT STATION ....Yes
MARINE REPAIRS: ....Close by	HAUL OUT: ....Close by
TOILETS: ....Yes	BOAT RAMP: ....None
HOT SHOWERS: ....Yes	LAUNDRY: ....Yes
RESTAURANT: ....Close by	LOUNGE: ....Close by
PICNIC AREA: ....None	POOL:......................................None
PLAY AREA: ....None	BBQ: ....None
BASIC STORE: ....Yes	GOLF: ....Close by
ELECTRICITY: ....$5.00 per day	OTHER: Chandlery, 24 hour
DAILY RATE: ....Appx. .75¢ per foot	security, close to some
	marine services.

CAUTION! This chartlet not intended for use in navigation.

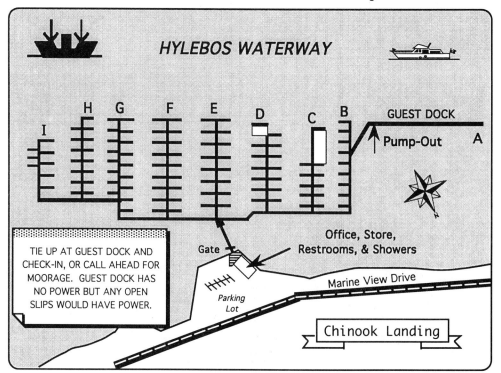

Tacoma

NAME OF YACHT CLUB: *CORINTHIAN YACHT CLUB OF TACOMA*

ADDRESS: 5624 Marine View Dr.   Tacoma,   WA   98422

TELEPHONE: 206-854-1476   PERSON IN CHARGE: Doug McLeod

SHORT DESCRIPTION & LOCATION:

47°17.70' - 122°25.00' Reciprocal moorage located within Tyee Marina on N. side of Commencement Bay about 1 mile SE of Browns Pt. Call above # or Ginny Leach at 206-862-6360 for available slips & combination. Also, moorage reservation may be made 24 hrs. in advance with Tyee Marina personnel Tues-Sat. (business hours) Tel: 206-383-5321.

RECIPROCAL BOAT CAPACITY .....Appx 2 boats	RECIPROCAL DOCK: ....Slips only
SEASON: ....All year	RECIPROCAL SLIPS: ....Varies
RESERVATION POLICY:........................Mandatory	WATER: ....Yes
TOILETS: ....Yes	AMT W/ELECTRICITY: ....All
HOT SHOWERS: ....Yes	AMPS: ....20 A
RESTAURANT:...One mile	LOUNGE: ....Close by
DAILY RATE: ....No Charge for 48 hours	OTHER: Puget Sound Sailing Institute next door.

NOTE: *THIS IS PRIVATE MOORAGE AND ONLY AVAILABLE TO MEMBERS OF RECIPROCAL YACHT CLUBS. YOUR CLUB MUST HAVE RECIPROCAL PRIVILEGES AND YOU MUST FLY YOUR BURGEE.*

CAUTION! This chartlet not intended for use in navigation.

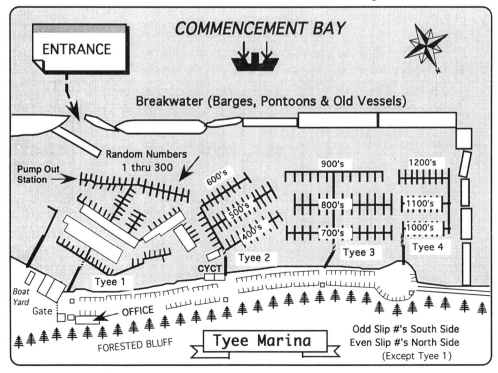

Tacoma

NAME OF YACHT CLUB: *DAY ISLAND YACHT CLUB*

ADDRESS: 2120 91st Ave W.   Tacoma,   WA   98466

TELEPHONE: 206-565-5794   PERSON IN CHARGE: Caretakers

SHORT DESCRIPTION & LOCATION:

47°14.40' - 122°33.50' DIYC lies in a lagoon w/several private marinas about 1 mi. S. of the Tacoma Narrows Bridge on the Tacoma side of the Narrows. Entry to lagoon is only possible at specific tide levels. Call ahead for reciprocal moorage and instructions.

RECIPROCAL BOAT CAPACITY ...Apx 4-6 boats

SEASON: ....All year

RESERVATION POLICY:....................None

TOILETS: ....Yes

HOT SHOWERS: ....Yes

RESTAURANT:.......................................None

DAILY RATE: ....No Charge
                      72 Hour Limit

RECIPROCAL DOCK: ..Appx. 100'

RECIPROCAL SLIPS: ...Dock only

WATER: ....Yes

AMT W/ELECTRICITY: ....All

AMPS: ....30 A

LOUNGE: ....None

OTHER: Register w/caretakers
                upon arrival. Marine
                supplies close by.

NOTE: THIS IS PRIVATE MOORAGE AND ONLY AVAILABLE TO MEMBERS OF RECIPROCAL YACHT CLUBS. YOUR CLUB MUST HAVE RECIPROCAL PRIVILEGES AND YOU MUST FLY YOUR BURGEE.

CAUTION! This chartlet not intended for use in navigation.

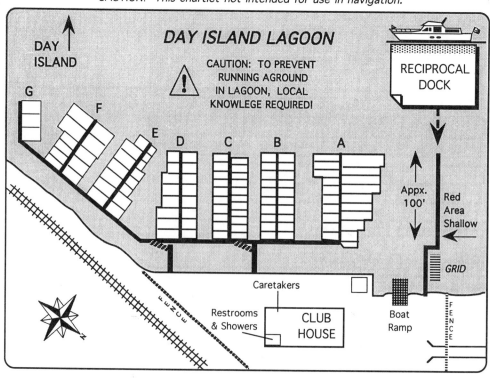

Tacoma

NAME OF MARINA: *JOHNNY'S DOCK RESTAURANT*   RADIO: None

ADDRESS: 1900 East D Street   Tacoma   WA 98421

TELEPHONE: 206-627-3186   MGR: Dave Bingham

SHORT DESCRIPTION & LOCATION:

48°14.80' - 122°25.80' Located on east side of downtown Tacoma's Thea Foss City Waterway about 1/2 mile south of bridge. Basic tie up float free of charge to restaurant patrons. No power or water. Restaurant personnel issues key to gate.

GUEST BOAT CAPACITY: ....Appx. 2-4 boats

SEASON: ....All year

RESERVATION POLICY: ....None

AMT W/ELECTRICITY: ....None

FUEL DOCK: ....Close by

MARINE REPAIRS: ....Close by

TOILETS: ....At restaurant

HOT SHOWERS: ....None

RESTAURANT: ....Yes

PICNIC AREA: ....None

PLAY AREA: ....None

BASIC STORE: ....Close by

ELECTRICITY: ....None

DAILY RATE: .....No charge to restaurant patrons

GUEST DOCK: ....Appx. 60 ft.

GUEST SLIPS: ....None

WATER: ....No

AMPS: ....None

PUMP OUT STATION ....None

HAUL OUT: ....None

BOAT RAMP: ....None

LAUNDRY: ....None

LOUNGE: ....Yes

POOL: ....None

BBQ: ....None

GOLF: ....Close by

OTHER: Sunday brunch, lunch and dinner daily, private rooms for groups.

CAUTION! This chartlet not intended for use in navigation.

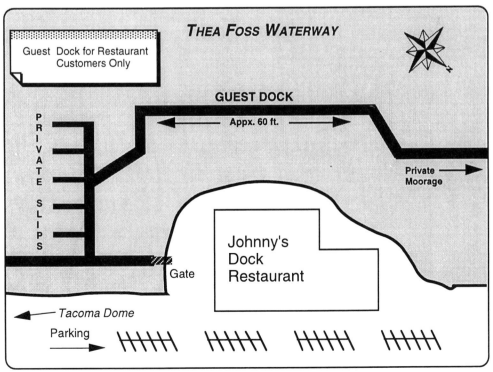

Tacoma

NAME OF PARK: *OLD TOWN DOCK, Metro Park District of Tacoma*
ADDRESS: 4702 S. 19th   Tacoma, WA   98405
TELEPHONE: 206-591-5325   **MGR:** Skip Larsen, Boathouse Marina

SHORT DESCRIPTION & LOCATION:

47°15.60' - 122°27.80' Located on SW shore of Commencement Bay about 2 miles NW of downtown Tacoma in Old Town Historic District. Guest moorage floats are situated behind the breakwater as well as one large float on N. side of Pier.

GUEST BOAT CAPACITY: ....Appx. 12 boats	GUEST DOCK: 2 lg. floats, 8 slips
SEASON: ....All year	MOORING BUOYS: 2
AMT W/ELECTRICITY: ....None	WATER: ....None
TOILETS: ....Yes	PAY PHONES: ....Yes
HOT SHOWERS: ....None	BOAT RAMP: ....None
PICNIC AREA: ....Close by	PICNIC SHELTER: ....None
PLAY AREA: ....Close by	BBQ: ....Close by
BASIC STORE: ....Close by	PUMP OUT STATION: ......None
DAILY RATE: ....$6 - $10 per night	OTHER: Fresh fish market, bus service, close to several restaurants on Ruston Way, park like setting.
72 Hour Limit	

CAUTION! This chartlet not intended for use in navigation.

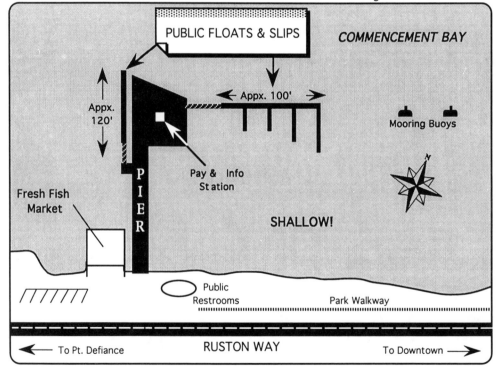

Tacoma

NAME OF MARINA: *15TH STREET DOCK,* *Tacoma Fire Dept.* RADIO: None
ADDRESS: 901 S. Fawcett   Tacoma   WA 98402
TELEPHONE: 206-591-5740   MGR: Harbormaster

SHORT DESCRIPTION & LOCATION:

47°14.90' - 122°25.80' This 240' public dock is situated on W. side of Thea Foss (City) Waterway 1/2 mi. S. of the 11th St. Bridge. The dock is in an industrial area of questionable security but within easy walking distance of downtown Tacoma attractions.

GUEST BOAT CAPACITY:.........Appx. 8-10 boats	GUEST DOCK:.....................240 ft.
SEASON: ....All year	GUEST SLIPS:.........................None
RESERVATION POLICY:...............................None	WATER: ....None
AMT W/ELECTRICITY: ....None	AMPS: ....None
FUEL DOCK: ....None	PUMP OUT STATION ....None
MARINE REPAIRS: ....Close by	HAUL OUT:...............................None
TOILETS: ....None	BOAT RAMP:.........................None
HOT SHOWERS: ....None	LAUNDRY: ....None
RESTAURANT: ....Close by	LOUNGE: ....Close by
PICNIC AREA: ....None	POOL:.....................................None
PLAY AREA: ....None	BBQ: ....None
BASIC STORE: ....None	GOLF: ....Close by
ELECTRICITY:......................................None	OTHER: NOTE: Official policy
DAILY RATE: ....No Charge - 24 Hour Limit	states no boats over 30'
Call harbormaster for approval for	without approval of the
longer stays if desired.	harbormaster at above
	number.

CAUTION! This chartlet not intended for use in navigation.

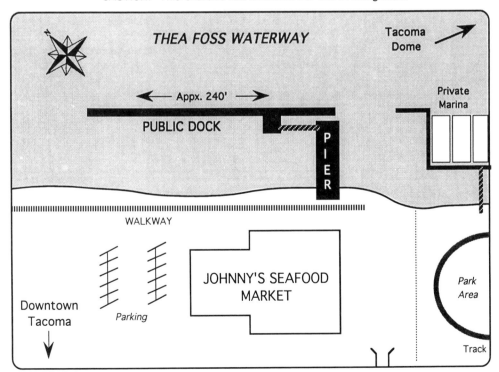

Tacoma

NAME OF MARINA: **TOTEM MARINA**   RADIO: None

ADDRESS: 821 Dock St.   Tacoma,   WA 98402

TELEPHONE: 206-272-4404   MGR: Eva Palka

SHORT DESCRIPTION & LOCATION:

47°15.35' - 122°26.03' This large 16 year old marina is located in downtown Tacoma on the W. side of Thea Foss (City) Waterway just before the 11th Street Bridge. The marina is walking distance to attractions and public services.

GUEST BOAT CAPACITY: ....Appx. 20 boats	GUEST DOCK:(2)....400' + slips
SEASON: ....All year	GUEST SLIPS: ....Appx. 12
RESERVATION POLICY: ....None	WATER:.......................................Yes
AMT W/ELECTRICITY: ....All	AMPS: ....20-30 A
FUEL DOCK: ....None	PUMP OUT STATION ....Yes
MARINE REPAIRS: ....Close by	HAUL OUT: ....Yes
TOILETS: ....Yes	BOAT RAMP:...........Sm. boat sling
HOT SHOWERS: ....Yes	LAUNDRY: ....Yes
RESTAURANT:...................................Close by	LOUNGE: ....Close by
PICNIC AREA: ....Yes	POOL:.......................................None
PLAY AREA: ....None	BBQ: ....None
BASIC STORE: ....Yes	GOLF: ....Close by
ELECTRICITY: ....$2-$5 per day	OTHER: Bait & tackle on
DAILY RATE: ....Appx. .50¢ per foot	premises. Marine store,
	parks, museum &
	shopping close by,

NAME OF YACHT CLUB: **TOTEM YACHT CLUB**

CLUB ADDRESS: 5045 N. Highland, Tacoma, WA 98407

CLUB TELEPHONE: 206-759-9062   PERSON IN CHARGE: Yeoman

LOCATION & SPECIAL NOTES

Totem Yacht Club provides moorage to members of reciprocal yacht clubs at the Totem Marina. The moorage is located within the general marina guest dock area on Piers 4 & 5. Please register in the marina office upon arrival.

RECIPROCAL BOAT CAPACITY:............Appx. 10	RECIPROCAL DOCK: ..Appx. 200'
RECIPROCAL SEASON:................................All year	RECIPROCAL SLIPS: ...Dock only
RESERVATION POLICY: ....None	WATER: ....Yes
TOILETS: ....At Marina	AMT W/ELECTRICITY: ....All
HOT SHOWERS: ....At Marina	AMPS: ....20-30 A
RESTAURANT: ....Close by	LOUNGE: ....Close by
DAILY RATE: ....$2-$5 daily charge for electricity	OTHER: ....Same as marina listing
Maximum stay is three days.	

NOTE: *THIS IS PRIVATE MOORAGE ONLY AVAILABLE TO MEMBERS OF RECIPROCAL YACHT CLUBS! YOUR CLUB MUST HAVE RECIPROCAL PRIVILEGES AND YOU MUST FLY YOUR BURGEE!*

Tacoma

CAUTION! This chartlet not intended for use in navigation.

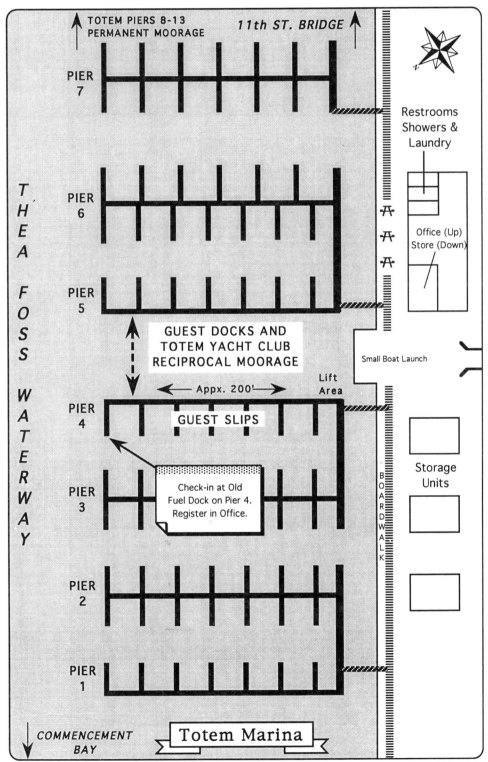

TOTEM PIERS 8-13
PERMANENT MOORAGE

11th ST. BRIDGE

PIER 7

PIER 6

PIER 5

Restrooms
Showers &
Laundry

Office (Up)
Store (Down)

GUEST DOCKS AND
TOTEM YACHT CLUB
RECIPROCAL MOORAGE

Small Boat Launch

Appx. 200'

Lift Area

PIER 4

GUEST SLIPS

Check-in at Old
Fuel Dock on Pier 4.
Register in Office.

PIER 3

Storage Units

BOARDWALK

PIER 2

PIER 1

THE A FOSS WATERWAY

COMMENCEMENT BAY

Totem Marina

Tacoma

NAME OF YACHT CLUB: *VIKING YACHT CLUB*

ADDRESS: P.O. Box 641 Tacoma, WA 98401

TELEPHONE: PERSON IN CHARGE: Yeoman

SHORT DESCRIPTION & LOCATION:

V.Y.C. offers up to 2 nights reciprocal moorage located at the **Totem Marina** Guest Dock. Visiting reciprocal yacht club members are requested to pay the moorage charges to the harbormaster & mail the moorage receipt to Viking for reimbursement.

RECIPROCAL BOAT CAPACITY ....Varies

SEASON: ....All year

RESERVATION POLICY:....................................None

TOILETS: ....At Totem Marina

HOT SHOWERS: ....At Totem Marina

RESTAURANT: ....Close by

DAILY RATE: No Charge for two nights moorage

RECIPROCAL DOCK: ....At marina

RECIPROCAL SLIPS: ...At marina

WATER: ....Yes

AMT W/ELECTRICITY: ....All

AMPS: ....20-30 A

LOUNGE: ....Close by

OTHER: Services same as Totem Marina listing on Page 46 & 47

NOTE: THIS IS PRIVATE MOORAGE AND ONLY AVAILABLE TO MEMBERS OF RECIPROCAL YACHT CLUBS. YOUR CLUB MUST HAVE RECIPROCAL PRIVILEGES AND YOU MUST FLY YOUR BURGEE.

SEE DATA & CHARTLET ON PAGE: 46 & 47

NOTES

Vashon Island

NAME OF PARK: *DOCKTON COUNTY PARK (King County)*
ADDRESS: 2500 Dock Streen   Dockton, WA   98070
TELEPHONE: 206-463-2947   MGR: N. Bush

SHORT DESCRIPTION & LOCATION:

47°22.4' - 122°27.4'   Actually located on Maury Is. in a bight on the E. side of Quartermaster Harbor about 2.5 miles N. of the Harbor entrance. The modern and well kept floats and facilities make this an excellent destination for a family or group cruise.

GUEST BOAT CAPACITY: ....Appx. 60 boats

SEASON: ....All year

AMT W/ELECTRICITY: ....None

TOILETS: ....Yes

HOT SHOWERS: ....Yes

PICNIC AREA: ....Yes

PLAY AREA: ....Yes

BASIC STORE: ....None

DAILY RATE: ....$8.00 Under 26'
.............................$11.00 26' & over
No Charge from Oct. 1 thru Apr.30

GUEST DOCK: ....Appx. 300 ft.

MOORING BUOYS: ....None

WATER: ....None

PAY PHONES: ....None

BOAT RAMP: ....Yes

PICNIC SHELTER: ....Yes

BBQ: ....Yes

PUMP OUT STATION: ....Yes

OTHER: Excellent anchorage,
cooking shelters,
unguarded beach,
kayaking, hiking trails.

CAUTION! This chartlet not intended for use in navigation.

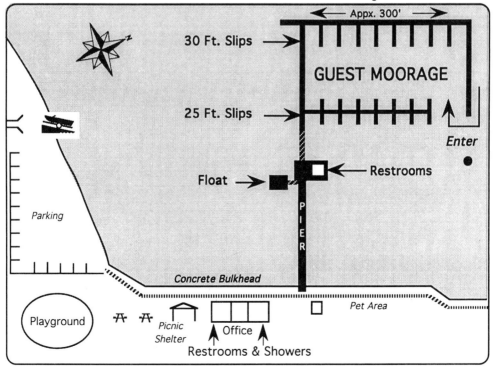

Vashon Island

NAME OF YACHT CLUB: *QUARTERMASTER YACHT CLUB*

ADDRESS: P.O. Box 13376   Vashon Island   WA   98013

TELEPHONE: 206-463-3309   PERSON IN CHARGE: Reciprocal Mgr.

SHORT DESCRIPTION & LOCATION:

47°23.60' - 122°27.80' The club is located on the S.W. side of inner Quartermaster Harbor. Reciprocal moorage is on the E. side of the float nearest to shore & approached from the port side of the facility when entering the club area. Use caution at low tide.

RECIPROCAL BOAT CAPACITY............Appx. 6-8

SEASON: ....All year

RESERVATION POLICY:...................................None

TOILETS: ....Yes

HOT SHOWERS: ....None

RESTAURANT: ....Close by

RECIPROCAL DOCK: ..Appx. 125'

RECIPROCAL SLIPS: ....Varies

WATER: ....Yes

AMT W/ELECTRICITY: ....All

AMPS: ....30 A

LOUNGE: ....Close by

DAILY RATE: Free for 48 hours- Add'l days- 20¢ per ft, - max. 4 days per month. Elect. $2-$4 day based on size.

OTHER: Rafting permitted, walking distance to store and restaurant in Burton.

NOTE: THIS IS PRIVATE MOORAGE AND ONLY AVAILABLE TO MEMBERS OF RECIPROCAL YACHT CLUBS. YOUR CLUB MUST HAVE RECIPROCAL PRIVILEGES AND YOU MUST FLY YOUR BURGEE.

CAUTION! This chartlet not intended for use in navigation.

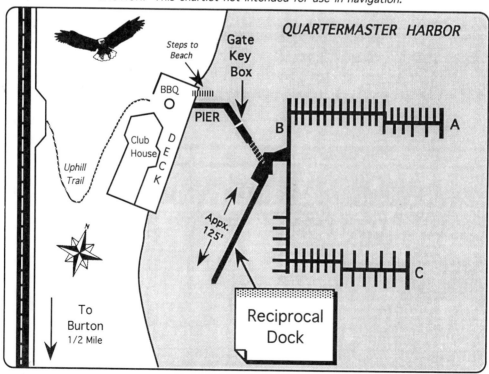

C H A P T E R

2

NORTH
PUGET SOUND

Bainbridge Island

NAME OF PARK: *EAGLE HARBOR WATERFRONT PARK*

ADDRESS: 625 Winslow Way E.   Bainbridge Island WA   98110

TELEPHONE: 206-842-2545   **MGR:** Public Works Director

SHORT DESCRIPTION & LOCATION:

47°37.00' - 122°31.00' Eagle Harbor indents the E. shore of Bainbridge Is., opposite Elliott Bay. The park float is located just W. of the State Ferry Shipyard in a typical park setting that is convenient to supermarket, shops, and restaurants in town of Winslow.

GUEST BOAT CAPACITY: ....Appx. 8-10 boats	**GUEST DOCK:** ....Appx. 225 ft.
SEASON: ....All year	**MOORING BUOYS:** ....None
AMT W/ELECTRICITY: ....None	**WATER:** ....None
TOILETS: ....Yes	**PAY PHONES:** ....Yes
HOT SHOWERS: ....None	**BOAT RAMP:** ....Yes
PICNIC AREA: ....Yes	**PICNIC SHELTER:** ....Yes
PLAY AREA: ....Yes	**BBQ:** ....None
BASIC STORE: ....Close by	**PUMP OUT STATION:** ....Yes
DAILY RATE: .... Appx. .25¢ per foot	**OTHER:** Great play area for kids,
.....................................48 Hour Limit	tennis courts, rafting OK - maximum 2 deep, walking distance to Seattle ferry.

CAUTION! This chartlet not intended for use in navigation.

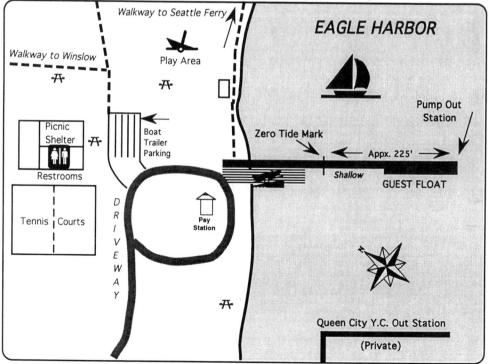

Bainbridge Island

NAME OF YACHT CLUB: *PORT MADISON YACHT CLUB*

ADDRESS: P.O. Box 10002   Bainbridge Island,   WA   98110

TELEPHONE: 206-842-2102/8826   PERSON IN CHARGE: Rear Commodore

SHORT DESCRIPTION & LOCATION:

47°41.80' - 122°32.30' Located on N end of Bainbridge Is. inside of Port Madison harbor immediately before (NE of) tug boat dock upon entering harbor. The guest float is inside of the large boat moorage. Please register in the clubhouse.

The electrical outlets are not adequate for shore power.

RECIPROCAL BOAT CAPACITY ....Appx. 2 or 3	RECIPROCAL DOCK: ....Appx. 75'
SEASON: ....All year	RECIPROCAL SLIPS: ...Dock only
RESERVATION POLICY:.......................None	WATER: ....Yes
TOILETS: ....Yes	AMT W/ELECTRICITY: ....None
HOT SHOWERS: ....None	AMPS: ....None
RESTAURANT:..None	LOUNGE: ....None
DAILY RATE: ....No Charge for 48 hours.	OTHER: Closest services are Rolling Bay 4 miles & Winslow 8 miles.

NOTE: THIS IS PRIVATE MOORAGE AND ONLY AVAILABLE TO MEMBERS OF RECIPROCAL YACHT CLUBS. YOUR CLUB MUST HAVE RECIPROCAL PRIVILEGES AND YOU MUST FLY YOUR BURGEE.

CAUTION! This chartlet not intended for use in navigation.

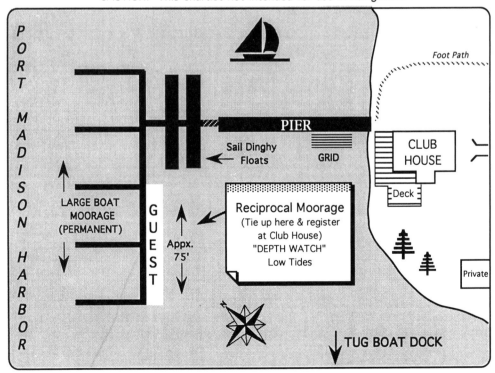

Bainbridge Island

NAME OF MARINA: **WINSLOW WHARF MARINA**   RADIO: VHF Ch. 09
ADDRESS: P.O. Box 10297   Bainbridge Island   WA 98110
TELEPHONE: 206-842-4202   MGR: David LaFave

SHORT DESCRIPTION & LOCATION:

47°37.40' - 122°31.20' Located on the N. side of Eagle Harbor which indents on the E. shore of Bainbridge Is. appx. 1/2 mile W. of the State Ferry Shipyard. Guest moorage is available by using open slips of condo moorage tenants. Best to call ahead for slip.

GUEST BOAT CAPACITY: ....Varies- up to 15	GUEST DOCK: ....Slips only
SEASON: ....All year	GUEST SLIPS: ....Varies
RESERVATION POLICY: ....Accepts	WATER: ....Yes
AMT W/ELECTRICITY: ....All	AMPS: ....20-30 A
FUEL DOCK: ....None	PUMP OUT STATION ....None
MARINE REPAIRS: ....Close by	HAUL OUT: ....Close by
TOILETS: ....Yes	BOAT RAMP: ....Close by
HOT SHOWERS: ....Yes	LAUNDRY: ....Yes
RESTAURANT: ....Yes	LOUNGE: ....Close by
PICNIC AREA: ....Yes	POOL: ....None
PLAY AREA: ....None	BBQ: ....None
BASIC STORE: ....Close by	GOLF: ....Close by
ELECTRICITY: ....Included in moorage	OTHER: Walking distance to
DAILY RATE: ....26' & under = $14.00	shopping center, shops,
....37'-32'=$17.00	& restaurants, marine
....33'-45'=$21.00	chandlery, close to
....Over 46' = .50¢/ft.	Seattle ferry.

NAME OF YACHT CLUB: *EAGLE HARBOR YACHT CLUB*   B

CLUB ADDRESS: P.O. Box 10905, Bainbridge Island, WA 98110

CLUB TELEPHONE: PERSON IN CHARGE: Recip. Chairman

LOCATION & SPECIAL NOTES

EHYC offers 1 slip per club per night (max. 3 slips or 100 ft.) at the Winslow Wharf Marina for members in good standing of reciprocal clubs. Check in with the Winslow Wharf harbormaster upon arrival although best to call ahead.

RECIPROCAL BOAT CAPACITY:..Appx. 3 boats	RECIPROCAL DOCK: ....Slips only
RECIPROCAL SEASON:................................All year	RECIPROCAL SLIPS: 3
RESERVATION POLICY: ....None	WATER: ....Yes
TOILETS: ....At Marina	AMT W/ELECTRICITY: ....All
HOT SHOWERS: ....At Marina	AMPS: ....20-30 A
RESTAURANT: ....Close by	LOUNGE: ....Close by
DAILY RATE: ....No charge	OTHER: ....Same as marina listing

NOTE: THIS IS PRIVATE MOORAGE _ONLY_ AVAILABLE TO MEMBERS OF RECIPROCAL YACHT CLUBS! YOUR CLUB _MUST_ HAVE RECIPROCAL PRIVILEGES AND YOU MUST FLY YOUR BURGEE!

Bainbridge Island

CAUTION! This chartlet not intended for use in navigation.

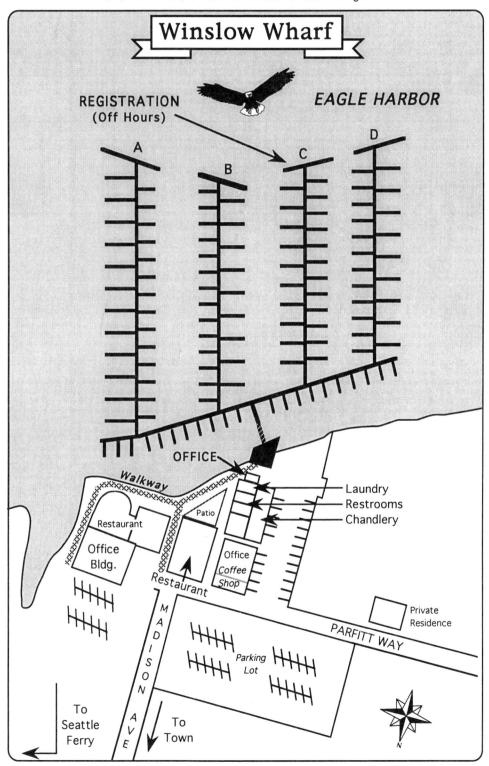

Winslow Wharf

REGISTRATION
(Off Hours)

EAGLE HARBOR

A

B

C

D

OFFICE

Walkway

Restaurant

Patio

Office
Bldg.

Office
Coffee
Shop

Restaurant

Laundry
Restrooms
Chandlery

Private
Residence

M
A
D
I
S
O
N

A
V
E

PARFITT WAY

*Parking
Lot*

To
Seattle
Ferry

To
Town

N

NOTES

Bellevue

NAME OF YACHT CLUB: *MEYDENBAUER BAY YACHT CLUB*

ADDRESS: P.O. Box 863   Bellevue   WA   98009

TELEPHONE: 206-454-8880   PERSON IN CHARGE: Club Manager

SHORT DESCRIPTION & LOCATION:

47°36.50'-122°12.40' MBYC invites reciprocal club members to use their moorage at <u>far</u> E. end of Meydenbauer Bay on Lake Washington. The reciprocal moorage is along the ends of their 3 piers, except where posted. Check in w/club manager upon arriving.

RECIPROCAL BOAT CAPACITY.............Appx 4-6

SEASON: ....All year

RESERVATION POLICY:.........................Accepts

TOILETS: ....Yes

HOT SHOWERS: ....None

RESTAURANT:...................................Close by

DAILY RATE: ....$2.00 per day for power.
48 Hour Limit. After 48 hours
moorage is $10.00 per day.

RECIPROCAL DOCK: 3-Appx. 60'

RECIPROCAL SLIPS: ....3 Docks

WATER: ....Yes

AMT W/ELECTRICITY: ....All

AMPS: ....30 A

LOUNGE: ....Close by

OTHER: Restaurants, shops, &
Bellevue Square close by.
Rafting OK up to 4 boats.

<u>NOTE:</u> THIS IS PRIVATE MOORAGE AND ONLY AVAILABLE TO MEMBERS OF RECIPROCAL YACHT CLUBS. YOUR CLUB <u>MUST</u> HAVE RECIPROCAL PRIVILEGES AND YOU MUST FLY YOUR BURGEE.

CAUTION! This chartlet not intended for use in navigation.

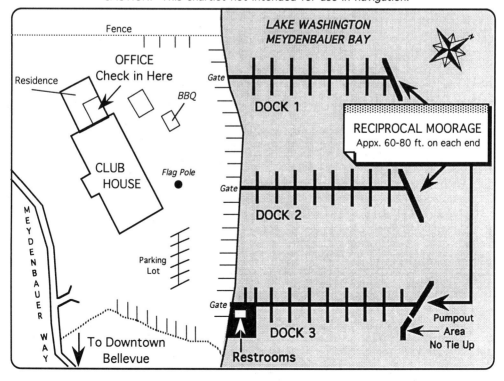

Bellevue

NAME OF YACHT CLUB: *NEWPORT YACHT CLUB*

ADDRESS: 81 Skagit Key   Bellevue,   WA   98006

TELEPHONE: 206-747-3291   **PERSON IN CHARGE:** Club Manager

SHORT DESCRIPTION & LOCATION:

47°34.50' - 122°11.30' NYC is located on the east shore, second marina south of the East Channel I-90 Bridge on Lake Washington. Upon arriving, tie up & check in with the Club Manager during working hours to obtain a slip and a gate key for dock access.

RECIPROCAL BOAT CAPACITY..........Appx. 6-10	RECIPROCAL DOCK: ....Slips only
SEASON: ....All year	RECIPROCAL SLIPS: ....Varies
RESERVATION POLICY:............................Accepts	WATER: ....Yes
TOILETS: ....Yes-during office hours	AMT W/ELECTRICITY: ....All
HOT SHOWERS: ....Yes-during office hours	AMPS: ....20-30 A
RESTAURANT: ....None	LOUNGE: ....None
DAILY RATE: ....Power - $2.00	OTHER: Quiet neighborhood location, close to Factoria Mall, pool, tennis

NOTE: THIS IS PRIVATE MOORAGE AND ONLY AVAILABLE TO MEMBERS OF RECIPROCAL YACHT CLUBS. YOUR CLUB MUST HAVE RECIPROCAL PRIVILEGES AND YOU MUST FLY YOUR BURGEE.

CAUTION! This chartlet not intended for use in navigation.

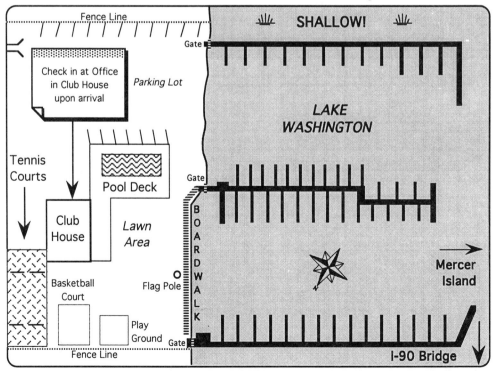

Blake Island

NAME OF PARK: *BLAKE ISLAND STATE MARINE PARK*

ADDRESS: P.O. Box 277   Manchester, WA   98353

TELEPHONE: 360-731-0770   MGR: Karen Patrick

SHORT DESCRIPTION & LOCATION:

47°32.75' - 122°28.50' Located 2 miles S. of Bainbridge Is. & 5 miles W. of Seattle, this 476 acre island park offers serene beauty & wildlife in the heart of Puget Sound. Island is densely wooded & only accessible by boat. *Tillicum Village open summer only.*

GUEST BOAT CAPACITY: ....Appx. 25 boats

SEASON: ....All year

AMT W/ELECTRICITY: ....None

TOILETS: ....Yes

HOT SHOWERS: ....Yes

PICNIC AREA: ....Yes

PLAY AREA: ....Yes

BASIC STORE: Snack bar/gift shop-summer only

DAILY RATE: Mooring Buoys................$5.00/night
Boats under 26 ft..........$8.00/night
Boats 26 ft. & Over.....$11.00/night
Subject to Change in 1997

GUEST DOCK: 3 Ea. - 100' floats

MOORING BUOYS: 22

WATER: ....Yes

PAY PHONES: ....None

BOAT RAMP: ....None

PICNIC SHELTER: ....Yes

BBQ: ....Yes

PUMP OUT STATION: ....Yes

OTHER: Beachcombing, camp-sites, hiking trails, Tillicum Village salmon dinner & auth. Indian stage show.

CAUTION! This chartlet not intended for use in navigation.

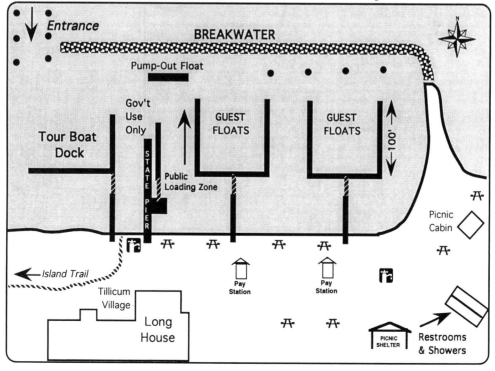

Bremerton

NAME OF YACHT CLUB: *BREMERTON YACHT CLUB*

ADDRESS: 2700 Yacht Haven Wy Bremerton, WA 98312

TELEPHONE: 206-479-2662 PERSON IN CHARGE: Caretakers

SHORT DESCRIPTION & LOCATION:

47°35.30' - 122°39.80' BYC moorage is located in Phinny Bay on the S. side of Port Washington Narrows. Register w/caretakers at clubhouse on Wed. thru Sun. (Mon. & Tue. contact any Bridge Officer-Info at gate). Current recip. Y.C. membership card required.

RECIPROCAL BOAT CAPACITY............Appx. 4-5	RECIPROCAL DOCK: ..Appx. 165'
SEASON: ....All year	RECIPROCAL SLIPS: ....Varies
RESERVATION POLICY:....................................None	WATER: ....Yes
TOILETS: ....Yes	AMT W/ELECTRICITY: ....All
HOT SHOWERS: ....Yes	AMPS: ....1 @30 A/ 4 @20 A
RESTAURANT: ....None	LOUNGE: ....None

DAILY RATE: 1st 72 hrs complimentary moorage
Add'l days - $5 each day,
Electricity - $1.00 every day.

OTHER: Coin laundry, Ice.
Security gate requires
$5.00 key deposit.

NOTE: THIS IS PRIVATE MOORAGE AND ONLY AVAILABLE TO MEMBERS OF RECIPROCAL YACHT CLUBS. YOUR CLUB MUST HAVE RECIPROCAL PRIVILEGES AND YOU MUST FLY YOUR BURGEE.

CAUTION! This chartlet not intended for use in navigation.

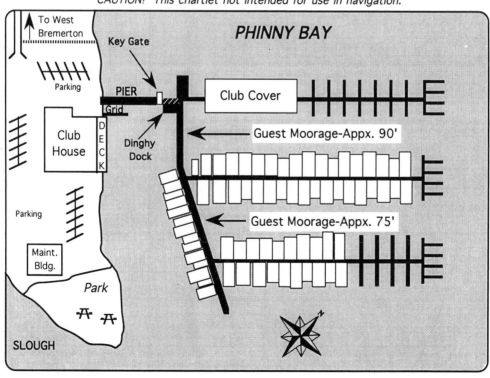

Bremerton

NAME OF PARK: *ILLAHEE STATE PARK*

ADDRESS: 3540 Bahia Vista N.E.   Bremerton, WA   98310

TELEPHONE: 360-478-6460   MGR: Norm Rockett

SHORT DESCRIPTION & LOCATION:

47°36.10'-122°35.50' Located in E. Bremerton on the W. shore of Port Orchard appx. 4 mi. S of Battle Pt. & 1 mi S of sm. town of Illahee. The 75 acre park contains park facilities in the wooded upland portion with a switchback road to the waterfront area.

GUEST BOAT CAPACITY: ....Appx. 4-6 boats	GUEST DOCK: ....Appx. 125 ft.
SEASON: ....All year	MOORING BUOYS: 5
AMT W/ELECTRICITY: ....None	WATER: ....Yes
TOILETS: ....Yes	PAY PHONES: ....Yes
HOT SHOWERS: ....Yes	BOAT RAMP: ....Yes
PICNIC AREA: ....Yes	PICNIC SHELTER: ....Yes
PLAY AREA: ....Yes	BBQ: ....Yes
BASIC STORE: ....None	PUMP OUT STATION: ......None

DAILY RATE: Mooring Buoys.................$5.00/night
Boats under 26 ft..........$8.00/night
Boats 26 ft. & Over.....$11.00/night
Subject to Change in 1997

OTHER: Campsites, fishing pier, hiking trails, horseshoes, baseball, swimming, beachcombing.

CAUTION! This chartlet not intended for use in navigation.

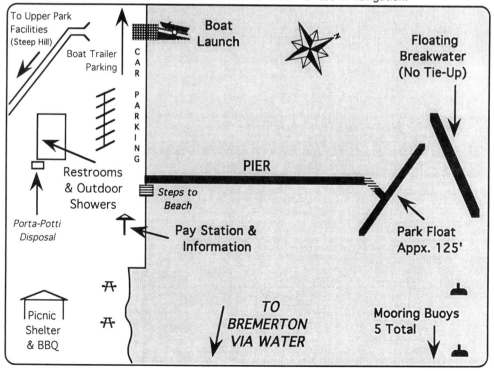

Bremerton

NAME OF MARINA: *THE BREMERTON MARINA*   **RADIO:** VHF Ch. 16

ADDRESS: 8850 SW State Hwy 3   Port Orchard,   WA 98366

TELEPHONE: 360-373-1035   **MGR:** Gene Baker

SHORT DESCRIPTION & LOCATION:

47°33.90' - 122°37.20' Located on N. side of Sinclair Inlet, N. of the ferry dock in downtown Bremerton adjacent to USS Turner Joy DD-951 floating museum. The new security protected facility is within walking distance to many shops & attractions.

GUEST BOAT CAPACITY: ....Appx. 55-60 boats	GUEST DOCK: ...Over 300' + slips
SEASON: ....All year	GUEST SLIPS: ....Appx. 45
RESERVATION POLICY: ....Accepts	WATER: ....Yes
AMT W/ELECTRICITY: ....All	AMPS: ....30 A
FUEL DOCK: ....Close by	PUMP OUT STATION ....Yes
MARINE REPAIRS: ....Close by	HAUL OUT: ....None
TOILETS: ....Yes	BOAT RAMP: ....None
HOT SHOWERS: ....Yes	LAUNDRY: ....Yes
RESTAURANT: ....Close by	LOUNGE: ....Close by
PICNIC AREA: ....Yes	POOL: ....None
PLAY AREA: ....None	BBQ: ....None
BASIC STORE: ....Close by	GOLF: ....Close by
ELECTRICITY: ....$ 2.30 per day	OTHER: Convenient to art galleries, downtown services, two Naval Museums & Ship's Store on boardwalk.
DAILY RATE: ....30¢ per foot	

NAME OF YACHT CLUB: *BREMERTON BOATING CLUB*   **B**

CLUB ADDRESS: P.O. Box 2003, Bremerton, WA 98310

CLUB TELEPHONE: **PERSON IN CHARGE:**   Secretary

LOCATION & SPECIAL NOTES

BBC offers reciprocal moorage in the Bremerton Marina. Three slips are provided in the general marina for recip. members. No more than 2 boats from same club at one time are permitted and there is a monthly limit of 10 reciprocal boats. 24 Hour reciprocal limit.

RECIPROCAL BOAT CAPACITY:............. 3 Boats	RECIPROCAL DOCK: ....Slips
RECIPROCAL SEASON:................................All year	RECIPROCAL SLIPS: .....3 Or less
RESERVATION POLICY: ....None	WATER: ....Yes
TOILETS: ....At Marina	AMT W/ELECTRICITY: ....All
HOT SHOWERS:..............................At Marina	AMPS: ....20-30 A
RESTAURANT: ....Close by	LOUNGE: ....Close by
DAILY RATE: ......$2.30 per day electricity charge	OTHER: ....Same as marina listing

NOTE: THIS IS PRIVATE MOORAGE *ONLY* AVAILABLE TO MEMBERS OF RECIPROCAL YACHT CLUBS! YOUR CLUB *MUST* HAVE RECIPROCAL PRIVILEGES AND YOU MUST FLY YOUR BURGEE!

CAUTION! This chartlet not intended for use in navigation.

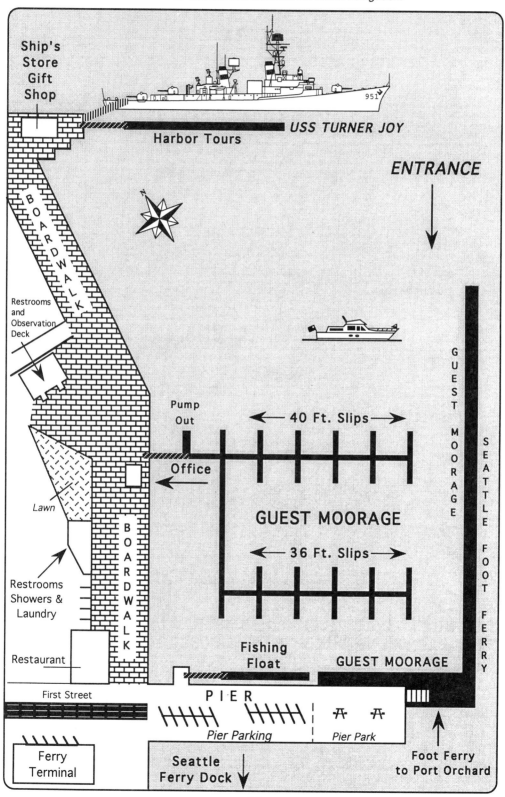

Ship's
Store
Gift
Shop

USS TURNER JOY

951

Harbor Tours

ENTRANCE

B O A R D W A L K

Restrooms
and
Observation
Deck

Pump
Out

40 Ft. Slips

Office

GUEST MOORAGE

36 Ft. Slips

Lawn

B O A R D W A L K

G U E S T   M O O R A G E

S E A T T L E   F O O T   F E R R Y

Restrooms
Showers &
Laundry

Restaurant

Fishing
Float

GUEST MOORAGE

First Street

P I E R

Pier Parking

Pier Park

Ferry
Terminal

Seattle
Ferry Dock

Foot Ferry
to Port Orchard

Brownsville

NAME OF MARINA: *PORT OF BROWNSVILLE MARINA* **RADIO:** VHF Ch. 16

ADDRESS: 9790 Ogle Rd. NE   Bremerton   WA 98311

TELEPHONE: 360-692-5498   **MGR:** Bill Bailey

SHORT DESCRIPTION & LOCATION:

47°39.10' - 122°36.65' Located on Kitsap Peninsula about 4 miles south of Agate Pass Bridge and 7 miles north of Bremerton in Port Orchard passage directly across from west side of Bainbridge Island. Full service marina in quiet neighborhood location.

GUEST BOAT CAPACITY: ....Appx, 60 boats	GUEST DOCK: ....530' plus slips
SEASON: ....All year	GUEST SLIPS: 34
RESERVATION POLICY: ....Accepts	WATER: ....Yes
AMT W/ELECTRICITY: ....All	AMPS: ....20-30 A
FUEL DOCK: ....Gas, Dsl, & LP	PUMP OUT STATION ....Yes
MARINE REPAIRS: ....Close by	HAUL OUT: ....None
TOILETS: ....Yes	BOAT RAMP: ....Yes
HOT SHOWERS: ....Yes	LAUNDRY: ....Yes
RESTAURANT: ....None	LOUNGE: ....None
PICNIC AREA: ....Yes	POOL: ....None
PLAY AREA: ....Yes	BBQ: ....Yes
BASIC STORE: ....Store & Deli	GOLF: ....Close by
ELECTRICITY: ....$ 2.75 per day	OTHER: Pump out station, Porta
DAILY RATE: ....Appx. .30¢ per foot	pump out, public shell-
	fish beaches close by,
	great group picnic area.

NAME OF YACHT CLUB: *BROWNSVILLE YACHT CLUB*

CLUB ADDRESS: 9756A Ogle Rd. N.E., Bremerton, WA 98310

CLUB TELEPHONE: **PERSON IN CHARGE:**   Commodore

LOCATION & SPECIAL NOTES

BYC provides 60 feet of guest moorage for reciprocal club visitors on the Port of Brownsville guest dock. Rafting is permitted. Tie up and check in with harbormaster. If your club is reciprocal, you will be granted reciprocal privileges. Limit 2 days.

RECIPROCAL BOAT CAPACITY:..........2-4 Boats	RECIPROCAL DOCK: .Guest dock
RECIPROCAL SEASON:................................All year	RECIPROCAL SLIPS: ...Dock only
RESERVATION POLICY: ....None	WATER: ....Yes
TOILETS: ....At Marina	AMT W/ELECTRICITY: ....All
HOT SHOWERS: ....At Marina	AMPS: ....20-30 A
RESTAURANT: ....None	LOUNGE: ....None
DAILY RATE: ....$2.75 electricity per day	OTHER: ......Same as marina listing

NOTE: *THIS IS PRIVATE MOORAGE _ONLY_ AVAILABLE TO MEMBERS OF RECIPROCAL YACHT CLUBS! YOUR CLUB _MUST_ HAVE RECIPROCAL PRIVILEGES AND YOU MUST FLY YOUR BURGEE!*

Brownsville

CAUTION! This chartlet not intended for use in navigation.

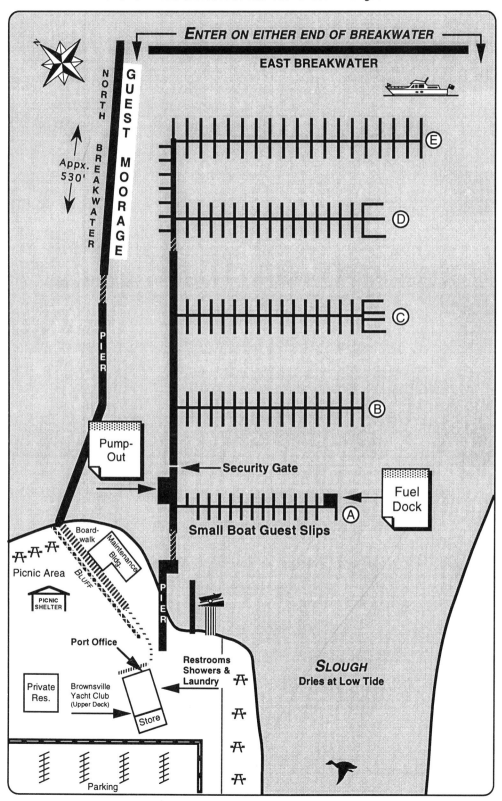

ENTER ON EITHER END OF BREAKWATER

EAST BREAKWATER

NORTH BREAKWATER

GUEST MOORAGE

Appx. 530'

PIER

E

D

C

B

Pump-Out

Security Gate

Fuel Dock

A

Small Boat Guest Slips

Board-walk

Maintenance Bldg.

BLUFF

Picnic Area

PICNIC SHELTER

PIER

Port Office

Restrooms Showers & Laundry

SLOUGH
Dries at Low Tide

Private Res.

Brownsville Yacht Club (Upper Deck)

Store

Parking

NOTES

Brownsville

NAME OF YACHT CLUB: *SEABACS - Boeing Employee Boat Club*

ADDRESS: M/S 4H-96, POB 3707 Seattle, WA 98124

TELEPHONE: PERSON IN CHARGE: Vice Commodore

SHORT DESCRIPTION & LOCATION:

SEABACS offers up to 2 nights reciprocal moorage located at the **Brownsville Marina** Guest Dock. Visiting reciprocal yacht club members are requested to pay the moorage charges to the harbormaster & mail the moorage receipt to SEABACS for reimbursement.

RECIPROCAL BOAT CAPACITY ....Varies

RECIPROCAL DOCK: ....At marina

SEASON: ....All year

RECIPROCAL SLIPS: ...At marina

RESERVATION POLICY:.................................None

WATER: ....Yes

TOILETS: ....At Brownsville Marina

AMT W/ELECTRICITY: ....All

HOT SHOWERS: ....At Brownsville Marina

AMPS: ....30 A

RESTAURANT: ....None

LOUNGE: ....None

DAILY RATE: No Charge for two nights moorage

OTHER: Services same as Brownsville Marina listing on Page 64 & 65.

NOTE: *THIS IS PRIVATE MOORAGE AND ONLY AVAILABLE TO MEMBERS OF RECIPROCAL YACHT CLUBS. YOUR CLUB MUST HAVE RECIPROCAL PRIVILEGES AND YOU MUST FLY YOUR BURGEE.*

SEE DATA & CHARTLET ON PAGE: 64 & 65

NOTES

Edmonds

NAME OF MARINA: *PORT OF EDMONDS MARINA*   RADIO: VHF Ch. 69

ADDRESS: 336 Admiral Way   Edmonds   WA 98020

TELEPHONE: 206-775-4588   MGR: Dave Howard

SHORT DESCRIPTION & LOCATION:

47°48.60' - 122°23.50' The Port of Edmonds is located north of Seattle on the east side of Puget Sound just NE of Point Edwards. Appx. 1000 ft. of guest moorage is available, however a Loan-A-Slip program provides expanded guest slips.

GUEST BOAT CAPACITY: ....Appx. 90 boats	GUEST DOCK: ..Appx. 100' + slips
SEASON: ....All year	GUEST SLIPS: ....Varies
RESERVATION POLICY: ....None	WATER: ....Yes
AMT W/ELECTRICITY: ....All	AMPS: ....20-30 A
FUEL DOCK: ....Gas & Diesel	PUMP OUT STATION ....Yes
MARINE REPAIRS: ....On premises	HAUL OUT: ....Travel-Lift
TOILETS: ....Yes	BOAT RAMP: ....Double sling
HOT SHOWERS: ....Yes	LAUNDRY: ....Close by
RESTAURANT: ....Several in area	LOUNGE: ....Yes
PICNIC AREA: ....Yes	POOL: ....None
PLAY AREA: ....Yes	BBQ: ....Yes
BASIC STORE: ....Close by	GOLF: ....Close by
ELECTRICITY: ....$2.00 per day	OTHER: Pump-out, waterfront
DAILY RATE: ....Appx. .40¢ per foot	shops & parks, fishing
The Port Offers Special	pier, several excellent
Accommodations for Boating Clubs.	restaurants close by, &
	city museum nearby.

NAME OF YACHT CLUB: *EDMONDS YACHT CLUB*   **B**

CLUB ADDRESS: Box 356, Edmonds, WA 98020

CLUB TELEPHONE: 206-778-5499   PERSON IN CHARGE: Rear Commo.

LOCATION & SPECIAL NOTES

Reciprocal moorage is located in the marina at the base of "G" Dock on north side. **Boats must be tied stern to dock - no exceptions.** There is a 48' boat length restriction & 48 hour limit. Please register at dock & post registration card on aft of boat.

RECIPROCAL BOAT CAPACITY: ....Appx. 4-6	RECIPROCAL DOCK: Appx 50 ft
RECIPROCAL SEASON:................................All year	RECIPROCAL SLIPS: Stern tie
RESERVATION POLICY: ....None	WATER: ....Yes
TOILETS: ....At Marina	AMT W/ELECTRICITY: ....All
HOT SHOWERS: ....At Marina	AMPS: ....20 A
RESTAURANT: ....Close by	LOUNGE: ....Close by
DAILY RATE: ....$2.00 per day for power	OTHER: ......Same as marina listing

NOTE: THIS IS PRIVATE MOORAGE ONLY AVAILABLE TO MEMBERS OF RECIPROCAL YACHT CLUBS! YOUR CLUB MUST HAVE RECIPROCAL PRIVILEGES AND YOU MUST FLY YOUR BURGEE!

Edmonds

CAUTION! This chartlet not intended for use in navigation.

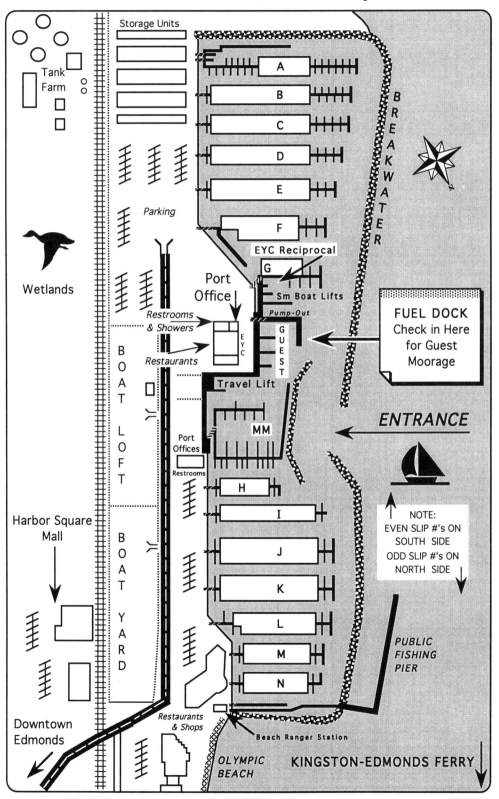

Everett

NAME OF MARINA: **DAGMAR'S LANDING**   RADIO: VHF Ch. 09

ADDRESS: 1871 Ross Ave.   Everett,   WA 98205

TELEPHONE: 206-259-6124   MGR: Kernan Manley

SHORT DESCRIPTION & LOCATION:

48°00.75' - 122°10.83' Located about 3 mi. up the Snohomish River from the Port of Everett. The marina caters primarliy to it's large 800 boat dry storage fleet, but offers guest moorage to the occasional boat that finds its way up the river.

GUEST BOAT CAPACITY: ....Appx. 20 boats	GUEST DOCK: ....Appx. 1000 ft.
SEASON: ....All year	GUEST SLIPS: ....Dock only
RESERVATION POLICY: ....None	WATER: ....Yes
AMT W/ELECTRICITY: ....All	AMPS: ....30 A
FUEL DOCK: ....None	PUMP OUT STATION ....None
MARINE REPAIRS: ....On premises	HAUL OUT: ....Up to appx. 36 ft.
TOILETS: ....Yes	BOAT RAMP: ....Yes
HOT SHOWERS: ....None	LAUNDRY: ....None
RESTAURANT: ....None	LOUNGE: ....None
PICNIC AREA: ....Yes	POOL: ....None
PLAY AREA: ....Yes	BBQ: ....Yes
BASIC STORE: ....None	GOLF: ....Close by
ELECTRICITY: ....Included in moorage	OTHER: Nice park area, ice,
DAILY RATE: ....$10.00/Night - Flat Rate	snacks, phone. Closest basic services are in Marysville or Everett.

CAUTION! This chartlet not intended for use in navigation.

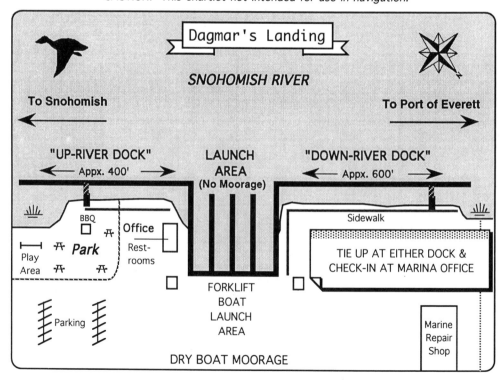

Everett

NAME OF YACHT CLUB: *DAGMAR'S YACHT CLUB*

ADDRESS: P.O. Box 1161   Everett,   WA   98201

TELEPHONE: PERSON IN CHARGE: Secretary

SHORT DESCRIPTION & LOCATION:

D.Y.C. offers 150 ft. of reciprocal moorage at Dagmars Landing on the Snohomish River. Tie up on either the Up-River or Down-River Dock & register at the marina office. In addition to River moorage, D.Y.C. also offers club members' private slips at the Port of Everett Marina, space available, on Fri. & Sat. Check w/harbormaster for availability.

RECIPROCAL BOAT CAPACITY ....Varies

SEASON: ....All year

RESERVATION POLICY:.................................None

TOILETS: ....Yes

HOT SHOWERS: .....Port of Everett location only

RESTAURANT: ....Port of Everett location only

DAILY RATE: ......No Charge for a two night stay. FIRST COME FIRST SERVE BASIS.

RECIPROCAL DOCK: ..Appx. 150'

RECIPROCAL SLIPS: ....Varies

WATER: ....Yes

AMT W/ELECTRICITY: ....All

AMPS: ....30 A

LOUNGE: .....Everett location only

OTHER: Port of Everett services same as listed on Pg. 74. Dagmars services-Pg70.

NOTE: THIS IS PRIVATE MOORAGE AND ONLY AVAILABLE TO MEMBERS OF RECIPROCAL YACHT CLUBS. YOUR CLUB MUST HAVE RECIPROCAL PRIVILEGES AND YOU MUST FLY YOUR BURGEE.

CAUTION! This chartlet not intended for use in navigation.

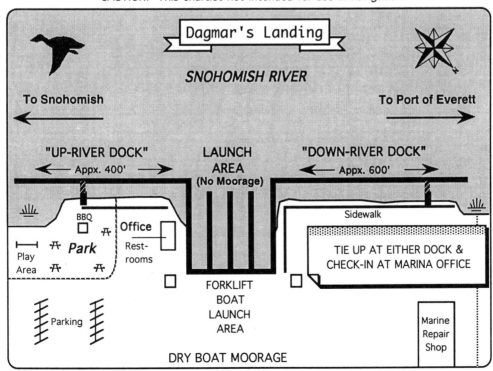

Everett

NAME OF PARK: *JETTY ISLAND MARINE PARK - Port of Everett*

ADDRESS:　　　P.O. Box 538　　　Everett, WA　　　98201

TELEPHONE:　　206-259-6001　　　MGR: Connie Bennett

SHORT DESCRIPTION & LOCATION:

48°00.20' - 122°13.80' Located across from Port of Everett Marina about 2 miles above mouth of and on west side of Snohomish River on Jetty Island. All natural river delta setting with great beach and picnic areas. No camping on shore allowed.

GUEST BOAT CAPACITY: ....Appx. 25-30 boats

GUEST DOCK: 3 Docks appx 100'

SEASON: ....All year

MOORING BUOYS: ....None

AMT W/ELECTRICITY: ....None

WATER: ....None

TOILETS:　　　.........................Summer only

PAY PHONES: ....None

HOT SHOWERS: ....None

BOAT RAMP: ....None

PICNIC AREA: ....Yes

PICNIC SHELTER: ....None

PLAY AREA: ....Yes

BBQ: ....None

BASIC STORE: ....None

PUMP OUT STATION: ......None

DAILY RATE: ....No Charge
　　　　Moorage limited to one night only.

OTHER:　Clam digging, swimming, campfires.

CAUTION! This chartlet not intended for use in navigation.

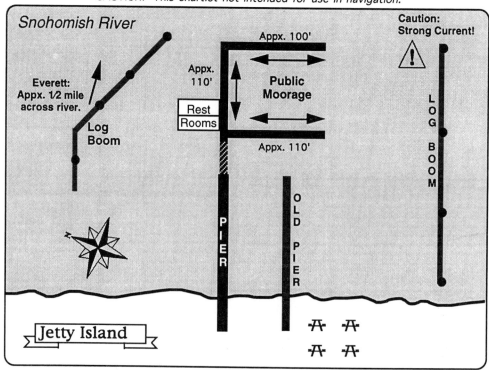

Everett

NAME OF YACHT CLUB: *MILLTOWN SAILING ASSOCIATION*

ADDRESS: P.O. BOX 2963   Everett,   WA   98203

TELEPHONE: 206-259-5275   PERSON IN CHARGE: Recip. Chairman

SHORT DESCRIPTION & LOCATION:

Milltown Sailing Assn. offers reciprocal moorage within the **Port of Everett Marina.** Present valid reciprocal club membership card at marina office and they will assign a slip. Gate key requires leaving driver's license for a deposit. Clubhouse located on north side of marina and open during Club functions, visitors welcome.

RECIPROCAL BOAT CAPACITY ....Ample

SEASON: ....All year

RESERVATION POLICY: ....None

TOILETS: ....At Everett Marina

HOT SHOWERS: ....At Everett Marina

RESTAURANT: ....Close by

DAILY RATE: ....No Charge
ONE STAY PER MONTH ALLOWED.
24 HOUR LIMIT

RECIPROCAL DOCK: ....At marina

RECIPROCAL SLIPS: ...At marina

WATER: ....Yes

AMT W/ELECTRICITY: ....All

AMPS: ....20-30 A

LOUNGE: ....Close by

OTHER: Services same as Port of Everett Marina listing on Page 74 & 75

NOTE: THIS IS PRIVATE MOORAGE AND ONLY AVAILABLE TO MEMBERS OF RECIPROCAL YACHT CLUBS. YOUR CLUB **MUST** HAVE RECIPROCAL PRIVILEGES AND YOU MUST FLY YOUR BURGEE.

SEE DATA & CHARTLET ON PAGE: 74 & 75

NOTES

Everett

NAME OF MARINA: *PORT OF EVERETT MARINA* **RADIO:** VHF Ch.16

ADDRESS: P.O. Box 538 Everett WA 98201

TELEPHONE: 206-259-6001 **MGR:** Connie Bennett

SHORT DESCRIPTION & LOCATION:

47°59.50' - 122°13.50' Located about 1 mile above mouth of and on east side of Snohomish River. Largest marina in the State and offers complete marine facilities. Note: Another guest dock is located 1 mile up river adjacent to boat launch for appx 15 boats.

GUEST BOAT CAPACITY: ....Appx . 50 boats	GUEST DOCK: ......1000' plus slips
SEASON: ....All year	GUEST SLIPS: 20
RESERVATION POLICY: ....Summer only	WATER: ....Yes
AMT W/ELECTRICITY: ....All	AMPS: ....20-30 A
FUEL DOCK: ....Gas & Diesel	PUMP OUT STATION ....Yes
MARINE REPAIRS: ....On premises	HAUL OUT: ....Travel-Lift
TOILETS: ....Yes	BOAT RAMP: ....Yes
HOT SHOWERS: ....Yes	LAUNDRY: ....Yes
RESTAURANT: ....Yes	LOUNGE: ....Yes
PICNIC AREA: ....Yes	POOL: ....None
PLAY AREA: ....Yes	BBQ: ....None
BASIC STORE: ....Yes	GOLF: ....Close by
ELECTRICITY: ....Included in moorage	OTHER: Many fine shops and
DAILY RATE: ....Appx .35¢ per foot	restaurants in Marina Village. Complete marine chandleries.

NAME OF YACHT CLUB: *EVERETT YACHT CLUB*

CLUB ADDRESS: 14th Street Dock, Everett, WA 98201

CLUB TELEPHONE: 206-259-8178 **PERSON IN CHARGE:** Commodore

LOCATION & SPECIAL NOTES

The EYC reciprocal float is located across form the fuel dock at the northwest corner of the marina. Nice modern float with ample electric service. Close to marina services. Maximum size boat allowable is 80 feet. Please register & pay at box.

RECIPROCAL BOAT CAPACITY:............Appx 15	RECIPROCAL DOCK: Appx. 150'
RECIPROCAL SEASON:................................All year	RECIPROCAL SLIPS: ....None
RESERVATION POLICY: ....None	WATER: ....No
TOILETS: ....At Marina	AMT W/ELECTRICITY: ....All
HOT SHOWERS: ....At Marina	AMPS: ....30 A
RESTAURANT: ....Close by	LOUNGE: ....Close by
DAILY RATE: ....First 2 days no charge. 25¢ per ft. after 2 days -Elec. $2 per night.	OTHER: ....Same as marina listing

NOTE: THIS IS PRIVATE MOORAGE ONLY AVAILABLE TO MEMBERS OF RECIPROCAL YACHT CLUBS! YOUR CLUB MUST HAVE RECIPROCAL PRIVILEGES AND YOU MUST FLY YOUR BURGEE!

Everett

CAUTION! This chartlet not intended for use in navigation.

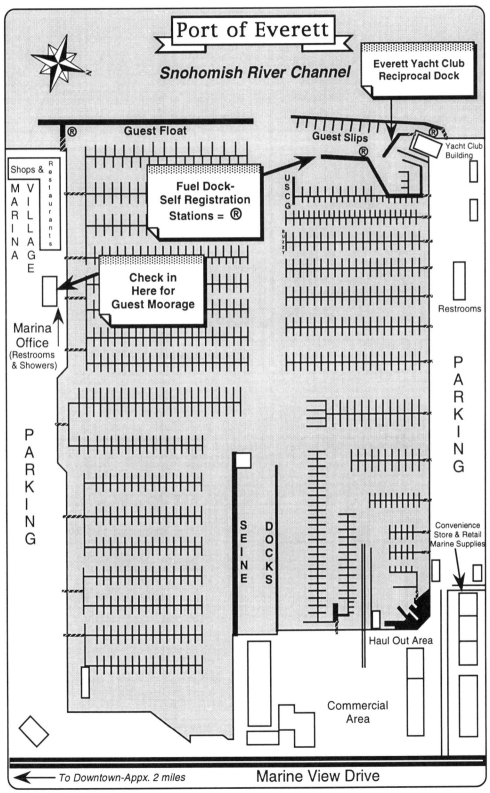

NOTES

Hat (Gedney) Island

NAME OF YACHT CLUB: *HAT ISLAND YACHT & GOLF CLUB*

ADDRESS: 1016 14th St. Suite A   Everett,   WA   98201

TELEPHONE: 360-444-6897   PERSON IN CHARGE: Harbormaster

SHORT DESCRIPTION & LOCATION:

48°01.20'-122°19.20' Hat Is. (Gedney Is. on chart) is located appx. 5 mi. NW of Everett. Club offers reciprocal moorage on a space avail. basis. Entire island is private & recip. guests are limited to immediate marina area unless escorted by an island resident. Call on Ch. 16 or land line telephone to arrange moorage. <u>BOAT SIZE IS LIMITED TO 45 FT</u>.

RECIPROCAL BOAT CAPACITY...........Appx . 2-6

SEASON: .....All year except holidays not available

RESERVATION POLICY:Call in advance,VHF/Tel

TOILETS: ....Yes

HOT SHOWERS: ....Yes

RESTAURANT:.......................................None

DAILY RATE: ....No Charge for 48 Hours
POWER CHARGE $2.00/DAY

RECIPROCAL DOCK: ....Appx.45'

RECIPROCAL SLIPS: ....Varies

WATER: ....None on docks

AMT W/ELECTRICITY: 6

AMPS: ....30 A

LOUNGE: ....None

OTHER: Quiet setting, very
limited services,
<u>no garbage facilities</u>.

<u>NOTE:</u> THIS IS PRIVATE MOORAGE AND ONLY AVAILABLE TO MEMBERS OF RECIPROCAL YACHT CLUBS. YOUR CLUB <u>MUST</u> HAVE RECIPROCAL PRIVILEGES AND YOU MUST FLY YOUR BURGEE.

CAUTION! This chartlet not intended for use in navigation.

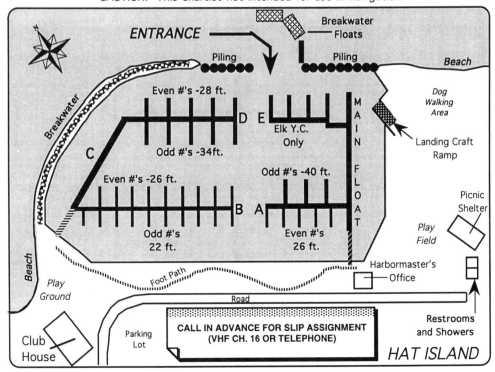

Kingston

NAME OF MARINA: *PORT OF KINGSTON*   RADIO: None

ADDRESS: P.O. Box 559   Kingston,   WA 98346

TELEPHONE: 360-297-3545   MGR: Gary Johnston

SHORT DESCRIPTION & LOCATION:

47°46.60' - 122°29.80' Located on the N. side of Appletree Cove, about 1.5 mi. S. of Apple Cove Pt adjacent to the Kingston-Edmonds Ferry Terminal. The modern & large marina is protected by a 340 yd. breakwater marked by a red light.

GUEST BOAT CAPACITY: ....Appx. 50 boats	GUEST DOCK: .....Guest slips only
SEASON: ....All year	GUEST SLIPS: ....Appx. 39
RESERVATION POLICY: ....None	WATER: ....Yes
AMT W/ELECTRICITY: ....All	AMPS: ....30 A
FUEL DOCK: ....Gas, Dsl, & LP	PUMP OUT STATION ....Yes
MARINE REPAIRS: ....None	HAUL OUT: ....None
TOILETS: ....Yes	BOAT RAMP:..........Sm. boat sling
HOT SHOWERS: ....Yes	LAUNDRY: ....Yes
RESTAURANT: ....Close by	LOUNGE: ....Close by
PICNIC AREA: ....Yes	POOL:..None
PLAY AREA: ....Yes	BBQ: ....Yes
BASIC STORE: ....Close by	GOLF: ....None
ELECTRICITY: ....$ 3.00 per day	OTHER: Adjacent to shops & restaurants, shopping center 1/2 mile, park, fishing & crabbing.
DAILY RATE: ....Appx. .35¢ per foot	

NAME OF YACHT CLUB: *KINGSTON COVE YACHT CLUB*

CLUB ADDRESS: P.O. Box 81, Kingston, WA 98346

CLUB TELEPHONE: 360-297-3371   PERSON IN CHARGE: Reciprocal Chmn

LOCATION & SPECIAL NOTES

The **new** KCYC reciprocal dock is located in the Kingston Marina at the head of the guest dock. Two 50 ft. slips are available on a first come first serve basis. After docking register at the Port Office, show your current Y.C. membership card & pay for power if needed. Note: New clubhouse available for clubs to rent for boating club functions. Call for info.

RECIPROCAL BOAT CAPACITY:..........Appx. 2-4	RECIPROCAL DOCK: 100' Total
RECIPROCAL SEASON:................................All year	RECIPROCAL SLIPS: 2-50' Slips
RESERVATION POLICY: ....None	WATER: ....Yes
TOILETS: ....At Marina	AMT W/ELECTRICITY: ....All
HOT SHOWERS: ....At Marina	AMPS: ....30 A
RESTAURANT: ....Close by	LOUNGE: ....Close by
DAILY RATE: ....Electricity - $4.00 per night	OTHER: ....Club open for Happy
48 HR. LIMIT	Hour Friday nights

NOTE: THIS IS PRIVATE MOORAGE *ONLY* AVAILABLE TO MEMBERS OF RECIPROCAL YACHT CLUBS! YOUR CLUB *MUST* HAVE RECIPROCAL PRIVILEGES AND YOU MUST FLY YOUR BURGEE!

Kingston

CAUTION! This chartlet not intended for use in navigation.

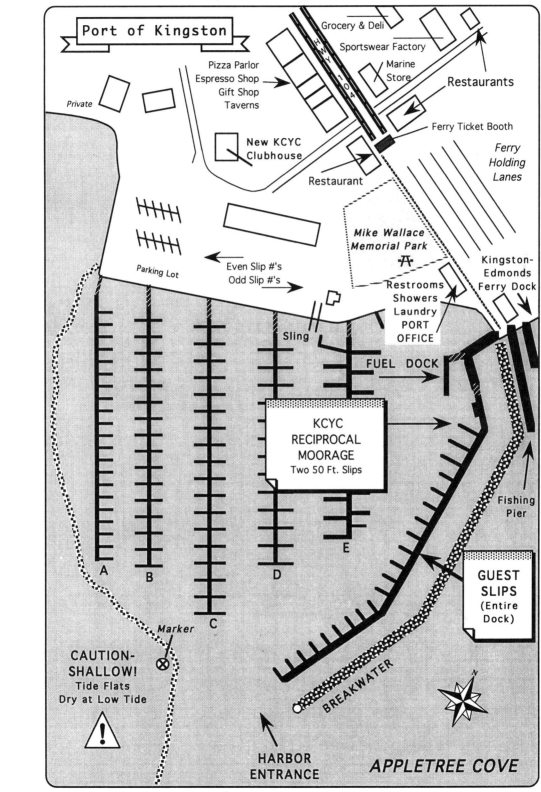

Port of Kingston

Grocery & Deli

Sportswear Factory

Pizza Parlor
Espresso Shop
Gift Shop
Taverns

Marine
Store

Hwy 104

Restaurants

Private

New KCYC
Clubhouse

Ferry Ticket Booth

*Ferry
Holding
Lanes*

Restaurant

*Mike Wallace
Memorial Park*

Kingston-
Edmonds
Ferry Dock

Parking Lot

Even Slip #'s
Odd Slip #'s

Restrooms
Showers
Laundry
PORT
OFFICE

Sling

FUEL DOCK

KCYC
RECIPROCAL
MOORAGE
Two 50 Ft. Slips

*Fishing
Pier*

E

GUEST
SLIPS
(Entire
Dock)

A

B

C

D

Marker

CAUTION-
SHALLOW!
Tide Flats
Dry at Low Tide

BREAKWATER

N

HARBOR
ENTRANCE

APPLETREE COVE

Kirkland

NAME OF PARK: *KIRKLAND MARINA PARK - Kirkland Parks Dept.*
ADDRESS: 123 5th Ave. Kirkland, WA 98033
TELEPHONE: 206-828-1213 **MGR:** Lynn Stokesbary
SHORT DESCRIPTION & LOCATION:

47°40.50' - 122°12.50' Located in downtown Kirkland on E. side of Lake Washington, this 2.5 acre park facility has 695' of lakefront beach. The marina is convenient to parks, shops, good restaurants, art galleries, and local summer festivals.

GUEST BOAT CAPACITY: ....Appx. 60 boats	GUEST DOCK: Appx 550' + slips
SEASON: ....All year	MOORING BUOYS: ....None
AMT W/ELECTRICITY: ....None	WATER: ....Yes
TOILETS: ....Yes	PAY PHONES: ....Yes
HOT SHOWERS: ....None	BOAT RAMP: ....Yes-(fee)
PICNIC AREA: ....Yes	PICNIC SHELTER: ....None
PLAY AREA: ....Yes	BBQ: ....None
BASIC STORE: ....Close by	PUMP OUT STATION: .....None
DAILY RATE: ....Appx. .25¢ per foot	OTHER: No rafting, gazebo pavilion in park for entertainment, waterfowl, fishing.

CAUTION! This chartlet not intended for use in navigation.

Tour Boat Ticket Booth

Pay/Info Station

Downtown Kirkland
•Shops
•Restaurants
•Services

Restrooms

Parking Lot

Park Area

Gazebo

LAKE WASHINGTON

Appx. 250'

Tour Boats

Appx. 100'

Appx. 200'

Small Boat Slips

Appx. 80'

Appx. 60'

B E A C H

Public Docks and Slips

Boat Launch

Kirkland

NAME OF MARINA: **YARROW BAY MARINA**   RADIO: VHF Ch. 68
ADDRESS: 5207 Lake Wash. Blvd.   Kirkland,   WA 98033
TELEPHONE: 206-822-6066   MGR: Don & Rose Marie Wilcox

SHORT DESCRIPTION & LOCATION:

47°39.20' - 122°12.50' Located 2 miles NE of the Evergreen Pt. Bridge and 1 mile S. of Kirkland on E. shore of Lake Washington. This convenient and established marina in Yarrow Bay has no designated guest moorage, but often has slips available for temp. use.

GUEST BOAT CAPACITY: ....Appx. 2-6 boats	GUEST DOCK: ....None
SEASON: ....All year	GUEST SLIPS: ....Varies
RESERVATION POLICY:........................Mandatory	WATER: ....Yes
AMT W/ELECTRICITY: ....All	AMPS: ....20-30 A
FUEL DOCK: ....Gas & Diesel	PUMP OUT STATION ....Yes
MARINE REPAIRS: ....On premises	HAUL OUT: ....Up to 32'
TOILETS: ....Yes	BOAT RAMP: ....None
HOT SHOWERS: ....None	LAUNDRY: ....None
RESTAURANT: ....Close by	LOUNGE: ....Close by
PICNIC AREA: ....None	POOL:...................................None
PLAY AREA: ....Close by	BBQ: ....None
BASIC STORE: ....Close by	GOLF:..................................Close by
ELECTRICITY: ....Included in moorage	OTHER: Adjacent to Carillon
DAILY RATE: ....Appx. $1.00 per foot	Point Marina & services
	incl. restaurants, shops,
	hotel, & espresso shop.

CAUTION! This chartlet not intended for use in navigation.

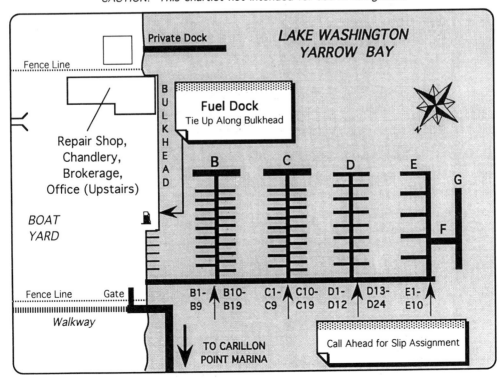

Kirkland

NAME OF YACHT CLUB: *YARROW BAY YACHT CLUB*

ADDRESS: P.O. Box 40   Kirkland,   WA   98003

TELEPHONE: 206-883-8147   PERSON IN CHARGE: Rear Commodore

SHORT DESCRIPTION & LOCATION:

47°39.30' - 122°12.50' Located at Carillon Point Marina 1 mi. S. of Kirkland. The marina offers deluxe amenities. YBYC moorage is slip D-56 plus 100' on the breakwater-<u>No Rafting.</u> A 24 hr. advance moorage request should be directed to the Rear Commodore.

RECIPROCAL BOAT CAPACITY ....Appx. 4

SEASON: ....All year

RESERVATION POLICY:...........................None

TOILETS: ....At marina

HOT SHOWERS: ....At marina

RESTAURANT: ....Yes

DAILY RATE: $2.00 per cord for power - Pay at slip D-56. $10.00 deposit for gate key available at Marina Office.

RECIPROCAL DOCK: Appx. 100'

RECIPROCAL SLIPS: ...Dock only

WATER: ....Yes

AMT W/ELECTRICITY: ....All

AMPS: ....30 A

LOUNGE: ....Yes

OTHER: 48 Hour limit. deli, store, restaurants, shops, bank, espresso, business ctr.

<u>NOTE:</u> THIS IS PRIVATE MOORAGE AND ONLY AVAILABLE TO MEMBERS OF RECIPROCAL YACHT CLUBS. YOUR CLUB <u>MUST</u> HAVE RECIPROCAL PRIVILEGES AND YOU MUST FLY YOUR BURGEE.

CAUTION! This chartlet not intended for use in navigation.

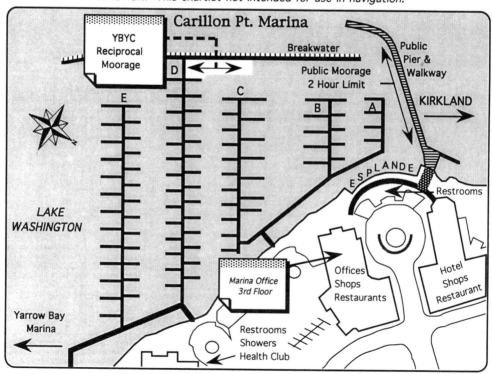

Port Orchard

NAME OF YACHT CLUB: *PORT ORCHARD YACHT CLUB*

ADDRESS: P.O. Box 3 Port Orchard, WA 98366

TELEPHONE: PERSON IN CHARGE: Commodore

SHORT DESCRIPTION & LOCATION:

47°32.30' - 122°38.50' Located about 1/4 mi. W. of downtown Port Orchard on the S. side of Sinclair Inlet. The reciprocal dock is on the outside of the breakwater float indicated by signs. See posted instructions on docks to register & obtain gate key.

RECIPROCAL BOAT CAPACITY.......Appx. 10-15	RECIPROCAL DOCK: Appx. 390'
SEASON: ....All year	RECIPROCAL SLIPS: Dock only
RESERVATION POLICY:....................None	WATER: ....Yes
TOILETS: ....Yes	AMT W/ELECTRICITY: ....All
HOT SHOWERS: ....Yes	AMPS: ....30 A
RESTAURANT:..................................Close by	LOUNGE: ....Close by
DAILY RATE: No charge for first 3 days. Add'l days @$5/day upon approval. Maximum days allowed - 14 per yr.	OTHER: Walking distance to down town Port Orchard shops, restaurants, museum.

NOTE: THIS IS PRIVATE MOORAGE AND ONLY AVAILABLE TO MEMBERS OF RECIPROCAL YACHT CLUBS. YOUR CLUB MUST HAVE RECIPROCAL PRIVILEGES AND YOU MUST FLY YOUR BURGEE.

CAUTION! This chartlet not intended for use in navigation.

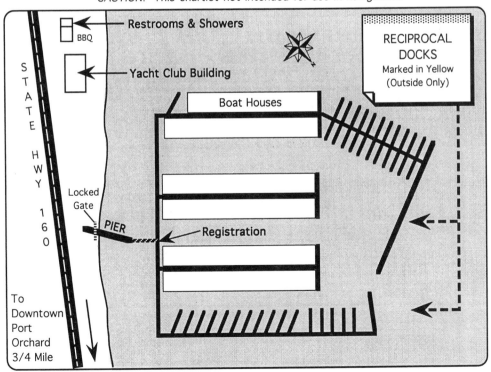

Port Orchard

NAME OF MARINA: *PORT ORCHARD MARINA*   RADIO: VHF Ch. 16

ADDRESS: 8850 State Hwy 3   Port Orchard   WA 98366

TELEPHONE: 360-876-5535   MGR: Gene Baker

SHORT DESCRIPTION & LOCATION:

47°32.80' - 122°38.30' Located on south shore of Sinclair Inlet directly across from City of Bremerton and adjacent to small Bremerton foot ferry. The marina is large and modern and close to many shops & restaurants in historic downtown Port Orchard.

GUEST BOAT CAPACITY: ....Appx. 180 boats	GUEST DOCK: ......3000' plus slips
SEASON: ....All year	GUEST SLIPS: 44
RESERVATION POLICY: ....Accepts	WATER: ....Yes
AMT W/ELECTRICITY: ....All	AMPS: ....30-50 A
FUEL DOCK: ....Gas & Diesel	PUMP OUT STATION ....Yes
MARINE REPAIRS: ....Close by	HAUL OUT: ....Close by
TOILETS: ....Yes	BOAT RAMP: ....Close by
HOT SHOWERS: ....Yes	LAUNDRY: ....Yes
RESTAURANT: ....Close by	LOUNGE: ....Close by
PICNIC AREA: ....Close by	POOL: ....None
PLAY AREA: ....Close by	BBQ: ....Yes
BASIC STORE: ....Close by	GOLF: ....Close by
ELECTRICITY: ....$2.30 per day	OTHER: Pump-out station, party
DAILY RATE: ....Appx. .30¢ per foot per day.	float for functions,
Winter Rate: $1.30 per ft. per wk.	portable BBQ, museum,
	art gallery, marine
	chandlery close by.

NAME OF YACHT CLUB: *SINCLAIR INLET YACHT CLUB*   **B**

CLUB ADDRESS: P.O. Box 1197, Port Orchard, WA 98366

CLUB TELEPHONE: PERSON IN CHARGE: Commodore

LOCATION & SPECIAL NOTES

SIYC provides three slips per night located in the general Port Orchard Marina guest dock area.. Tie up anywhere & check in with harbormaster. If your club is reciprocal and SIYC's monthly budget limit not reached, you will be granted reciprocal privileges.

RECIPROCAL BOAT CAPACITY: Apx 5 per mo.	RECIPROCAL DOCK: ..See above
RECIPROCAL SEASON:................................All year	RECIPROCAL SLIPS: .See above
RESERVATION POLICY: ....None	WATER: ....Yes
TOILETS: ....At Marina	AMT W/ELECTRICITY: ....All
HOT SHOWERS: ....At Marina	AMPS: ....30-50 A
RESTAURANT: ....Close by	LOUNGE: ....Close by
DAILY RATE: ....$2.30 per day for electricity	OTHER: ....Same as marina listing

NOTE: THIS IS PRIVATE MOORAGE *ONLY* AVAILABLE TO MEMBERS OF RECIPROCAL YACHT CLUBS! YOUR CLUB *MUST* HAVE RECIPROCAL PRIVILEGES AND YOU MUST FLY YOUR BURGEE!

Port Orchard

CAUTION! This chartlet not intended for use in navigation.

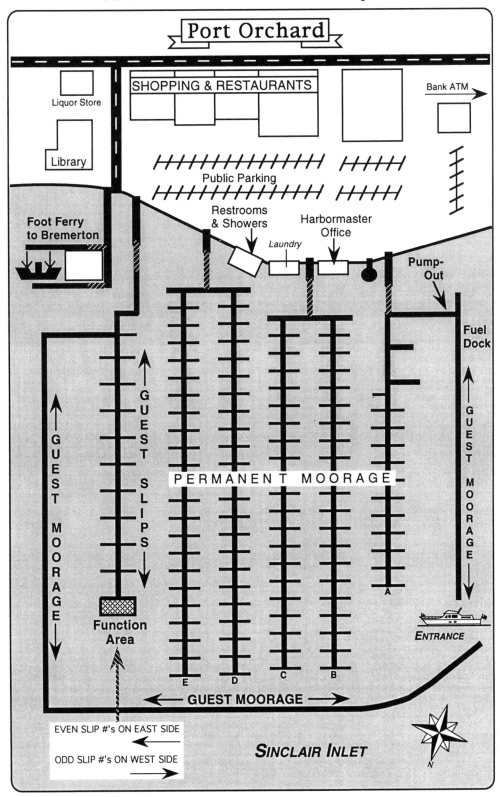

Port Orchard

SHOPPING & RESTAURANTS

Bank ATM

Liquor Store

Library

Public Parking

Foot Ferry to Bremerton

Restrooms & Showers

Laundry

Harbormaster Office

Pump-Out

Fuel Dock

GUEST MOORAGE

GUEST SLIPS

PERMANENT MOORAGE

GUEST MOORAGE

A

Function Area

ENTRANCE

E   D   C   B

← GUEST MOORAGE →

EVEN SLIP #'s ON EAST SIDE
←

ODD SLIP #'s ON WEST SIDE
→

SINCLAIR INLET

N

Poulsbo

NAME OF MARINA: *PORT OF POULSBO MARINA* RADIO: VHF Ch. 16
ADDRESS: P.O. Box 732 Poulsbo, WA 98370
TELEPHONE: 360-779-3505 MGR: Gary Proutt

SHORT DESCRIPTION & LOCATION:

47°44.00' - 122°38.60' Located at head of Liberty Bay on north side of bay in heart of downtown Poulsbo. Picturesque town with Norwegian theme and heritage. Full boating amenities including speciality shops and restaurants. Many seasonal festivals.

GUEST BOAT CAPACITY: ....Appx. 130 boats	GUEST DOCK: ......60 ft. plus slips
SEASON: ....All year	GUEST SLIPS: 130
RESERVATION POLICY:........................None	WATER: ....Yes
AMT W/ELECTRICITY: ....All	AMPS: ....20 A
FUEL DOCK: ....Gas & Diesel	PUMP OUT STATION ....Yes
MARINE REPAIRS: ....Close by	HAUL OUT: ....None
TOILETS: ....Yes	BOAT RAMP: ....Yes
HOT SHOWERS: ....Yes	LAUNDRY: ....Yes
RESTAURANT: ....Close by	LOUNGE: ....Close by
PICNIC AREA: ....Yes	POOL:..None
PLAY AREA: ....Yes	BBQ: ....None
BASIC STORE: ....Close by	GOLF: ....Close by
ELECTRICITY: ....$ 3.00 per day	OTHER: Marine chandlery close
DAILY RATE: ....Appx. .25¢ per foot	by, many shops, bakery, walking trails.

CAUTION! This chartlet not intended for use in navigation.

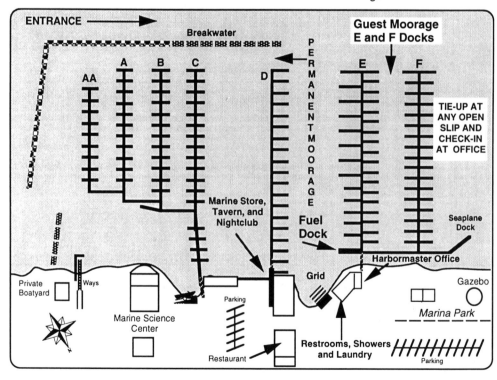

Poulsbo

NAME OF YACHT CLUB: *POULSBO YACHT CLUB*

ADDRESS: 18129 Fjord Dr. NE #T   Poulsbo   WA   98370

TELEPHONE: 360-779-3116   PERSON IN CHARGE: Commodore

SHORT DESCRIPTION & LOCATION:

47°43.60' - 122°38.30' Modern facility and clubhouse located appx. 3/4 mile SE of downtown Poulsbo, a picturesque town with a Norwegian theme and heritage. Reciprocal moorage inside of breakwater float. Key pad on marina gate & restrooms.

RECIPROCAL BOAT CAPACITY...........Appx 8-10	RECIPROCAL DOCK: Appx. 225'
SEASON: ....All year	RECIPROCAL SLIPS: Dock only
RESERVATION POLICY:......................Groups only	WATER: ....Yes
TOILETS: ....Yes	AMT W/ELECTRICITY: ....All
HOT SHOWERS: ....Yes	AMPS: ....30 A
RESTAURANT:.......................................None	LOUNGE: ....None

DAILY RATE: Electricity $2.00 per day. Moorage N/C for 48 consecutive hrs. with a maximum of 4 days in 3 mo. period

OTHER: Groups of 3 or more need advance notice.

NOTE: THIS IS PRIVATE MOORAGE AND ONLY AVAILABLE TO MEMBERS OF RECIPROCAL YACHT CLUBS. YOUR CLUB MUST HAVE RECIPROCAL PRIVILEGES AND YOU MUST FLY YOUR BURGEE.

CAUTION! This chartlet not intended for use in navigation.

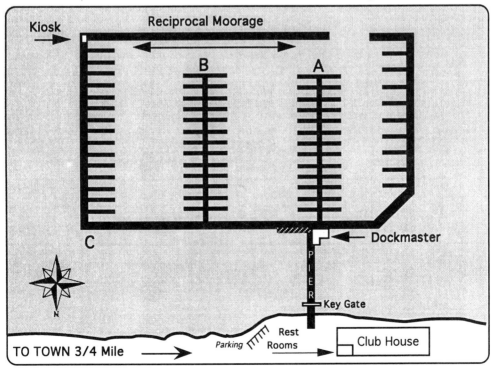

Renton

NAME OF PARK: *GENE COULON MEMORIAL PARK - Renton Parks Dept.*
ADDRESS: 200 Mill Ave. So.   Renton, WA   98055
TELEPHONE: 206-235-2560   **MGR:** T. Higashiyama/R. Weiss

SHORT DESCRIPTION & LOCATION:

47°30.30' - 122°13.20'   Located 2 miles N. of downtown Renton at the S.E. end of Lake Washington. The 1 1/2 mi. waterfront park has many recreational activities for both boaters and non-boaters. Twelve 30' slips are available for boaters plus guest dock.

GUEST BOAT CAPACITY: ....Appx. 20 boats

SEASON: ....Moorage closed during winter

AMT W/ELECTRICITY: ....None

TOILETS: ....Yes

HOT SHOWERS: ....Yes (summer only)

PICNIC AREA: ....Yes

PLAY AREA: ....Yes

BASIC STORE: ....None

DAILY RATE: ....$10.00 per night
................ONE NIGHT MAXIMUM STAY

GUEST DOCK: ....Appx. 75 ft.

MOORING BUOYS: ....None

WATER: ....None

PAY PHONES: ....Yes

BOAT RAMP: ....Yes

PICNIC SHELTER: ....Yes

BBQ: ....Yes

PUMP OUT STATION: ......None

OTHER: <u>NO PETS</u>. Fishing pier, swimming beach, interpretive trails, tennis courts, & 2 restaurants.

CAUTION! This chartlet not intended for use in navigation.

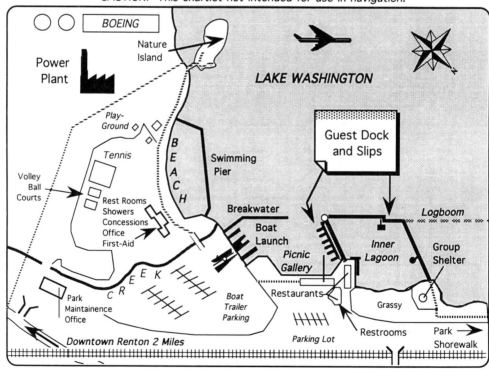

Seattle

NAME OF MARINA: *BELL STREET PIER MARINA*	**RADIO:** VHF Ch. 66
ADDRESS: P.O. Box 1209. Pier 69 Seattle, WA 98111	
TELEPHONE: 206-728-3000 **MGR:** Marla Kleiven	

SHORT DESCRIPTION & LOCATION:

47°36.65'-122°21.10' This is the Port of Seattle's new "short stay" marina at Pier 69 on Seattle's waterfront just opened during the summer of 1996. The marina accents & complements an entire waterfront community w/ business, transp., & retail centers.

GUEST BOAT CAPACITY: ....Appx. 50-60 boats	GUEST DOCK: 125 ft. plus slips
SEASON: ....All year	GUEST SLIPS: ....Appx. 50
RESERVATION POLICY:................................None	WATER: ....Yes
AMT W/ELECTRICITY: ....All	AMPS: ....30-50 A
FUEL DOCK: ....Close by	PUMP OUT STATION ....Yes
MARINE REPAIRS: ....Close by	HAUL OUT: ....None
TOILETS: ....Yes	BOAT RAMP: ....None
HOT SHOWERS: ....Yes	LAUNDRY: ....None
RESTAURANT: ....Yes	LOUNGE: ....Yes
PICNIC AREA: ....Yes	POOL:..None
PLAY AREA: ....Yes	BBQ: ....None
BASIC STORE: ....Yes	GOLF: ....None
ELECTRICITY: Rate not determined at presstime	OTHER: 24 Hour security, museum, fish market & processor, close to Pike Place Mkt & many downtown Seattle attractions.
DAILY RATE: Not determined at presstime but will be set at general market rates.	
72 HOURS MAXIMUM STAY	

CAUTION! This chartlet not intended for use in navigation.

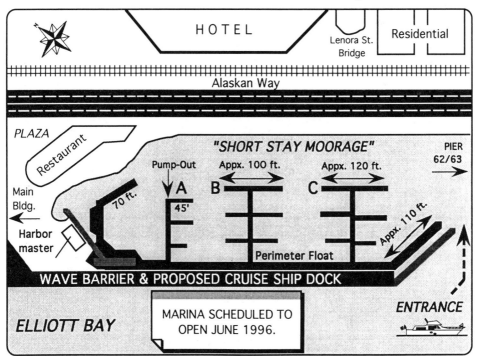

Seattle

NAME OF YACHT CLUB: *BELLEVUE YACHT CLUB (AT LAKE UNION)*

ADDRESS: P.O. Box 5641   Bellevue,   WA   98006

TELEPHONE: 206-284-6236   PERSON IN CHARGE: Al Hartman

SHORT DESCRIPTION & LOCATION:

47°38.25' - 122°20.28' BYC offers moorage for clubs holding a current reciprocal agreement for boats up to 40 ft. in the Hunan Harbor Marina adjacent to the former Elk Yacht Club located on west side of Lake Union at 2040 Westlake Ave. N..

RECIPROCAL BOAT CAPACITY ....Appx. 2 boats

RECIPROCAL DOCK: ....Appx. 80'

SEASON: ....All year

RECIPROCAL SLIPS: ...Dock only

RESERVATION POLICY:....................................None

WATER: ....Yes

TOILETS: ....None

AMT W/ELECTRICITY: ....All

HOT SHOWERS: ....None

AMPS: ....30 A

RESTAURANT:.....................................Close by

LOUNGE: ....Close by

DAILY RATE: First- come-first-serve with a maximum of two nights stay.

OTHER: Located close to many marine oriented businesses and services.

<u>NOTE:</u> THIS IS PRIVATE MOORAGE AND ONLY AVAILABLE TO MEMBERS OF RECIPROCAL YACHT CLUBS. YOUR CLUB <u>MUST</u> HAVE RECIPROCAL PRIVILEGES AND YOU MUST FLY YOUR BURGEE.

CAUTION! This chartlet not intended for use in navigation.

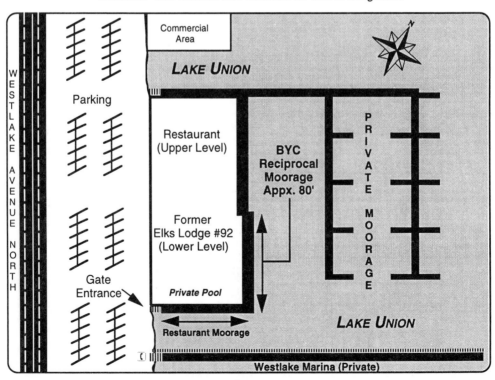

Seattle

NAME OF MARINA: *CHANDLER'S COVE MARINA*   RADIO: None
ADDRESS: 901 Fairview Ave N.   Seattle,   WA 98109
TELEPHONE: 206-628-0838   MGR: Brad Olson
SHORT DESCRIPTION & LOCATION:
47°37.70' - 122°19.90' Located at the very south end of Lake Union in an upscale public area with deluxe amenities. Excellent restaurants, shops, and marine services in the neighborhood.

GUEST BOAT CAPACITY: ....Appx. 15 boats	GUEST DOCK: 2 Docks-600' total
SEASON: ....All year	GUEST SLIPS: ....Docks only
RESERVATION POLICY:..................Accepts	WATER: ....Yes
AMT W/ELECTRICITY: ....All	AMPS: ....30-50 A
FUEL DOCK: ....Close by	PUMP OUT STATION ....Yes
MARINE REPAIRS: ....Close by	HAUL OUT: ....Close by
TOILETS: ....Yes	BOAT RAMP:...........................None
HOT SHOWERS: ....None	LAUNDRY: ....None
RESTAURANT: ....Yes	LOUNGE: ....Yes
PICNIC AREA: ....Yes	POOL:......................................None
PLAY AREA: ....Yes	BBQ: ....None
BASIC STORE: ....Yes	GOLF: ....Close by
ELECTRICITY: ....$2.00 per day	OTHER: No rafting. Maritime
DAILY RATE: ....Overnight: $1.00 per ft.	museum, tour & charter
..............................3 Hours - no charge	boats, yacht dive shop,
	brokerage, shopping,
	art gallery, & hair salon.

CAUTION! This chartlet not intended for use in navigation.

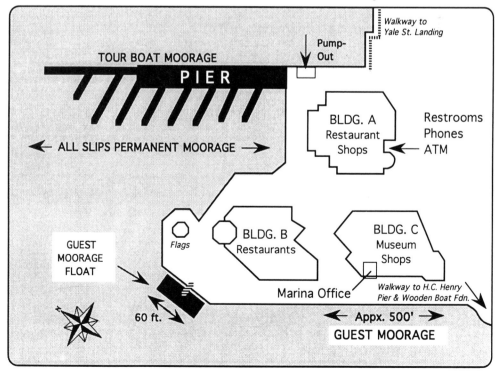

Seattle

NAME OF YACHT CLUB: *DUWAMISH YACHT CLUB*

ADDRESS: 1801 South 93rd St. Seattle, WA 98108

TELEPHONE: 206-767-9330 PERSON IN CHARGE: Office Manager

SHORT DESCRIPTION & LOCATION:

47°31.02' - 122°18.50' Located in the Duwamish River appx. 40 minutes cruising time from Elliott Bay, 1/2 mile past the 14th Ave. bridge. Vacant member slips are available for boats up to 50 ft. Small shopping center w/in walking distance. Best to call ahead for moorage arrangements to club office 767-9330 (Tues./Thur. only, 10 AM-4 PM).

RECIPROCAL BOAT CAPACITY..........Appx . 2-4

SEASON: ....All year

RESERVATION POLICY:................Recommended

TOILETS: ....Yes

HOT SHOWERS: ....Yes

RESTAURANT:..Close by

DAILY RATE: ....No charge for 48 hours. Thereafter .35¢ per ft. **Power is $2.00 per day.**

RECIPROCAL DOCK: ....45-50'

RECIPROCAL SLIPS: ....Varies

WATER: ....Yes

AMT W/ELECTRICITY: ....All

AMPS: ....30 A

LOUNGE: ....Close by

OTHER: Clubhouse w/showers & laundry, fuel close by, pump out station.

NOTE: THIS IS PRIVATE MOORAGE AND ONLY AVAILABLE TO MEMBERS OF RECIPROCAL YACHT CLUBS. YOUR CLUB MUST HAVE RECIPROCAL PRIVILEGES AND YOU MUST FLY YOUR BURGEE.

CAUTION! This chartlet not intended for use in navigation.

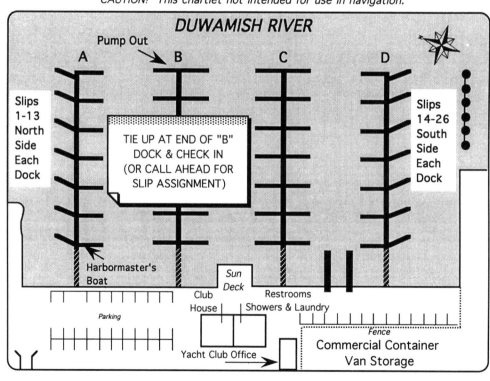

Seattle

NAME OF YACHT CLUB: *ELK YACHT CLUB*

ADDRESS: P.O. Box 33990 Seattle, WA 98133

TELEPHONE: PERSON IN CHARGE: Commodore

SHORT DESCRIPTION & LOCATION:

Elk Yacht Club offers reciprocal moorage located at the **Shilshole Bay Marina** Guest Dock. Visiting yacht club members are to request reciprocal moorage forms from the moorage office & pay the moorage fee. Please mail forms to E.Y.C. for reimbursement.

RECIPROCAL BOAT CAPACITY ....2 boats

RECIPROCAL DOCK: ....At marina

SEASON: ....All year

RECIPROCAL SLIPS: ...At marina

RESERVATION POLICY:...................................None

WATER: ....Yes

TOILETS: ....At Shilshole Bay Marina

AMT W/ELECTRICITY: ....All

HOT SHOWERS: ....At Shilshole Bay Marina

AMPS: ....30 A

RESTAURANT:...Close by

LOUNGE: ....Close by

DAILY RATE: ....No Charge
<u>2 NIGHT LIMIT FOR A MAXIMUM OF</u>
<u>2 VISITING MEMBERS PER NIGHT</u>

OTHER: Services same as
Shilshole Bay Marina
listing on Pg. 108 & 109

<u>NOTE:</u> THIS IS PRIVATE MOORAGE AND ONLY AVAILABLE TO MEMBERS OF RECIPROCAL YACHT CLUBS. YOUR CLUB <u>MUST</u> HAVE RECIPROCAL PRIVILEGES AND YOU MUST FLY YOUR BURGEE.

SEE DATA & CHARTLET ON PAGE: 108 & 109

NOTES

Seattle

NAME OF MARINA: *ELLIOTT BAY MARINA* **RADIO:** VHF Ch.78A
ADDRESS: 2601 West Marina   Seattle   WA   98199
TELEPHONE: 206-285-4817   **MGR:** Martin Harder

SHORT DESCRIPTION & LOCATION:

47°37.80' - 122°23.80' One of Seattle's newest marinas offers spacious guest moorage w/complete amenities. Located on N side of Elliott Bay at base of Magnolia Bluff about 3 mi. N of downtown Seattle. *Call ahead via VHF or land line for slip assignment.*

GUEST BOAT CAPACITY: ....Appx. 200 boats	GUEST DOCK: ....400' plus slips
SEASON: ....All year	GUEST SLIPS: ....Appx. 60
RESERVATION POLICY: ....Accepts	WATER: ....Yes
AMT W/ELECTRICITY: ....All	AMPS: ....30-50 A & 3 Phase
FUEL DOCK: ....Gas & Diesel	PUMP OUT STATION ....Yes
MARINE REPAIRS: ....On premises	HAUL OUT: ....Close by
TOILETS: ....Yes	BOAT RAMP: ....None
HOT SHOWERS: ....Yes (Free)	LAUNDRY: ....Yes
RESTAURANT: ....Yes - 3	LOUNGE: ....Yes
PICNIC AREA: ....Yes	POOL: ....Close-by
PLAY AREA: ....Yes	BBQ: ....None
BASIC STORE: ....Yes	GOLF: ....Close by
ELECTRICITY: ....$3.00-30A/$5.00-50A per day	OTHER: 24 Hr. security, shops,
DAILY RATE: .... .50¢ per ft. - winter	boat brokerages,
....................75¢ per ft. - spring/fall	canvas repair, diving
.........................$1.00 per ft. - summer	services, concierge, line
	handlers upon request.

CAUTION! This chartlet not intended for use in navigation.

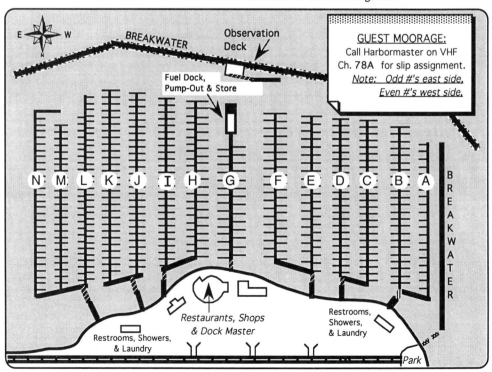

Seattle

NAME OF MARINA: *H.C. HENRY MARINA*   RADIO: None

ADDRESS: 809 Fairview Pl. N.   Seattle,   WA 98109

TELEPHONE: 206-621-1142   MGR: Sam Roland

SHORT DESCRIPTION & LOCATION:

47°37.60' -122°20.00' Located at the very S. end of Lake Union between the Naval Reserve Center on the W. and Chandler's Cove Marina on the E. The upscale neighborhood has deluxe amenities w/ample shops, fine restaurants, and marine services nearby.

GUEST BOAT CAPACITY: ....Appx. 2-4 boats	GUEST DOCK: ....Appx. 80 ft.
SEASON: ....All year	GUEST SLIPS: ....Dock only
RESERVATION POLICY:..........Resv. Encouraged!	WATER: ....Yes
AMT W/ELECTRICITY: ....All	AMPS: ....30 & 50 A
FUEL DOCK: ....Close by	PUMP OUT STATION ....Yes
MARINE REPAIRS: ....Close by	HAUL OUT: ....Close by
TOILETS: ....Yes	BOAT RAMP:...........................None
HOT SHOWERS: ....Yes	LAUNDRY: ....None
RESTAURANT: ....Yes	LOUNGE: ....Yes
PICNIC AREA: ....Yes	POOL:..None
PLAY AREA: ....Yes	BBQ: ....None
BASIC STORE: ....Close by	GOLF: ....Close by
ELECTRICITY: ....$ 2.00 per day	OTHER: Rafting OK. fitness
DAILY RATE: ....Appx. .50¢ per foot	center, maritime
<u>YOU SHOULD CALL AHEAD</u>	museum & Wooden Boat
<u>FOR OVERNIGHT MOORAGE</u>	Foundation next door.

CAUTION! This chartlet not intended for use in navigation.

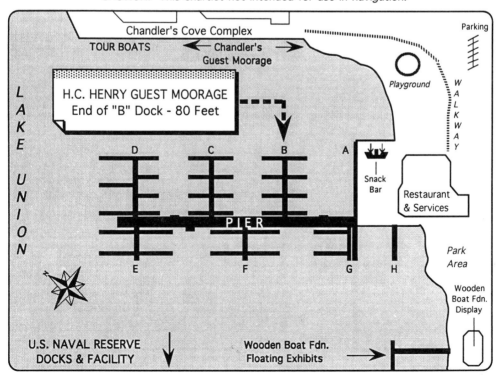

Seattle

NAME OF MARINA: *HARBOR ISLAND MARINA*   RADIO: None
ADDRESS: 1001 S.W. Klickitat Way   Seattle,   WA 98134
TELEPHONE: 206-467-9400   MGR: Doug Starup
SHORT DESCRIPTION & LOCATION:
47°34.20' - 122°20.70' Located on the West Waterway of the Duwamish River, just S. of the Spokane St. Bridge & at the southern tip of Harbor Island. The modern marina has a large guest dock plus rents available open slips of permanent moorage tenants.

GUEST BOAT CAPACITY: ....Appx. 15 boats	GUEST DOCK: ....225' plus slips
SEASON: ....All year	GUEST SLIPS: ....Varies
RESERVATION POLICY: ....Accepts	WATER: ....Yes
AMT W/ELECTRICITY: ....All	AMPS: ....30 A
FUEL DOCK: ....Gas & Diesel	PUMP OUT STATION ....Yes
MARINE REPAIRS: ....Close by	HAUL OUT: ....None
TOILETS: ....Yes	BOAT RAMP: ....None
HOT SHOWERS: ....Yes	LAUNDRY: ....None
RESTAURANT: ....Deli open on weekdays only	LOUNGE: ....Close by
PICNIC AREA: ....Yes	POOL: ....None
PLAY AREA: ....Close by	BBQ: ....None
BASIC STORE: ....Yes	GOLF: ....Close by
ELECTRICITY: ....$3.00 per day	OTHER: Ice & bait in store,
DAILY RATE: ....Up to 20 ft.- $8.00	pump-out, bus service
+ $2.00 for every 5 ft. over 20 ft.	to downtown Seattle.
............................Deposit for gate key	
..........................MAXIMUM SIZE 65'	

NAME OF YACHT CLUB: *WEST SEATTLE YACHT CLUB* **B**
CLUB ADDRESS: Box 16905, Seattle, WA 98116
CLUB TELEPHONE: PERSON IN CHARGE: Yeoman
LOCATION & SPECIAL NOTES
WSYC offers reciprocal moorage at the Harbor Island Marina to members in good standing of reciprocal clubs holding current membership cards. Upon arrival check in with the dock master to be assigned moorage. Moorage is limited to 4 boats in a 24 hour period.

RECIPROCAL BOAT CAPACITY:...............4 Boats	RECIPROCAL DOCK: ....At marina
RECIPROCAL SEASON:................................All year	RECIPROCAL SLIPS: ...At marina
RESERVATION POLICY: ....None	WATER: ....Yes
TOILETS: ....At Marina	AMT W/ELECTRICITY: ....All
HOT SHOWERS: ....At Marina	AMPS: ....30 A
RESTAURANT: ....Close by	LOUNGE: ....Close by
DAILY RATE: ...Electricity charge - $3.00 per day	OTHER: ....Same as marina listing
..Moorage - No charge for 48 hours	

NOTE: THIS IS PRIVATE MOORAGE ONLY AVAILABLE TO MEMBERS OF RECIPROCAL YACHT CLUBS! YOUR CLUB MUST HAVE RECIPROCAL PRIVILEGES AND YOU MUST FLY YOUR BURGEE!

CAUTION! This chartlet not intended for use in navigation.

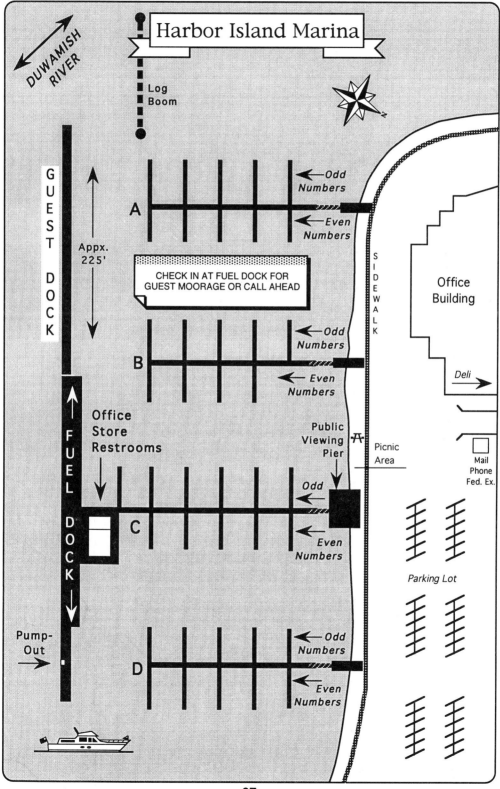

Harbor Island Marina

DUWAMISH RIVER

Log Boom

GUEST DOCK

Appx. 225'

A

Odd Numbers

Even Numbers

CHECK IN AT FUEL DOCK FOR GUEST MOORAGE OR CALL AHEAD

B

Odd Numbers

Even Numbers

Office Store Restrooms

FUEL DOCK

C

Odd

Even Numbers

Pump-Out

D

Odd Numbers

Even Numbers

SIDEWALK

Office Building

Deli

Public Viewing Pier

Picnic Area

Mail Phone Fed. Ex.

Parking Lot

Seattle

NAME OF MARINA: *LAKE UNION LANDING*   RADIO: None

ADDRESS: 1171 Fairview Ave. N.   Seattle   WA 98109

TELEPHONE: 206-623-4924   MGR: Max Heller/Tom Cooper

SHORT DESCRIPTION & LOCATION:

47°37.90' - 122°19.70' Located on S.E. side of Lake Union about 1/2 mi. N of Chandler's Cove. Although marina has no designated guest moorage, it may have 1-2 vacant slips to rent to overnight boaters. Call ahead on weekdays to arrange moorage.

GUEST BOAT CAPACITY:	Appx. 1-2 boats	GUEST DOCK:	None
SEASON:	All year	GUEST SLIPS:	Varies
RESERVATION POLICY:	Mandatory	WATER:	Yes
AMT W/ELECTRICITY:	All	AMPS:	20-30 A
FUEL DOCK:	Close by	PUMP OUT STATION	None
MARINE REPAIRS:	Close by	HAUL OUT:	Travel-Lift next door
TOILETS:	Yes	BOAT RAMP:	None
HOT SHOWERS:	Yes	LAUNDRY:	None
RESTAURANT:	Yes	LOUNGE:	Close by
PICNIC AREA:	None	POOL:	None
PLAY AREA:	None	BBQ:	None
BASIC STORE:	Close by	GOLF:	None
ELECTRICITY:	$5.00 per day	OTHER:	Walking distance to Chandler's Cove amenities, shops, restaurants, chandleries.
DAILY RATE:	$25.00 per day		

CAUTION! This chartlet not intended for use in navigation.

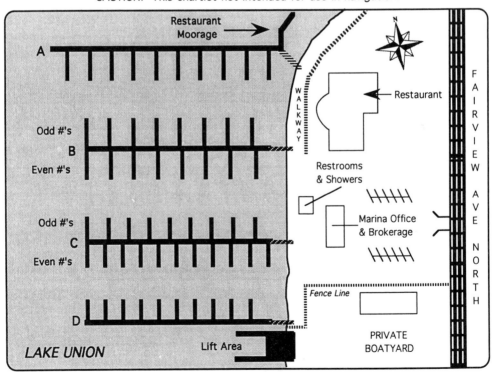

Seattle

NAME OF MARINA: *LAKEWOOD MOORAGE* RADIO: None

ADDRESS: 4500 Lake Wash. Blvd S Seattle WA 98118

TELEPHONE: 206-722-3887 MGR: Rick Camerer

SHORT DESCRIPTION & LOCATION:

47°33.80' - 122°15.80' Small older marina in quiet park like setting located on W. side of Lake Washington about a mile N. of Seward Park close to the entrance of Andrews Bay. Moorage is available on small guest dock.

GUEST BOAT CAPACITY: ....Appx. 3-5 boats
GUEST DOCK: ....40 ft.
SEASON: ....All year
GUEST SLIPS: ....Dock only
RESERVATION POLICY: ....Preferred
WATER: ....Yes
AMT W/ELECTRICITY: ....Limited
AMPS: ....20 A
FUEL DOCK: ....None
PUMP OUT STATION ....None
MARINE REPAIRS: ....None
HAUL OUT: ....None
TOILETS: ....Yes
BOAT RAMP: ....None
HOT SHOWERS: ....None
LAUNDRY: ....None
RESTAURANT: ....None
LOUNGE: ....None
PICNIC AREA: ....Yes
POOL: ....None
PLAY AREA: ....None
BBQ: ....None
BASIC STORE: ....Yes
GOLF: ....Close by
ELECTRICITY: ....Limited
OTHER: Bus service in front, waterfowl, close to Seward Park, gift & convenience store.
DAILY RATE: ....Appx. .50¢ per foot

CAUTION! This chartlet not intended for use in navigation.

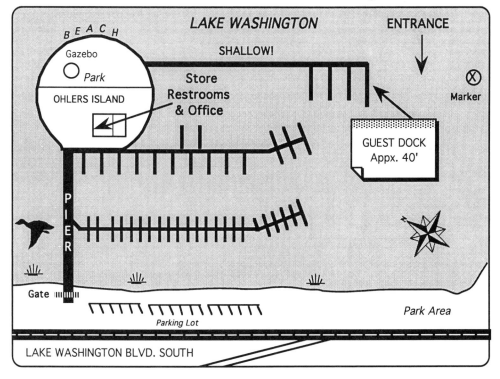

Seattle

NAME OF MARINA: *LESCHI YACHT BASIN*   RADIO: None
ADDRESS: 120 Lakeside Ave. #330   Seattle,   WA 98122
TELEPHONE: 206-328-6777   MGR: Judy Maccarrone

SHORT DESCRIPTION & LOCATION:

47°36.10' - 122°16.97' Located on W. side of Lake Wash. between the 2 floating bridges and situated between the lg. sailboat moorage and Seattle Police Dock. Although no designated guest moorage, the marina often has slips available for overnight moorage.

GUEST BOAT CAPACITY:	Appx. 1-4 boats	GUEST DOCK:	None
SEASON:	All year	GUEST SLIPS:	Varies
RESERVATION POLICY:	Mandatory	WATER:	Yes
AMT W/ELECTRICITY:	All	AMPS:	30 A
FUEL DOCK:	Gas only	PUMP OUT STATION	None
MARINE REPAIRS:	None	HAUL OUT:	None
TOILETS:	Yes	BOAT RAMP:	None
HOT SHOWERS:	None	LAUNDRY:	None
RESTAURANT:	Yes	LOUNGE:	Yes
PICNIC AREA:	Close by	POOL:	None
PLAY AREA:	Close by	BBQ:	Close by
BASIC STORE:	Yes	GOLF:	Close by
ELECTRICITY:	Included in moorage	OTHER:	Good security, deli,
DAILY RATE:	$25.00 per night		excellent restaurants, video rental, bike shop, supermarket, parks close by, bus service to town.

CAUTION! This chartlet not intended for use in navigation.

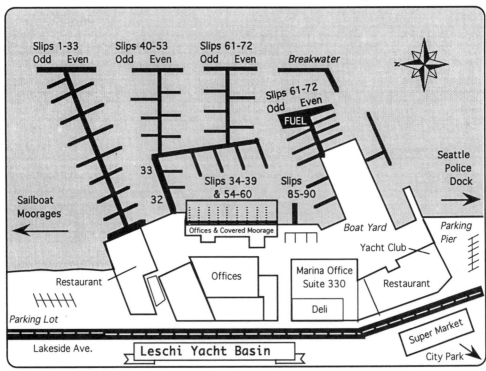

Seattle

NAME OF YACHT CLUB: *PUGET SOUND YACHT CLUB*

ADDRESS: 2321 N Northlake Way   Seattle   WA   98103

TELEPHONE: 206-634-3733   PERSON IN CHARGE: Dockmaster

SHORT DESCRIPTION & LOCATION:

47°39.00' -122°19.60' The PSYC facility is located 1/4 mi. E. of Gasworks Park on the N side of Lake Union. The reciprocal moorage is on the E. side & at the end of the dock. Please register w/Dockmaster for Security Gate key.

RECIPROCAL BOAT CAPACITY ....Appx. 2 boats

SEASON: ....All year

RESERVATION POLICY:................................None

TOILETS: ....Yes

HOT SHOWERS: ....None

RESTAURANT:.....................................Close by

DAILY RATE: ....$2.00 Electricity charge
THREE DAY LIMIT

RECIPROCAL DOCK: ....Appx. 40'

RECIPROCAL SLIPS: ...Dock only

WATER: ....Yes

AMT W/ELECTRICITY: ....All

AMPS: ....30 A

LOUNGE: ....Close

OTHER: Close to many marine services and chandleries on N. side of Lake Union.

NOTE: THIS IS PRIVATE MOORAGE AND ONLY AVAILABLE TO MEMBERS OF RECIPROCAL YACHT CLUBS. YOUR CLUB MUST HAVE RECIPROCAL PRIVILEGES AND YOU MUST FLY YOUR BURGEE.

CAUTION! This chartlet not intended for use in navigation.

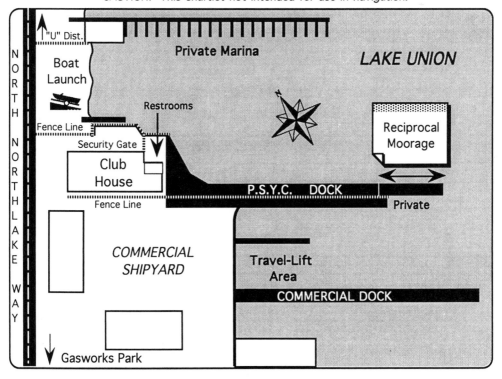

Seattle

NAME OF MARINA: *PARKSHORE MARINA*   RADIO: None
ADDRESS: 9050 Seward Park Ave S. Seattle   WA 98118
TELEPHONE: 206-725-3330   MGR: Dean Kelley

SHORT DESCRIPTION & LOCATION:

47°31.40' - 122°15.60' Located on W. side of Lake Washington adjacent to Seward Park in the Rainier Beach area, this well secured marina offers a guest dock for overnight moorage plus rents any available open slips of permanent marina tenants.

GUEST BOAT CAPACITY: ....Appx. 5 boats	GUEST DOCK: ....Appx. 100 ft.
SEASON: ....All year	GUEST SLIPS: ....Varies
RESERVATION POLICY: ....Accepts	WATER: ....Yes
AMT W/ELECTRICITY: ....All	AMPS: ....15-30 A
FUEL DOCK: ....Close by	PUMP OUT STATION ....Yes
MARINE REPAIRS: ....None	HAUL OUT: ....None
TOILETS: ....Yes	BOAT RAMP: ....Close by
HOT SHOWERS: ....Yes	LAUNDRY: ....Yes
RESTAURANT: ....Close by	LOUNGE: ....Close by
PICNIC AREA: ....Close by	POOL: ....None
PLAY AREA: ....Close by	BBQ: ....None
BASIC STORE: ....Close by	GOLF: ....Close by
ELECTRICITY: ....Included in moorage	OTHER: Close to Seward Park facilities, bus service close by, pump-out.
DAILY RATE: ....$10.00 per night-any size boat	

NAME OF YACHT CLUB: *RAINIER YACHT CLUB* **B**
CLUB ADDRESS: 9094 Seward Park Ave. S.,   Seattle, WA   98118
CLUB TELEPHONE: 206-722-9576   PERSON IN CHARGE: Secretary

LOCATION & SPECIAL NOTES

RYC offers one 30' & one 40' slip for members in good standing of reciprocal yacht clubs. If you wish to leave the marina, a gate key is available in a lock box. Check w/your home club's reciprocal information & correspondence for combination & location of lock box.

RECIPROCAL BOAT CAPACITY: Apx 2-3 boats	RECIPROCAL DOCK: ....Slips only
RECIPROCAL SEASON:................................All year	RECIPROCAL SLIPS: 2
RESERVATION POLICY: ....None	WATER: ....Yes
TOILETS: ....At Marina	AMT W/ELECTRICITY: ....All
HOT SHOWERS: ....At Marina	AMPS: ....15-30 A
RESTAURANT: ....Close by	LOUNGE: ....Close by
DAILY RATE: No charge for 48 hours. Over 48 hrs. must be approved (@$3/day).	OTHER: ....Same as marina listing

<u>NOTE:</u> THIS IS PRIVATE MOORAGE <u>ONLY</u> AVAILABLE TO MEMBERS OF RECIPROCAL YACHT CLUBS! YOUR CLUB <u>MUST</u> HAVE RECIPROCAL PRIVILEGES AND YOU MUST FLY YOUR BURGEE!

Seattle

CAUTION! This chartlet not intended for use in navigation.

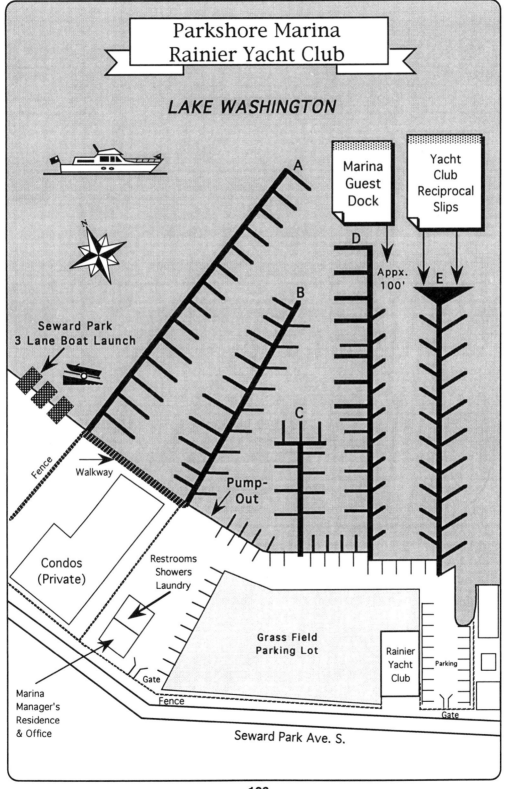

Parkshore Marina
Rainier Yacht Club

LAKE WASHINGTON

A

Marina Guest Dock

Yacht Club Reciprocal Slips

D

Appx. 100'

E

B

Seward Park
3 Lane Boat Launch

C

Fence

Walkway

Pump-Out

Condos
(Private)

Restrooms
Showers
Laundry

Grass Field
Parking Lot

Rainier Yacht Club

Parking

Gate

Marina Manager's Residence & Office

Fence

Gate

Seward Park Ave. S.

Seattle

NAME OF YACHT CLUB: *QUEEN CITY YACHT CLUB*

ADDRESS: 2608 Boyer Ave. E.   Seattle   WA   98102

TELEPHONE: 206-323-9602   PERSON IN CHARGE: Caretaker on duty

SHORT DESCRIPTION & LOCATION:

47°38.60' - 122°18.90' QCYC is located on the S. end of the W. shore of Portage Bay. The reciprocal moorage is on the S.E. side of Dock 3 at the outer end. Vacated member slips may also be available upon checking with the Caretaker at the Club House. <u>7 Day reciprocal moorage maximum & skipper (or family) must be on board overnight.</u>

RECIPROCAL BOAT CAPACITY.................Varies	RECIPROCAL DOCK: ....150 ft.
SEASON: ....All year	RECIPROCAL SLIPS: ....Varies
RESERVATION POLICY:....................................None	WATER: ....Yes
TOILETS: ....Yes	AMT W/ELECTRICITY: ....All
HOT SHOWERS: ....Yes	AMPS: ....30 A
RESTAURANT:...Close by	LOUNGE: ....Close by
DAILY RATE: ....$2.00 Per day utility fee ....$5.00 Gate key deposit	OTHER: Small grocery store 3 blocks west, city bus service at front door.

<u>NOTE:</u> THIS IS PRIVATE MOORAGE AND ONLY AVAILABLE TO MEMBERS OF RECIPROCAL YACHT CLUBS. YOUR CLUB <u>MUST</u> HAVE RECIPROCAL PRIVILEGES AND YOU MUST FLY YOUR BURGEE.

CAUTION! This chartlet not intended for use in navigation.

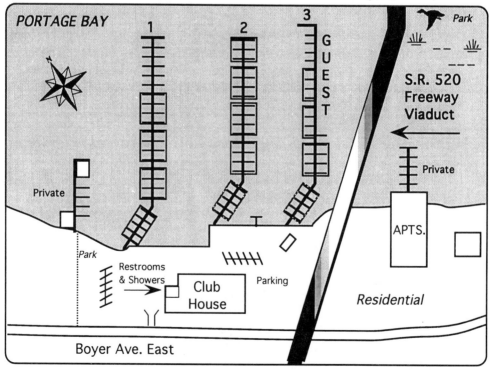

Seattle

NAME OF YACHT CLUB: *ROCHE HARBOR YACHT CLUB*

ADDRESS: P.O. Box 24022   Seattle,   WA   98124

TELEPHONE: PERSON IN CHARGE: Vice Commodore

SHORT DESCRIPTION & LOCATION:

RHYC offers 2 days reciprocal moorage at the **Harbor Island Marina.** Upon arrival check in with the dock master & show current membership card to be assigned moorage. Moorage is limited to 2 club members at one visit. A gate key may be obtained from the dock master for a $10.00 deposit.

RECIPROCAL BOAT CAPACITY...............2 Boats

SEASON: ....All year

RESERVATION POLICY:....................................None

TOILETS: ....At Harbor Island Marina

HOT SHOWERS: ....At Harbor Island Marina

RESTAURANT:...Close by

DAILY RATE: Electricity charge - $3.00 per day
.....................Moorage - No charge for
two consecutive days

RECIPROCAL DOCK: ....At marina

RECIPROCAL SLIPS: ...At marina

WATER: ....Yes

AMT W/ELECTRICITY: ....All

AMPS: ....30 A

LOUNGE: ....Close by

OTHER: Services same as
Harbor Island Marina
listing on Page 96 & 97

NOTE: THIS IS PRIVATE MOORAGE AND ONLY AVAILABLE TO MEMBERS OF RECIPROCAL YACHT CLUBS. YOUR CLUB MUST HAVE RECIPROCAL PRIVILEGES AND YOU MUST FLY YOUR BURGEE.

SEE DATA & CHARTLET ON PAGE: 96 & 97

NOTES

Seattle

NAME OF YACHT CLUB: *SEATTLE YACHT CLUB*

ADDRESS: 1807 E. Hamlin   Seattle   WA   98112

TELEPHONE: 206-325-1000   PERSON IN CHARGE: Manager

SHORT DESCRIPTION & LOCATION:

47°38.80' - 122°18.60' Located on the W. side of Portage Bay near the entrance to Portage Cut. This *historic and stately facility* offers reciprocal amenities, incl. moorage on end of Pier 2, to members of all yacht clubs <u>outside of a 30 mile radius</u> of Seattle.

RECIPROCAL BOAT CAPACITY Appx. 4 boats	RECIPROCAL DOCK: Appx. 160'
SEASON: ....All year	RECIPROCAL SLIPS: Dock only
RESERVATION POLICY:.....................None	WATER: ....Yes
TOILETS: ....Yes	AMT W/ELECTRICITY: ....All
HOT SHOWERS: ....Yes	AMPS: ....30 A
RESTAURANT:..................................Yes	LOUNGE: ....Yes

DAILY RATE: Reciprocal guests are entitled to two nights free per calendar year. Add'l nights are .30¢ per ft/night.

OTHER: Park area nearby. SYC sponsors the big annual Opening Day Boat Parade.

NOTE: THIS IS PRIVATE MOORAGE AND ONLY AVAILABLE TO MEMBERS OF RECIPROCAL YACHT CLUBS. YOUR CLUB MUST HAVE RECIPROCAL PRIVILEGES AND YOU MUST FLY YOUR BURGEE.

CAUTION! This chartlet not intended for use in navigation.

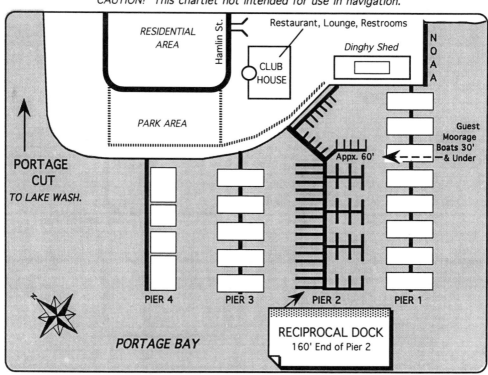

Seattle

NAME OF YACHT CLUB: *SHILSHOLE BAY YACHT CLUB*

ADDRESS: 2442 NW Market St. Box 98 Seattle, WA 98107

TELEPHONE: PERSON IN CHARGE: Secretary

SHORT DESCRIPTION & LOCATION:

Shilshole Bay Yacht Club offers reciprocal moorage located at the **Shilshole Bay Marina** Guest Dock. Visiting yacht club members are to request reciprocal moorage forms from the moorage office & pay the moorage fee. Please mail forms to SBYC for reimbursement w/copy of current yacht club membership card.

RECIPROCAL BOAT CAPACITY ....Varies

SEASON: ....All year

RESERVATION POLICY:....................None

TOILETS: ....At Shilshole Bay Marina

HOT SHOWERS: ....At Shilshole Bay Marina

RESTAURANT:....................................Close by

DAILY RATE: Power charge per Marina Rate. One night maximum limited to 3 members per club per month.

RECIPROCAL DOCK: ....At marina

RECIPROCAL SLIPS: ...At marina

WATER: ....Yes

AMT W/ELECTRICITY: ....All

AMPS: ....30 A

LOUNGE: ....Close by

OTHER: Services same as Shilshole Bay Marina listing on Page 108 & 109

NOTE: *THIS IS PRIVATE MOORAGE AND ONLY AVAILABLE TO MEMBERS OF RECIPROCAL YACHT CLUBS. YOUR CLUB MUST HAVE RECIPROCAL PRIVILEGES AND YOU MUST FLY YOUR BURGEE.*

SEE DATA & CHARTLET ON PAGE: 108 & 109

NOTES

Seattle

NAME OF MARINA: *SHILSHOLE BAY MARINA*   **RADIO:** VHF Ch. 17

ADDRESS: 7001 Seaview Ave. N.W. Seattle   WA 98117

TELEPHONE: 206-728-3006   **MGR:** Darlene Robertson

SHORT DESCRIPTION & LOCATION:

47°42.00' - 122°24.25' Shilshole is one of the largest marinas on the Pacific Coast and located between Meadow Point and West Point just N. of the open bight from which the Lake Washington Ship Canal is entered. Here full services abound for the boater.

GUEST BOAT CAPACITY: ....Appx. 200 boats	**GUEST DOCK:** Total 1900 lin. ft.
SEASON: ....All year	**GUEST SLIPS:** Appx. 40 + docks
RESERVATION POLICY: ....None	**WATER:** ....Yes
AMT W/ELECTRICITY: ....All	**AMPS:** ....30 A
FUEL DOCK: ....Gas & Diesel	**PUMP OUT STATION** ....Yes
MARINE REPAIRS: ....Yes	**HAUL OUT:** ....Yes
TOILETS: ....Yes	**BOAT RAMP:** ....Yes
HOT SHOWERS: ....Yes	**LAUNDRY:** ....Yes
RESTAURANT: ....Yes	**LOUNGE:** ....Yes
PICNIC AREA: ....Close by	**POOL:** ....None
PLAY AREA: ....Close by	**BBQ:** ....Close by at City Park
BASIC STORE: ....Yes - At Fuel Dock	**GOLF:** ....Close by
ELECTRICITY: ....Included in moorage	**OTHER:** Restaurants & night life,
DAILY RATE: ....Appx. .40¢ per foot	marine chandlery.
	pump-out station,
	garbage, recycling, haz.
	waste & oil stations.

NAME OF YACHT CLUB: *CORINTHIAN YACHT CLUB OF SEATTLE*   (B)

CLUB ADDRESS: 7755 Seaview Ave. NW, Seattle, WA 98117

CLUB TELEPHONE: 206-789-1919   **PERSON IN CHARGE:**   Shane Moore

LOCATION & SPECIAL NOTES

CYC is located at the base of "S" dock in a modern and unique large 2 story house boat. The 60 ft. reciprocal float is on the N. side of the club house and occasionally "S" dock member slips may be available. Best to call ahead to get the check-in box combination.

RECIPROCAL BOAT CAPACITY: Appx. 2 Boats	**RECIPROCAL DOCK:** ....60 ft.
RECIPROCAL SEASON:................................All year	**RECIPROCAL SLIPS:** ....Varies
RESERVATION POLICY: ....None	**WATER:** ....Yes
TOILETS: ....At Marina	**AMT W/ELECTRICITY:** ....All
HOT SHOWERS: ....At Marina	**AMPS:** ....30 A
RESTAURANT: ....Close by	**LOUNGE:** ....Close by
DAILY RATE: ....No charge	**OTHER:** ....Same as marina
	listing

NOTE: THIS IS PRIVATE MOORAGE _ONLY_ AVAILABLE TO MEMBERS OF RECIPROCAL YACHT CLUBS! YOUR CLUB _MUST_ HAVE RECIPROCAL PRIVILEGES AND YOU MUST FLY YOUR BURGEE!

Seattle

CAUTION! This chartlet not intended for use in navigation.

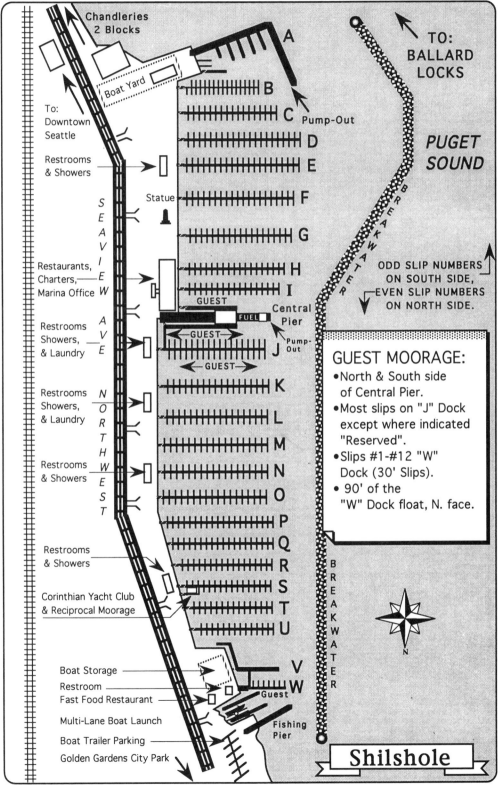

Chandleries 2 Blocks

Boat Yard

To: Downtown Seattle

Restrooms & Showers

Statue

SEAVIEW AVE

Restaurants, Charters, Marina Office

Restrooms Showers, & Laundry

Restrooms Showers, & Laundry

NORTHWEST

Restrooms & Showers

Restrooms & Showers

Corinthian Yacht Club & Reciprocal Moorage

Boat Storage

Restroom

Fast Food Restaurant

Multi-Lane Boat Launch

Boat Trailer Parking

Golden Gardens City Park

A
B
C — Pump-Out
D
E
F
G
H
I
GUEST
Central Pier
FUEL
Pump-Out
GUEST
J
GUEST
K
L
M
N
O
P
Q
R
S
T
U
V
W — Guest
Fishing Pier

TO: BALLARD LOCKS

PUGET SOUND

BREAKWATER

ODD SLIP NUMBERS ON SOUTH SIDE, EVEN SLIP NUMBERS ON NORTH SIDE.

GUEST MOORAGE:
- North & South side of Central Pier.
- Most slips on "J" Dock except where indicated "Reserved".
- Slips #1-#12 "W" Dock (30' Slips).
- 90' of the "W" Dock float, N. face.

BREAKWATER

N

Shilshole

Seattle

NAME OF YACHT CLUB: *TYEE YACHT CLUB*

ADDRESS: 3229 Fairview Ave. E.   Seattle   WA   98102

TELEPHONE: 206-324-0200 Clubhse   **PERSON IN CHARGE:** Commodore

SHORT DESCRIPTION & LOCATION:

47°39.10' - 122°19.30' Nice yacht club facility conveniently located on E. side of Lake Union almost directly under I-5 bridge. Close to restaurants and marine services. The busy club house is frequently rented out and catered for groups and special occasions. Please call Event Manager 206-323-9440 for information.

RECIPROCAL BOAT CAPACITY...........Appx 6-10

SEASON: ....All year

RESERVATION POLICY:...................................None

TOILETS: ....None

HOT SHOWERS: ....None

RESTAURANT:..Close by

DAILY RATE: ....No Charge
THREE DAY LIMIT

RECIPROCAL DOCK: Appx. 100'

RECIPROCAL SLIPS: ...Dock only

WATER: ....Yes

AMT W/ELECTRICITY: ....All

AMPS: ....30A &110

LOUNGE: ....Close by

OTHER: Rafting permitted. Nice dest. for boating clubs.

NOTE: THIS IS PRIVATE MOORAGE AND ONLY AVAILABLE TO MEMBERS OF RECIPROCAL YACHT CLUBS. YOUR CLUB **MUST** HAVE RECIPROCAL PRIVILEGES AND YOU MUST FLY YOUR BURGEE.

CAUTION! This chartlet not intended for use in navigation.

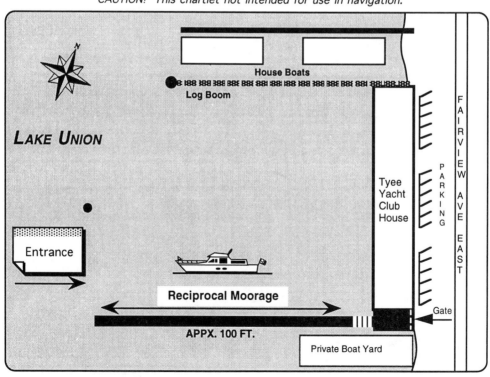

Seattle

NAME OF MARINA: *YALE STREET LANDING*	RADIO: None

ADDRESS: 1001 Fairview Ave. N. Seattle WA 98109

TELEPHONE: 206-682-3160 MGR: Sheila Samuelson

SHORT DESCRIPTION & LOCATION:

47°37.80' - 122°19.80' Located on S.E. side of Lake Union and was formerly St. Vincent De Paul marina. Although marina has no designated guest moorage, between June and October, it generally has 1 or 2 vacant slips to rent out to overnight boaters.

GUEST BOAT CAPACITY:	Appx. 1-2 boats	GUEST DOCK:	None
SEASON:	Summer only	GUEST SLIPS:	Varies
RESERVATION POLICY:	Mandatory	WATER:	Yes
AMT W/ELECTRICITY:	All	AMPS:	30-50 A
FUEL DOCK:	Close by	PUMP OUT STATION	None
MARINE REPAIRS:	Close by	HAUL OUT:	Close by
TOILETS:	Yes	BOAT RAMP:	None
HOT SHOWERS:	None	LAUNDRY:	None
RESTAURANT:	Yes	LOUNGE:	Yes
PICNIC AREA:	None	POOL:	None
PLAY AREA:	Yes	BBQ:	None
BASIC STORE:	Close by	GOLF:	Close by
ELECTRICITY:	Included in moorage	OTHER:	Walking distance to Chandler's Cove amenities, shops, restaurants, chandleries, Marriott Residence Inn.
DAILY RATE:	Appx. .50¢ per foot		

NOTE: CALL AHEAD DURING WEEKDAY OFFICE HOURS FOR SLIP ASSIGNMENT (IF AVAILABLE.).

CAUTION! This chartlet not intended for use in navigation.

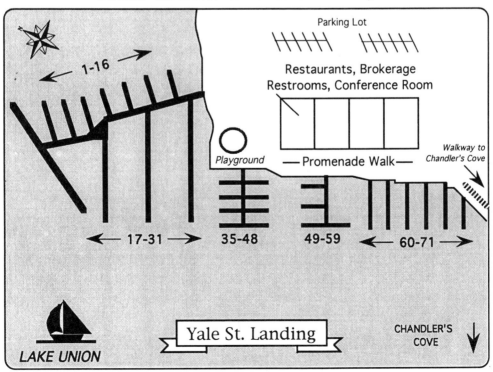

Silverdale

NAME OF MARINA: *SILVERDALE WATERFRONT PARK*   RADIO: None
ADDRESS: P.O. Box 310   Silverdale   WA 98383
TELEPHONE: 360-698-4918   MGR: Clyde Ford

SHORT DESCRIPTION & LOCATION:

47°38.50' - 122°41.70' Located at the head of Dyes Inlet on the W. side about 4.5 miles NNW of Bremerton. The marina features a waterfront park with gazebo & picnic area which is within walking distance to many shops and restaurants.

GUEST BOAT CAPACITY: ....Appx. 40-50 boats	GUEST DOCK: ....300' plus slips
SEASON: ....All year	GUEST SLIPS: ....4 large slips
RESERVATION POLICY: ....None	WATER: ....Yes
AMT W/ELECTRICITY: ....None	AMPS: ....None
FUEL DOCK: ....None	PUMP OUT STATION ....None
MARINE REPAIRS: ....None	HAUL OUT: ....None
TOILETS: ....Yes	BOAT RAMP: ....Yes
HOT SHOWERS: ....None	LAUNDRY: ....Close by
RESTAURANT: ....Close by	LOUNGE: ....Close by
PICNIC AREA: ....Yes	POOL: ....None
PLAY AREA: ....Yes	BBQ: ....None
BASIC STORE: ....Close by	GOLF: ....Close by
ELECTRICITY: ....None	OTHER: No rafting. Fishing pier,
DAILY RATE: ....$3.00 - Under 28'	swimming, historical
..............................$5.00 - 28' & over	display & museum,
........Three nights maximum	horseshoe pits, close
	to Oldtown attractions.

CAUTION! This chartlet not intended for use in navigation.

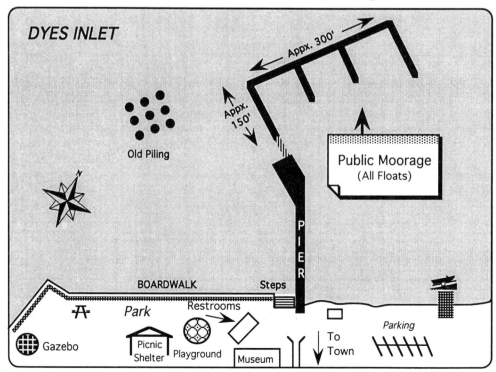

C H A P T E R

3

HOOD CANAL
&
OLYMPIC PENINSULA

NOTES

Belfair

NAME OF PARK: *TWANOH STATE PARK*

ADDRESS: E 12190 Hwy 106   Union, WA   98592

TELEPHONE: 360-275-2222   **MGR:** Larry Otto

SHORT DESCRIPTION & LOCATION:

47°22.70' - 122°50.20'   Located about 6 miles E. of Union on the S. shore at the bottom of Hood Canal. This full service park offers many activities for family boating and camping. Use caution at low tide on mooring float. Buoys recommended for larger boats.

GUEST BOAT CAPACITY: ....Appx. 5-10 boats	GUEST DOCK: ....Appx. 100 ft.
SEASON: ....Closed winter	MOORING BUOYS: ....7 buoys
AMT W/ELECTRICITY: ....None	WATER: ....Yes
TOILETS: ....Yes	PAY PHONES: ....Yes
HOT SHOWERS: ....Yes	BOAT RAMP: ....Yes
PICNIC AREA: ....Yes	PICNIC SHELTER: ....Yes
PLAY AREA: ....Yes	BBQ: ....Yes
BASIC STORE: ....Summer only	PUMP OUT STATION: ....Yes

DAILY RATE: Mooring Buoys................$5.00/night
                    Boats under 26 ft...........$8.00/night
                    Boats 26 ft. & Over.....$11.00/night
                    Subject to Change in 1997

OTHER: Summer snack bar,
campsites, swimming area,
hiking trails, sports area,
salmon creek.

CAUTION! This chartlet not intended for use in navigation.

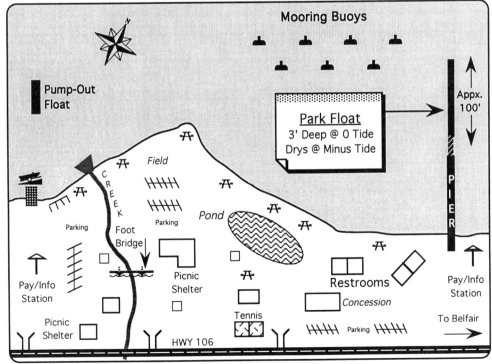

Brinnon

NAME OF MARINA: **PLEASANT HARBOR MARINA**   RADIO: VHF Ch.16/9

ADDRESS: 308913 Highway 101   Brinnon   WA   98320

TELEPHONE: 360-796-4611   MGR: Chuck & Betty Finnila

SHORT DESCRIPTION & LOCATION:

47°39.70' - 122°54.80' Family oriented marina resort located in lovely cove on Hood Canal 2 miles S. of town of Brinnon. Well protected marina caters to recreational boaters and boating clubs. ***Check in at fuel dock or call ahead for slip assignment.***

GUEST BOAT CAPACITY: ....Appx. 30 boats	GUEST DOCK: ....240' plus slips
SEASON: ....All year	GUEST SLIPS: 25
RESERVATION POLICY:............................Accepts	WATER: ....Yes
AMT W/ELECTRICITY: ....All	AMPS: ....20-30 A
FUEL DOCK: ....Gas & Diesel	PUMP OUT STATION ....Yes
MARINE REPAIRS: ....Close by	HAUL OUT: ....None
TOILETS: ....Yes	BOAT RAMP: ....Close by
HOT SHOWERS: ....Yes	LAUNDRY: ....Yes
RESTAURANT: ....Pizza Deli	LOUNGE: ....None
PICNIC AREA: ....Yes	POOL: ....Yes
PLAY AREA: ....None	BBQ: ....Yes
BASIC STORE: ....Yes	GOLF: ....Close by
ELECTRICITY: ....Up to 35' $2.00/over 35' $2.50	OTHER: Hot tub, boater lounge,
DAILY RATE: ....Appx. .45¢ per foot	crabbing, shrimping in
	season, great dinghy
	area in harbor.

CAUTION! This chartlet not intended for use in navigation.

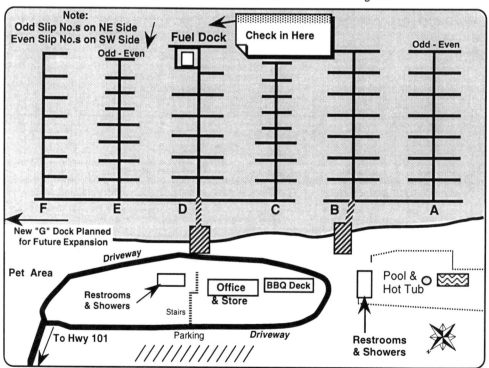

Brinnon

NAME OF PARK:	*PLEASANT HARBOR STATE MARINE PARK*
ADDRESS:	P.O. Box K Brinnon WA 98320
TELEPHONE:	360-796-4415 **MGR:** Harry Louch

SHORT DESCRIPTION & LOCATION:

47°39.90' - 122°54.60' Located just inside the Pleasant Harbor entrance behind the sand & gravel spit on the N. side of the harbor. No upland facilities but nice wide float in beautiful and serene harbor location. Popular location during shrimping season.

GUEST BOAT CAPACITY: ....Appx. 6 boats

GUEST DOCK: ....Appx. 100 ft.

SEASON: ....All year

MOORING BUOYS: ....None

AMT W/ELECTRICITY: ....None

WATER: ....None

TOILETS: ....Vault toilet

PAY PHONES: ....Close by

HOT SHOWERS: ....None

BOAT RAMP: ....None

PICNIC AREA: ....None

PICNIC SHELTER: ....None

PLAY AREA: ....None

BBQ: ....None

BASIC STORE: ....Close by

PUMP OUT STATION: Close by

DAILY RATE: Mooring Buoys................$5.00/night
Boats under 26 ft..........$8.00/night
Boats 26 ft. & Over.....$11.00/night
Subject to Change in 1997

OTHER: Great dinghy area, crabbing, shrimping (in season), fishing, close to Pls. Hbr. Marina services.

CAUTION! This chartlet not intended for use in navigation.

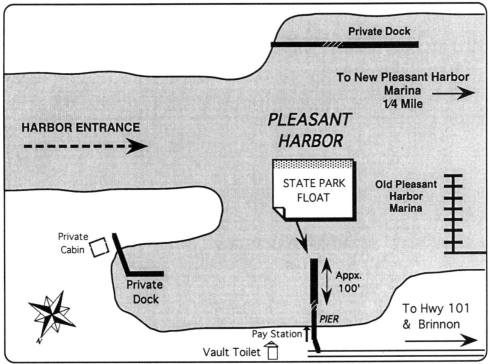

Marrowstone Is.

NAME OF PARK: *FORT FLAGLER STATE PARK*

ADDRESS: 8 Mi. N.E. of Hadlock   Nordland WA   98358

TELEPHONE: 360-385-1259   **MGR:** Al Giersch

SHORT DESCRIPTION & LOCATION:

48°05.55' - 122°43.17' The park floats are located on the N. side of the first bend of the winding entrance to Kilisut Harbor which lies between Indian Is. on the W. and Marrowstone Is. on the E.. The park is a historic former Army fort & consists of 783 acres.

GUEST BOAT CAPACITY: ....Appx. 5-7 boats

SEASON: ....Closed winter

AMT W/ELECTRICITY: ....None

TOILETS: ....Yes

HOT SHOWERS: ....Yes-By Park H.Q.

PICNIC AREA: ....Yes

PLAY AREA: ....Yes

BASIC STORE: ....Yes - summer only

DAILY RATE: Mooring Buoys................$5.00/night
Boats under 26 ft..........$8.00/night
Boats 26 ft. & Over.....$11.00/night
Subject to Change in 1997

GUEST DOCK: ....Appx. 132 ft.

MOORING BUOYS: 7-Avail. all yr.

WATER: ....Yes

PAY PHONES: ....Yes

BOAT RAMP: ....Yes

PICNIC SHELTER: ....Yes

BBQ: ....Yes

PUMP OUT STATION: ......None

OTHER: Lodging, campsites, hiking, swimming, scuba diving, underwater park, fishing close by, porta-potty dump station.

CAUTION! This chartlet not intended for use in navigation.

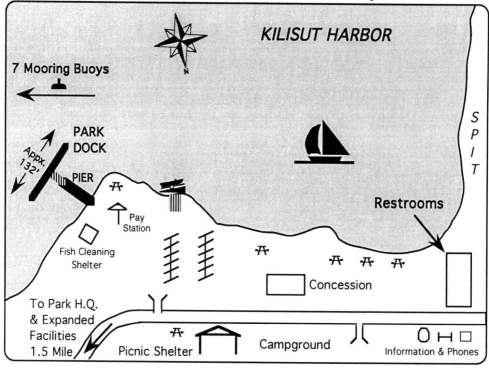

Marrowstone Is.

NAME OF PARK: *MYSTERY BAY STATE PARK*

ADDRESS: 6 Mi. N.E. of Hadlock   Nordland WA   98358

TELEPHONE: 360-385-1259   **MGR:** Al Giersch

SHORT DESCRIPTION & LOCATION:

48°03.50' - 122°41.60' Located in northeastern portion of Mystery Bay in Kilisut Harbor adjacent to west side of Marrowstone Island. Ten acre day use park in quiet rural setting. The park is affiliated with Ft. Flagler State Park 3 miles north.

GUEST BOAT CAPACITY: ....Appx. 15-20 boats	**GUEST DOCK:** ....Appx. 320 ft.
SEASON: ....All year	**MOORING BUOYS:** 7
AMT W/ELECTRICITY: ....None	**WATER:** ....On shore
TOILETS: ....Yes	**PAY PHONES:** ....No
HOT SHOWERS: ....None	**BOAT RAMP:** ....Yes
PICNIC AREA: ....Yes	**PICNIC SHELTER:** ....Yes
PLAY AREA: ....Yes	**BBQ:** ....Yes
BASIC STORE: ....Close by	**PUMP OUT STATION:** ....Yes

DAILY RATE: Mooring Buoys.................$5.00/night
Boats under 26 ft..........$8.00/night
Boats 26 ft. & Over.....$11.00/night
Subject to Change in 1997

OTHER: Clam beaches, unguarded swimming beach, bicycling, and great shoreside picnic area.

CAUTION! This chartlet not intended for use in navigation.

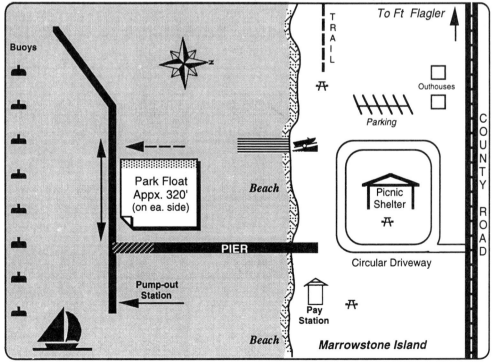

Port Angeles

NAME OF MARINA: *PORT OF PORT ANGELES Boat Haven* RADIO: None

ADDRESS: 832 Boathaven Drive   Port Angeles   WA 98362

TELEPHONE: 360-457-4505   MGR: Chuck Faires

SHORT DESCRIPTION & LOCATION:

48°07.60' - 123°27.08' Marina is located at southwest corner of Port Angeles Harbor just west of downtown Port Angeles. The well protected facility offers full services for the boater. Additional moorage is located at the Municipal Pier, east of the ferry dock.

GUEST BOAT CAPACITY: ....Appx. 20-30 boats	GUEST DOCK: ....700 feet
SEASON: ....All year	GUEST SLIPS: ....Guest dock only
RESERVATION POLICY: ....None	WATER: ....Yes
AMT W/ELECTRICITY: ....All	AMPS: ....20 A
FUEL DOCK: ....Gas & Diesel	PUMP OUT STATION ....Yes
MARINE REPAIRS: ....On premises	HAUL OUT: ....Travel-Lift
TOILETS: ....Yes	BOAT RAMP: ....Yes
HOT SHOWERS: ....Yes	LAUNDRY: ....Close by
RESTAURANT: ....Yes	LOUNGE: ....Close by
PICNIC AREA: ....None	POOL: ....None
PLAY AREA: ....None	BBQ: ....None
BASIC STORE: ....Close by	GOLF: ....Close by
ELECTRICITY: ....Included in moorage	OTHER: Customs port-of-entry,
DAILY RATE: ....$10.00 up to 30 feet	city tours, close to
................20¢ per foot over 30 feet	good fishing grounds,
	walking distance to
	shops and restaurants.

NAME OF YACHT CLUB: *PORT ANGELES YACHT CLUB* Ⓑ

CLUB ADDRESS: Box 692, Port Angeles, WA 98362

CLUB TELEPHONE: PERSON IN CHARGE: Commodore

LOCATION & SPECIAL NOTES

The club house is located on west side of boat harbor entrance. PAYC provides one reciprocal slip per night in the <u>P.A. Boat Haven</u> and offer one night's free moorage for members of reciprocating clubs. Check in with harbor master at fuel dock for instructions.

RECIPROCAL BOAT CAPACITY:.....................One	RECIPROCAL DOCK: Guest dock
RECIPROCAL SEASON:................................All year	RECIPROCAL SLIPS: ...Dock only
RESERVATION POLICY: ....None	WATER: ....Yes
TOILETS: ....At Marina	AMT W/ELECTRICITY: ....All
HOT SHOWERS: ....At Marina	AMPS: ....20 A
RESTAURANT: ....Close by	LOUNGE: ....Close by
DAILY RATE: ....No Charge	OTHER: ....Same as marina listing
Marina rates apply after first night	

NOTE: *THIS IS PRIVATE MOORAGE ONLY AVAILABLE TO MEMBERS OF RECIPROCAL YACHT CLUBS! YOUR CLUB MUST HAVE RECIPROCAL PRIVILEGES AND YOU MUST FLY YOUR BURGEE!*

Port Angeles

CAUTION! This chartlet not intended for use in navigation.

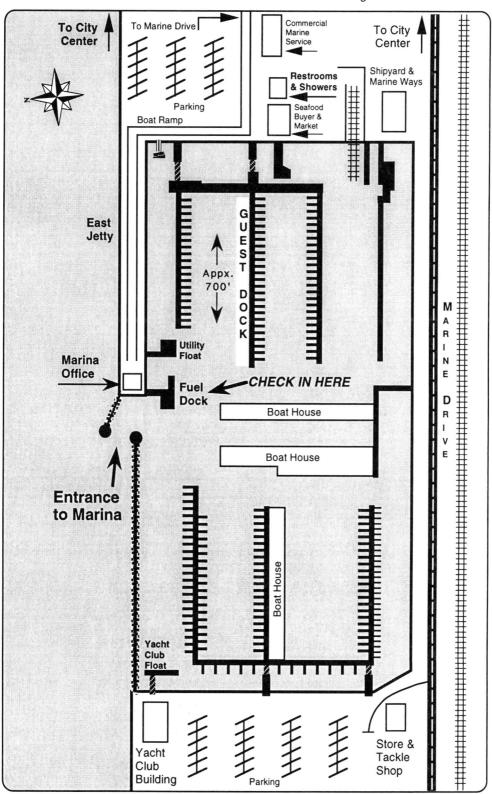

NOTES

Port Angeles

NAME OF PARK: *PORT ANGELES MUNICIPAL PARK & CITY PIER*

ADDRESS: City Hall 321 E. 5th St. Port Angeles, WA 98362

TELEPHONE: 360-457-0411 Ext. 227 MGR: City of Port Angeles

SHORT DESCRIPTION & LOCATION:

48°07.30' - 123°25.65' Located in downtown Port Angeles in a 2 acre waterfront park. A 50' tall observation tower provides a good landmark. Full services for boaters can be found as well as historic and tourist related activities. Maximum boat size is 40'.

GUEST BOAT CAPACITY: ....Appx. 20 boats

SEASON: ....Closed winter

AMT W/ELECTRICITY: ....None

TOILETS: ....Yes

HOT SHOWERS: ....None

PICNIC AREA: ....Yes

PLAY AREA: ....Yes

BASIC STORE: ....Close by

DAILY RATE: ....$8.00 per 24 hours

GUEST DOCK: ....4/Appx. 80 ft.

MOORING BUOYS: ....None

WATER: ....None

PAY PHONES: ....Yes

BOAT RAMP: ....None

PICNIC SHELTER: ....Yes

BBQ: ....Yes-Pits

PUMP OUT STATION: ......None

OTHER: Marine laboratory on Pier open to public, sandy beach, fishing close by, close to many restaurants & shops.

CAUTION! This chartlet not intended for use in navigation.

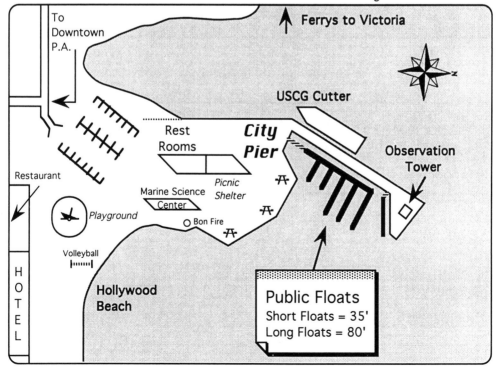

Port Hadlock

NAME OF MARINA: **PORT HADLOCK MARINA**   RADIO: None

ADDRESS: 310 Alcohol Loop   Port Hadlock,   WA 98339

TELEPHONE: 360-385-7030   MGR: Ed Hanson

SHORT DESCRIPTION & LOCATION:

48°01.80' - 122°44.60' Located about 5 mi. S. of Port Townsend just W. of entrance to Pt. Townsend Canal. The marina was ravaged by the great storms of 1991 but is re-built and open. Although no designated guest dock, open slips are rented out as needed.

GUEST BOAT CAPACITY: ....Appx. 2-6 boats	GUEST DOCK: ....Slips only
SEASON: ....All year	GUEST SLIPS: ....Varies
RESERVATION POLICY:............................Accepts	WATER: ....Yes
AMT W/ELECTRICITY: ....All	AMPS: ....30 A
FUEL DOCK: ....None	PUMP OUT STATION ....None
MARINE REPAIRS: ....Close by	HAUL OUT: ....None
TOILETS: ....Yes	BOAT RAMP: ....Close by
HOT SHOWERS: ....Yes	LAUNDRY: ....Close by
RESTAURANT: ....Yes	LOUNGE: ....Yes
PICNIC AREA: ....Yes	POOL:..None
PLAY AREA: ....Yes	BBQ: ....None
BASIC STORE: ....Close by	GOLF: ....Close by
ELECTRICITY:.........................$2.50 per day	OTHER: Historic Alcohol Plant
DAILY RATE: ....Appx. .50¢ per foot	Restaurant & Lodge.
MOST BOATS $15.00/NIGHT	Walking distance to
	Hadlock shopping
	centers & services.

CAUTION! This chartlet not intended for use in navigation.

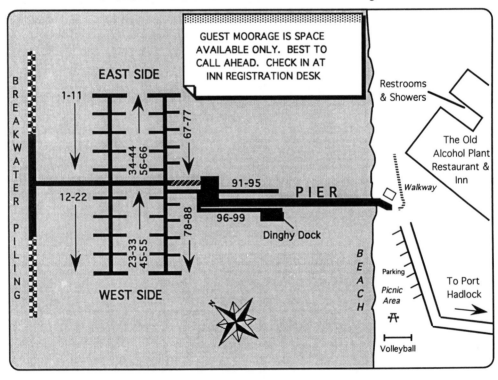

Port Hadlock

NAME OF YACHT CLUB: *PORT HADLOCK YACHT CLUB*

ADDRESS: P.O. Box 248   Port Hadlock,   WA   98339

TELEPHONE: 360-385-7377   PERSON IN CHARGE: Port Captain

SHORT DESCRIPTION & LOCATION:

48°01.90' - 122°44.70' Located appx. 5 mi. S. of Port Townsend just W. of entrance to Port Townsend Canal & N. of Skunk Is., PHYC offers 2 reciprocal buoys adjacent to the Old Alcohol Plant Inn & Marina.. Tie your tender to PHYC dinghy dock at marina & see PHYC registration info on bulletin board at head of pier.

RECIPROCAL BOAT CAPACITY............... 2 boats   RECIPROCAL DOCK: Buoys only

SEASON: ....All year   RECIPROCAL SLIPS: Buoys only

RESERVATION POLICY:.......................Groups only   WATER: ....At marina

TOILETS: ....At marina   AMT W/ELECTRICITY: ....None

HOT SHOWERS: ....At marina   AMPS: ....None

RESTAURANT:..................................At marina   LOUNGE: ....At marina

DAILY RATE: ....No charge for 3 nights   OTHER: Walking distance to Port
of moorage. Thereafter $5/night   Hadlock shopping centers
with max. of 7 consecutive nights.   restaurants, & services.

NOTE: THIS IS PRIVATE MOORAGE AND ONLY AVAILABLE TO MEMBERS OF RECIPROCAL YACHT CLUBS. YOUR CLUB MUST HAVE RECIPROCAL PRIVILEGES AND YOU MUST FLY YOUR BURGEE.

CAUTION! This chartlet not intended for use in navigation.

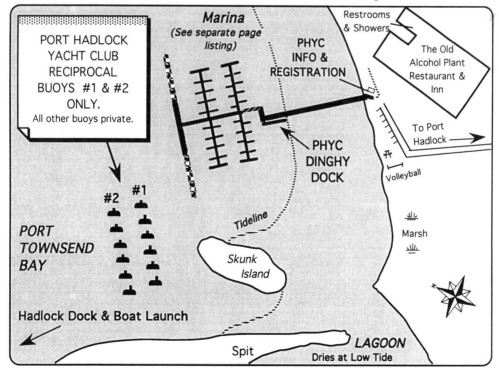

Port Ludlow

NAME OF MARINA: **PORT LUDLOW MARINA**   RADIO: VHF Ch.16
ADDRESS: 1 Gull Drive   Port Ludlow   WA 98365
TELEPHONE: 360-437-0513   MGR: Dean Kelley

SHORT DESCRIPTION & LOCATION:

47°55.30' - 122°41.10' Located about 12 mi. S. of Port Townsend on N. side of Port Ludlow Bay. The upscale resort & marina offer full marine services in a well protected harbor. There is a large guest dock plus open slips are rented out to overnighters.

GUEST BOAT CAPACITY: ....Appx. 60 boats	GUEST DOCK: ...Appx.300' + slips
SEASON: ....All year	GUEST SLIPS: ....Varies
RESERVATION POLICY: ....Accepts	WATER: ....Yes
AMT W/ELECTRICITY: ....All	AMPS: ....30-50 A
FUEL DOCK: ....Gas & Diesel	PUMP OUT STATION ....Yes
MARINE REPAIRS: ....None	HAUL OUT: ....None
TOILETS: ....Yes	BOAT RAMP: ....None
HOT SHOWERS: ....Yes	LAUNDRY: ....Yes
RESTAURANT: ....Yes	LOUNGE: ....Yes
PICNIC AREA: ....Yes	POOL: ....For hotel guests only
PLAY AREA: ....Yes	BBQ: ....Yes
BASIC STORE: ....Yes	GOLF: ....Yes
ELECTRICITY: ....$3.00 30 Amp/$6.00 50 Amp	OTHER: Hotel, boat and bicycle
DAILY RATE: ....Appx. 60¢/ft. per day - summer	rentals, tennis, gifts &
.........Appx. 50¢/ft. per day - winter	marine supplies, free
10% DISCOUNT FOR GROUPS	shuttle to golf course.

NAME OF YACHT CLUB: *PORT LUDLOW YACHT CLUB*   (B)
CLUB ADDRESS: P.O. Box 65338, Port Ludlow, WA 98365
CLUB TELEPHONE: PERSON IN CHARGE: Commodore

LOCATION & SPECIAL NOTES

PLYC offers 150 feet of reciprocal moorage located just on the inside of the first pier (A) near the fuel dock. Visiting reciprocal yachtsmen are allowed 48 hours of free moorage with 5 days per year maximum. *Your current Y.C. membership card is required.*

RECIPROCAL BOAT CAPACITY:...........3-6 Boats	RECIPROCAL DOCK: ....150 ft.
RECIPROCAL SEASON:................................All year	RECIPROCAL SLIPS: ...Dock only
RESERVATION POLICY: ....None	WATER: ....Yes
TOILETS: ....At Marina	AMT W/ELECTRICITY: ....All
HOT SHOWERS: ....At Marina	AMPS: ....30-50 A
RESTAURANT: ....Close by	LOUNGE: ....Close by
DAILY RATE: ....No charge	OTHER: ....Same as marina listing
...........CHECK IN W/HARBORMASTER	

<u>NOTE:</u> *THIS IS PRIVATE MOORAGE <u>ONLY</u> AVAILABLE TO MEMBERS OF RECIPROCAL YACHT CLUBS! YOUR CLUB <u>MUST</u> HAVE RECIPROCAL PRIVILEGES AND YOU MUST FLY YOUR BURGEE!*

Port Ludlow

CAUTION! This chartlet not intended for use in navigation.

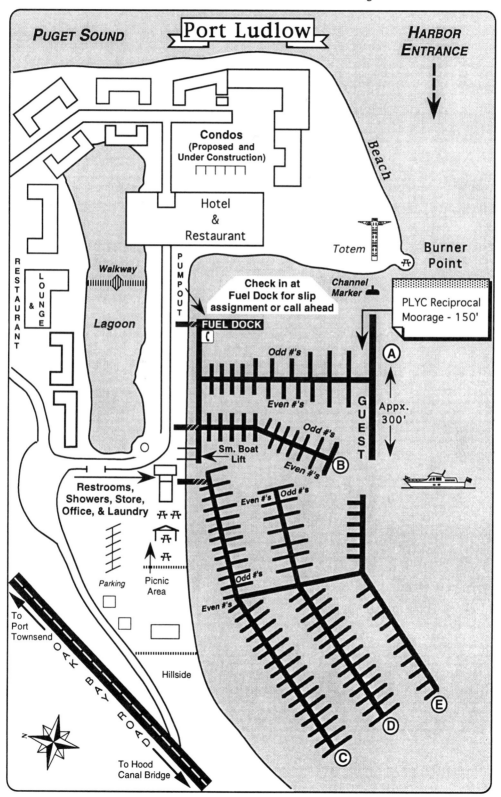

PUGET SOUND

Port Ludlow

HARBOR ENTRANCE

Condos
(Proposed and Under Construction)

Beach

Hotel & Restaurant

Totem

Burner Point

RESTAURANT

LOUNGE &

Walkway

PUMPOUT

Channel Marker

PLYC Reciprocal Moorage - 150'

Check in at Fuel Dock for slip assignment or call ahead

FUEL DOCK

Lagoon

Odd #'s

Even #'s

A

GUEST

Appx. 300'

Odd #'s

Sm. Boat Lift

Even #'s

B

Restrooms, Showers, Store, Office, & Laundry

Even #'s   Odd #'s

Parking

Picnic Area

Odd #'s

Even #'s

To Port Townsend

OAK BAY ROAD

Hillside

E

D

C

To Hood Canal Bridge

Port Townsend

NAME OF PARK: *FORT WORDEN STATE PARK*

ADDRESS: 200 Battrey Way   Port Townsend, WA   98368

TELEPHONE: 360-385-4730   MGR: Jim Farmer

SHORT DESCRIPTION & LOCATION:

48°08.20' - 122°45.50' The park floats are located about 1.5 mi. N. of Pt. Hudson and .5 mi. S. of Pt. Wilson. The large 443 acre park was once a military installation and the landscaped and historic grounds offer many attractions for visitors.

GUEST BOAT CAPACITY: ....Appx. 2-4 boats

GUEST DOCK: ....Appx. 60 ft.

SEASON: ....All year

MOORING BUOYS: 8

AMT W/ELECTRICITY: ....None

WATER: ....Yes

TOILETS: ....Yes

PAY PHONES: ....Yes

HOT SHOWERS: ....Yes

BOAT RAMP: ....Yes - $4.00 fee

PICNIC AREA: ....Yes

PICNIC SHELTER: ....Yes

PLAY AREA: ....Yes

BBQ: ....Yes

BASIC STORE: ....Summer only

PUMP OUT STATION: ......None

DAILY RATE: Mooring Buoys................$5.00/night
Boats under 26 ft..........$8.00/night
Boats 26 ft. & Over.....$11.00/night
Subject to Change in 1997

OTHER: Marine Science Center, tennis courts, athletic fields, scuba diving, fishing, swimming.

CAUTION! This chartlet not intended for use in navigation.

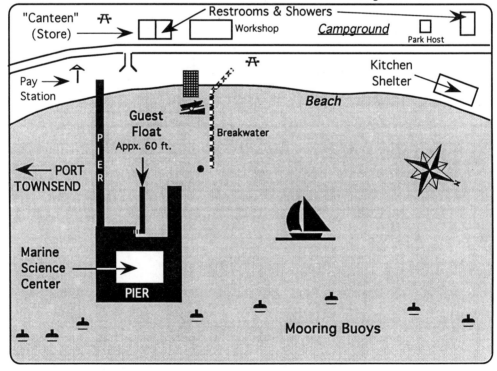

Port Townsend

NAME OF MARINA: *POINT HUDSON RESORT & MARINA*   RADIO: None

ADDRESS: Point Hudson Harbor   Port Townsend,   WA 98368

TELEPHONE: 800-826-3854   MGR: Forrest Rambo, General Manager

SHORT DESCRIPTION & LOCATION:

48°07.00'-122°44.90' Located about 2 blocks north of downtown Port Townsend in a protected dredged harbor which was formerly a Coast Guard station. This older marina is very well maintained and convenient to shops, galleries, restaurants, and historic sights.

GUEST BOAT CAPACITY: ......Appx. 60-75 boats	GUEST DOCK: ....800' plus slips
SEASON: ....All year	GUEST SLIPS: ....Appx. 46
RESERVATION POLICY: ....Accepts	WATER: ....Yes
AMT W/ELECTRICITY: ....All	AMPS: ....15-30 A
FUEL DOCK: ....Close by	PUMP OUT STATION Close by
MARINE REPAIRS: ....On premises	HAUL OUT: ....Travel-Lift
TOILETS: ....Yes	BOAT RAMP: ....Yes-free
HOT SHOWERS: ....Yes	LAUNDRY: ....Yes
RESTAURANT: ....3 On premises	LOUNGE: ....Close by
PICNIC AREA: ....Yes	POOL: ....None
PLAY AREA: ....Close by	BBQ: ....None
BASIC STORE: ....Yes	GOLF: ....Close by
ELECTRICITY: ....$ 3.00 per day	OTHER: Customs Port-of-Entry,
DAILY RATE: ....Appx. .50¢- -.75¢ per foot	motel, guest house,
	RV Park, group event
	facility, charts, bait, ice,
	athletic club facilities.

CAUTION! This chartlet not intended for use in navigation.

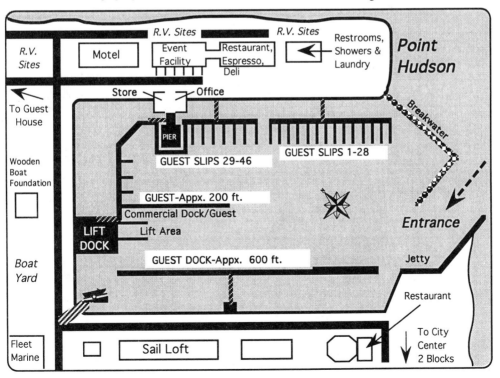

Port Townsend

NAME OF MARINA: *PORT TOWNSEND BOAT HAVEN*   **RADIO:** VHF Ch.9
ADDRESS: P.O. Box 1180   Port Townsend   WA 98368
TELEPHONE: 360-385-2355   **MGR:** Ken Radon

SHORT DESCRIPTION & LOCATION:
48°06.50' - 122°46.20' Located one mile SSW of Point Hudson in Port Townsend. Largest public boat yard on west coast. *Tie up at Fuel Dock & register at port office immediately for slip.* After hours open slip list posted nightly at Port Office.

GUEST BOAT CAPACITY: ....Varies	GUEST DOCK: ....No
SEASON: ....All year	GUEST SLIPS: ....Varies
RESERVATION POLICY: ....None	WATER: ....Yes
AMT W/ELECTRICITY: ....All	AMPS: ....30 A
FUEL DOCK: ....Gas & Diesel	PUMP OUT STATION ....Yes
MARINE REPAIRS: ....On premises	HAUL OUT: ....Travel-Lift
TOILETS: ....Yes	BOAT RAMP: ....Yes
HOT SHOWERS: ....Yes	LAUNDRY: ....Yes
RESTAURANT: ....Close by	LOUNGE: ....Close by
PICNIC AREA: ....Yes	POOL: ....None
PLAY AREA: ....None	BBQ: ....None
BASIC STORE: ....Yes	GOLF: ....Close by
ELECTRICITY: ....$ 3.00 per day	OTHER: Close to P.T. attractions

DAILY RATE: 20' slip = $9.00 / 30' slip = $12.00   & services, dry storage,
40' slip = $13.00 /50' slip = $15.00   large boatyard, 70 ton
Over 52' = .50 cents per foot.   lifts, many chandleries
and skilled shipwrights.

NAME OF YACHT CLUB: *PORT TOWNSEND YACHT CLUB*
CLUB ADDRESS: P.O. Box 75, Port Townsend, WA 98368
CLUB TELEPHONE: **PERSON IN CHARGE:** Vice Commodore

LOCATION & SPECIAL NOTES
PTYC offers slips on "D" Dock in Boat Haven for reciprocal yacht club members. Slip #281 (40 ft.) is available all year long while Slip #282 (50 ft.) is also available from June through Labor Day. Pls register at Port Office, present your current club card & check out by noon.

RECIPROCAL BOAT CAPACITY: Apx.1-4 boats	RECIPROCAL DOCK: See above
RECIPROCAL SEASON:..................All year	RECIPROCAL SLIPS: ....1 or 2
RESERVATION POLICY: ....None	WATER: ....Yes
TOILETS: ....At Marina	AMT W/ELECTRICITY: ....All
HOT SHOWERS: ....At Marina	AMPS: ....30 A
RESTAURANT: ....Close by	LOUNGE: ....Close by
DAILY RATE: No Charge. Limit: 1 night/yr. May-Sept. & 1 night/mo. Oct-Apr.	OTHER: NO RAFTING ALLOWED. POWER SUBJECT TO FEE.

NOTE: THIS IS PRIVATE MOORAGE ONLY AVAILABLE TO MEMBERS OF RECIPROCAL YACHT CLUBS! YOUR CLUB MUST HAVE RECIPROCAL PRIVILEGES AND YOU MUST FLY YOUR BURGEE!

Port Townsend

CAUTION! This chartlet not intended for use in navigation.

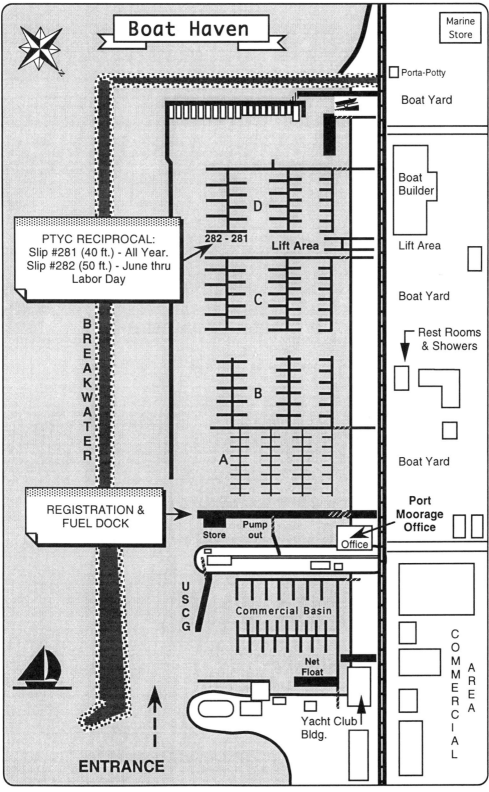

Boat Haven

Marine Store

Porta-Potty

Boat Yard

Boat Builder

Lift Area

PTYC RECIPROCAL:
Slip #281 (40 ft.) - All Year.
Slip #282 (50 ft.) - June thru Labor Day

D

282 - 281   **Lift Area**

Boat Yard

Rest Rooms & Showers

C

B

B R E A K W A T E R

A

Boat Yard

REGISTRATION & FUEL DOCK

Port Moorage Office

Store   Pump out   Office

U S C G

Commercial Basin

Net Float

Yacht Club Bldg.

C O M M E R C I A L   A R E A

ENTRANCE

Quilcene

NAME OF MARINA: *QUILCENE BOAT HAVEN*   RADIO: None
ADDRESS: 1731 Linger Longer   Quilcene   WA 98376
TELEPHONE: 360-765-3131   MGR: Don Dicken

SHORT DESCRIPTION & LOCATION:

47°48.00' - 122°49.60' Located in Quilcene Bay, a small inlet on the W. side of Dabob Bay N. of Whitney Point. The small marina is on the W. side of the bay about 1.4 mi. S. of the Town of Quilcene, famous for oysters and seafood.

GUEST BOAT CAPACITY: ....Appx 5-6 boats	GUEST DOCK: 70 ft.+ open slips
SEASON: ....All year	GUEST SLIPS: ....Varies
RESERVATION POLICY:.....................Accepts	WATER: ....Yes
AMT W/ELECTRICITY: ....All	AMPS: ....20 A
FUEL DOCK: ....Gas & Diesel	PUMP OUT STATION ....Yes
MARINE REPAIRS: ....None	HAUL OUT: ....None
TOILETS: ....Yes	BOAT RAMP:...............................Yes
HOT SHOWERS: ....Yes	LAUNDRY: ....Close by
RESTAURANT: ....In Quilcene	LOUNGE: ....In Quilcene
PICNIC AREA: ....Yes	POOL:...None
PLAY AREA: ....None	BBQ: ....Yes
BASIC STORE: ....None	GOLF: ....None
ELECTRICITY: ....$2.00 per day	OTHER: Swimming beach,
DAILY RATE: ....Up to 24' - $12.00	clam & oyster beach,
....24'-36' - $14.00	shuttle to town, bike
....36'-50' - $14.00	loaners by harbormaster

CAUTION! This chartlet not intended for use in navigation.

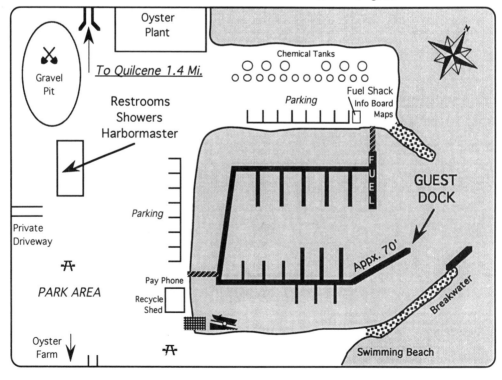

Seabeck

NAME OF MARINA: **SEABECK MARINA**   RADIO: VHF Ch. 16

ADDRESS: P.O. Box 177   Seabeck   WA   98380

TELEPHONE: 360-830-5179   MGR: Mark Sjostrom

SHORT DESCRIPTION & LOCATION:

47°38.50' - 122°49.60' Located in Seabeck Bay, a sm. cove about 6 miles SW of Bangor on E. shore of Hood Canal. The marina & historic sm. settlement is on the S. side of the bay. New management is currently redesigning & upgrading the docks & facilities.

GUEST BOAT CAPACITY: ....Appx. 12 boats	GUEST DOCK: ....Appx. 200 ft.
SEASON: ....All year	GUEST SLIPS: ....Varies
RESERVATION POLICY: ....Accepts	WATER: ....At fuel dock
AMT W/ELECTRICITY: ....None	AMPS: ....None
FUEL DOCK: ....Gas only	PUMP OUT STATION ....None
MARINE REPAIRS: ....On premises	HAUL OUT: ....Sm. boat sling
TOILETS: ....Yes	BOAT RAMP: ....Close by
HOT SHOWERS: ....None	LAUNDRY: ....None
RESTAURANT: ....Pizza & snack bar	LOUNGE: ....None
PICNIC AREA: ....Yes	POOL: ....None
PLAY AREA: ....None	BBQ: ....None
BASIC STORE: ....Yes	GOLF: ....None
ELECTRICITY: ....None	OTHER: Historic mosquito fleet
DAILY RATE: ....Appx. .30¢ per foot	pier, general store, post office, spectacular view of Olympics, fishing, oysters, & shrimping.

CAUTION! This chartlet not intended for use in navigation.

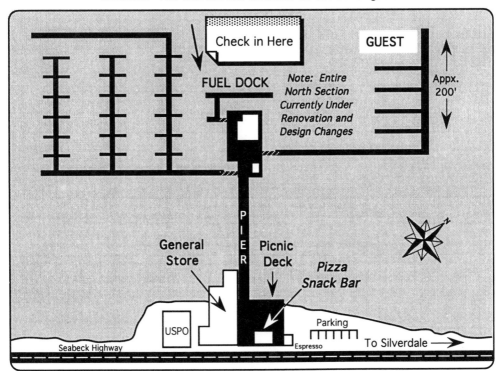

Sequim

NAME OF MARINA: *JOHN WAYNE MARINA*   **RADIO:** None

ADDRESS: 2577 W. Sequim Bay Rd. Sequim   WA 98382

TELEPHONE: 360-417-3440   **MGR:** Jan Hardin

SHORT DESCRIPTION & LOCATION:

48°03.99' -123°2.22' Located in Sequim Bay, 6 mi. S.E. of Dungeness Bay. The bay is accessed via a well marked channel at N.W. corner & marina is marked by nav. lights at the E. ends of the breakwaters at Pitship Pt. The modern facility offers full boater services.

GUEST BOAT CAPACITY: ....Appx. 40 boats	GUEST DOCK: ....160' plus slips
SEASON: ....All year	GUEST SLIPS: ....Varies
RESERVATION POLICY: ....None	WATER:...Yes
AMT W/ELECTRICITY: ....All	AMPS: ....20-30 A
FUEL DOCK: ....Gas & Diesel	PUMP OUT STATION ....Yes
MARINE REPAIRS: ....Close by	HAUL OUT: ....None
TOILETS: ....Yes	BOAT RAMP: ....Yes
HOT SHOWERS: ....Yes	LAUNDRY: ....Yes
RESTAURANT: ....Yes	LOUNGE: ....None
PICNIC AREA: ....Yes	POOL:.....................................None
PLAY AREA: ....Yes	BBQ: ....None
BASIC STORE: ....Yes + marine gifts & supplies	GOLF: ....Close by
ELECTRICITY: ....$3.00 per day	OTHER: Bus service to town of
DAILY RATE: ....Up to 30 ft. - $15.00	Sequim 3 mi. away,
..................................31-40 ft. - $19.00	boat rentals, fishing,
..........................40 ft. & over - $23.00	clamming, crabbing,
	groceries, bait & tackle.

NAME OF YACHT CLUB: *THE SEQUIM BAY YACHT CLUB*

CLUB ADDRESS: P.O. Box 1261, Sequim, WA 98382

CLUB TELEPHONE: 360-683-1338   **PERSON IN CHARGE:**   Secretary

LOCATION & SPECIAL NOTES

One day moorage in the John Wayne Marina is extended to members of reciprocal clubs on a space available basis. Check in with the Harbormaster to be assigned guest moorage. Moorage includes power hook-ups as available.

RECIPROCAL BOAT CAPACITY:.................Varies	RECIPROCAL DOCK: ....None
RECIPROCAL SEASON:.................................All year	RECIPROCAL SLIPS: ....Varies
RESERVATION POLICY: ....None	WATER:...Yes
TOILETS: ....At Marina	AMT W/ELECTRICITY: .....Varies
HOT SHOWERS: ....At Marina	AMPS: ....20-30 A
RESTAURANT: ....At Marina	LOUNGE: ....None
DAILY RATE: ....No charge	OTHER: ....Same as marina listing

NOTE: THIS IS PRIVATE MOORAGE ONLY AVAILABLE TO MEMBERS OF RECIPROCAL YACHT CLUBS! YOUR CLUB MUST HAVE RECIPROCAL PRIVILEGES AND YOU MUST FLY YOUR BURGEE!

Sequim

CAUTION! This chartlet not intended for use in navigation.

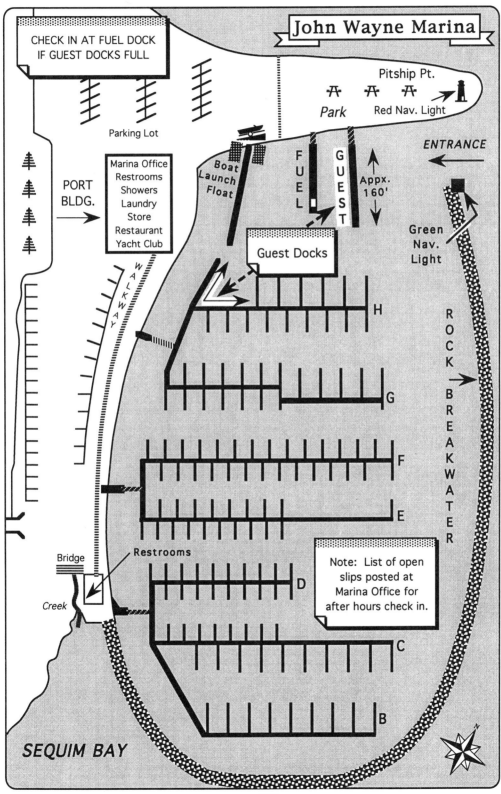

John Wayne Marina

CHECK IN AT FUEL DOCK
IF GUEST DOCKS FULL

Pitship Pt.

Park   Red Nav. Light

Parking Lot

ENTRANCE

PORT
BLDG.

Marina Office
Restrooms
Showers
Laundry
Store
Restaurant
Yacht Club

Boat
Launch
Float

F
U
E
L

G
U
E
S
T

Appx.
160'

Green
Nav.
Light

WALKWAY

Guest Docks

H

G

R
O
C
K

B
R
E
A
K
W
A
T
E
R

F

E

Bridge   Restrooms

Creek

D

Note: List of open
slips posted at
Marina Office for
after hours check in.

C

B

SEQUIM BAY

Sequim

NAME OF PARK: **SEQUIM BAY STATE PARK**

ADDRESS: 269035 Hwy 101 Sequim WA 98382

TELEPHONE: 360-683-4235 MGR: Mike Reichner

SHORT DESCRIPTION & LOCATION:

48°02.45' -123°01.50' Located in Sequim Bay, 6 mi. S.E. of Dungeness Bay. The 3.8 mi. long bay is landlocked and the park is at the S.W. end of the bay N. of Schoolhouse Point. At low tide the water shallows at the float & buoys recommended for large boats.

GUEST BOAT CAPACITY: ....Appx. 15-20 boats

SEASON: ....All year

AMT W/ELECTRICITY: ....None

TOILETS: ....Yes

HOT SHOWERS: ....Yes

PICNIC AREA: ....Yes

PLAY AREA: ....Yes

BASIC STORE: ....Close by

DAILY RATE: Mooring Buoys.................$5.00/night
Boats under 26 ft..........$8.00/night
Boats 26 ft. & Over.....$11.00/night
Subject to Change in 1997

GUEST DOCK: ....Appx. 200 ft.

MOORING BUOYS: 6

WATER: ....Yes

PAY PHONES: ....Yes

BOAT RAMP: ....Yes

PICNIC SHELTER: ....Yes

BBQ: ....Yes

PUMP OUT STATION: Planned

OTHER: ....92 Acre park, campsites, fishing, tennis, hiking, swimming, games, scuba diving.

CAUTION! This chartlet not intended for use in navigation.

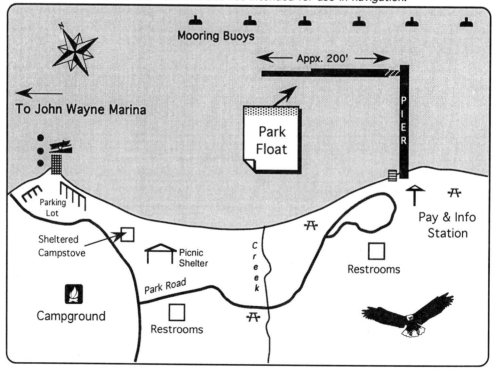

Mooring Buoys

Appx. 200'

To John Wayne Marina

Park Float

PIER

Parking Lot

Sheltered Campstove

Picnic Shelter

Creek

Pay & Info Station

Restrooms

Campground

Park Road

Restrooms

Union

NAME OF MARINA: *ALDERBROOK INN MARINA*   RADIO: None

ADDRESS: E. 7101 Hwy 106   Union   WA 98592

TELEPHONE: 360-898-2200   MGR: Lee Cameron

SHORT DESCRIPTION & LOCATION:

47°21.00' - 123°04.00' Located in a cove on S. shore of The Great Bend of Hood Canal about 1.3 miles E. of the town of Union. The resort has a large "T" Pier with ample float space and many world class amenities for boaters in a quiet and serene setting.

GUEST BOAT CAPACITY: ....Appx. 40 boats	GUEST DOCK: ....Appx. 580 ft.
SEASON: ....All year	GUEST SLIPS: ....Dock only
RESERVATION POLICY: ....None	WATER: ....Yes
AMT W/ELECTRICITY: ....All	AMPS: ....30 A
FUEL DOCK: ....Close by	PUMP OUT STATION ....Yes
MARINE REPAIRS: ....Close by	HAUL OUT: ....None
TOILETS: ....Yes	BOAT RAMP: ....Close by
HOT SHOWERS: ....Yes	LAUNDRY: ....Close by
RESTAURANT: ....Yes	LOUNGE: ....Yes
PICNIC AREA: ....Yes	POOL: ....Yes
PLAY AREA: ....Yes	BBQ: ....Yes
BASIC STORE: ....Close by	GOLF: ....Yes
ELECTRICITY: ....**$6.00 per day	OTHER: Hotel and cottages,
DAILY RATE: ....Appx.. 40¢ per foot	jacuzzi, sm. boat rentals,
......................**INCLUDES USE	tennis, scuba diving,
OF THE SHORE FACILITIES.	water skiing, gift shop,
	beauty salon, boutique.

CAUTION! This chartlet not intended for use in navigation.

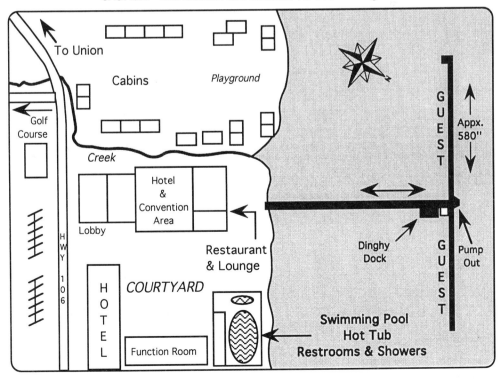

Union

NAME OF MARINA: *HOOD CANAL MARINA*   **RADIO:** VHF Ch. 16

ADDRESS: E. 5101 Hwy 106,   Union,   WA   98592

TELEPHONE: 360-898-2252   **MGR:** Martin Sun

SHORT DESCRIPTION & LOCATION:

47°21.40' - 122°06.00' Located on the S. shore of The Great Bend of Hood Canal, the marina and town offer many services for boaters. The town of Union is a historic railway stop and the marina is well protected from south winds.

GUEST BOAT CAPACITY: ....Appx 10 boats	**GUEST DOCK:** ....Appx. 300 ft.
SEASON: ....All year	**GUEST SLIPS:** ....Dock only
RESERVATION POLICY:.............................Accepts	**WATER:** ....Yes
AMT W/ELECTRICITY: ....None	**AMPS:** ....30 A
FUEL DOCK: ....Gas only	**PUMP OUT STATION** ....None
MARINE REPAIRS: ....On premises	**HAUL OUT:** ....None
TOILETS: ....Yes	**BOAT RAMP:**...............................Yes
HOT SHOWERS: ....None	**LAUNDRY:** ....None
RESTAURANT: ....Yes	**LOUNGE:** ....None
PICNIC AREA: ....Yes	**POOL:**...None
PLAY AREA: ....None	**BBQ:** ....Yes
BASIC STORE: ....Close by	**GOLF:** ....Close by
ELECTRICITY: ....$2.50 per day	**OTHER:** Charming country store
DAILY RATE: ....Appx. .50¢ per foot	across street, oysters,
	clams, & crabbing close
	by, marine supplies.

CAUTION! This chartlet not intended for use in navigation.

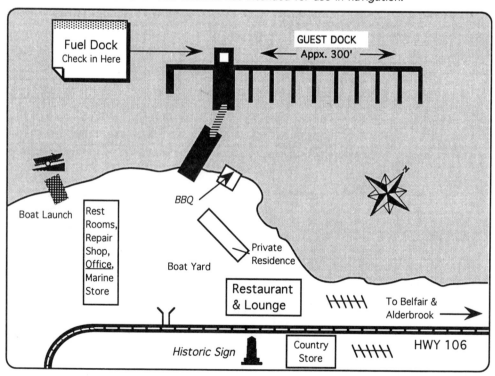

C H A P T E R

4

WHIDBEY ISLAND
&
SKAGIT COUNTY

Cornet Bay

NAME OF MARINA: *DECEPTION PASS MARINA*   RADIO: VHF Ch.16
ADDRESS: 5191 N Cornet Bay Rd   Oak Harbor   WA   98277
TELEPHONE: 360-675-5411   MGR: Dundee Woods

SHORT DESCRIPTION & LOCATION:

48°23.90' - 122°37.60'   (FORMERLY CORNET BAY MARINA) Cornet Bay indents into the N. end of Whidbey Is. off the S.E. side of Deception Pass. Guest moorage consists of open slips of perm. marina tenants. Usually can accommodate 5-10 boats.

GUEST BOAT CAPACITY: ....Varies	GUEST DOCK: ....None
SEASON: ....All year	GUEST SLIPS: ....Varies
RESERVATION POLICY: ....None	WATER: ....Yes
AMT W/ELECTRICITY: 90%	AMPS: ....30 A
FUEL DOCK: ....Gas, Dsl, & LP	PUMP OUT STATION Close by
MARINE REPAIRS: ....Close by	HAUL OUT: ....None
TOILETS: ....Yes	BOAT RAMP: ....Close by
HOT SHOWERS: ....Close by	LAUNDRY: ....Close by
RESTAURANT: ....Close by	LOUNGE: ....None
PICNIC AREA: ....Yes	POOL: ....None
PLAY AREA: ....Yes	BBQ: ....Close by
BASIC STORE: ....Yes	GOLF: ....Close by
ELECTRICITY: ....Included in moorage	OTHER: Close to Deception Pass
DAILY RATE: ....Appx. .65¢ per foot	State Park, well stocked store with propane, marine & fishing supplies.

CAUTION! This chartlet not intended for use in navigation.

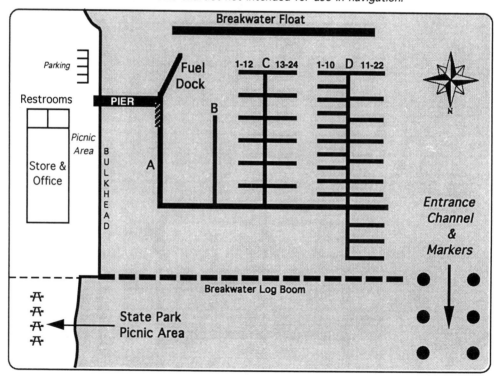

Cornet Bay

NAME OF PARK: *DECEPTION PASS STATE PARK*

ADDRESS: 5175 N. Cornet Rd.   Oak Harbor WA   98277

TELEPHONE: 360-675-2417   **MGR:**   W.M. Overby

SHORT DESCRIPTION & LOCATION:

48°24.10' - 122°37.40' Located about 1/4 mile east of Cornet Bay marina on north end of Whidbey off southeast side of Deception Pass. Large boat launching area with parking for 70 boat trailers is convenient for boaters cruising to San Juan Islands.

GUEST BOAT CAPACITY: ....Appx. 30-40	GUEST DOCK: ......300 ft. + floats
SEASON: ....All year	MOORING BUOYS: 11
AMT W/ELECTRICITY: ....None	WATER: ....Shoreside
TOILETS: ....Yes	PAY PHONES: ....None
HOT SHOWERS: ....Yes	BOAT RAMP: ....Yes
PICNIC AREA: ....Yes	PICNIC SHELTER: ....Yes
PLAY AREA: ....Yes	BBQ: ....Yes
BASIC STORE: ....Close by	PUMP OUT STATION: ....Yes

DAILY RATE: Mooring Buoys.................$5.00/night
Boats under 26 ft...........$8.00/night
Boats 26 ft. & Over.....$11.00/night
Subject to Change in 1997

OTHER: Scenic walking trail in the Hoypus point area of the park, fishing, beachcombing, crabbing.

CAUTION! This chartlet not intended for use in navigation.

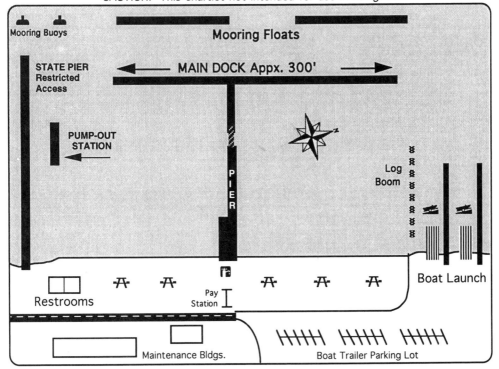

Coupeville

NAME OF MARINA: *PORT OF COUPEVILLE FLOATS*   RADIO: None

ADDRESS: P.O. Box 577   Coupeville   WA 98239

TELEPHONE: 360-678-5020   MGR: Jack Parker

SHORT DESCRIPTION & LOCATION:

48°13.30' - 122°41.10' Located on E. Whidbey Is. on the S. shore of Penn Cove, about 2 miles from head of Cove. Moorage is on the floats adjacent to the historic city pier. Coupeville's waterfront Front St. offers picturesque shops, restaurants & museum..

GUEST BOAT CAPACITY: ....Appx. 8-12 boats	GUEST DOCK: ....Appx. 160 ft.
SEASON: ....All year	GUEST SLIPS: ....Dock only
RESERVATION POLICY:....................................None	WATER: ....None
AMT W/ELECTRICITY: ....None	AMPS: ....None
FUEL DOCK: ....Gas & Diesel	PUMP OUT STATION ....None
MARINE REPAIRS: ....Close by	HAUL OUT: ....None
TOILETS: ....Yes	BOAT RAMP: ....Close by
HOT SHOWERS: ....Yes	LAUNDRY: ....None
RESTAURANT: ....Close by	LOUNGE: ....Close by
PICNIC AREA: ....Yes	POOL:..None
PLAY AREA: ....Close by	BBQ: ....None
BASIC STORE: ....Yes	GOLF: ....Close by
ELECTRICITY: ....None	OTHER: Liquor store, grocery
DAILY RATE: ....Appx. .20¢ per ft. nightly	store, bank, deli, Sat.
	Farmers Market,
	Victorian homes.

CAUTION! This chartlet not intended for use in navigation.

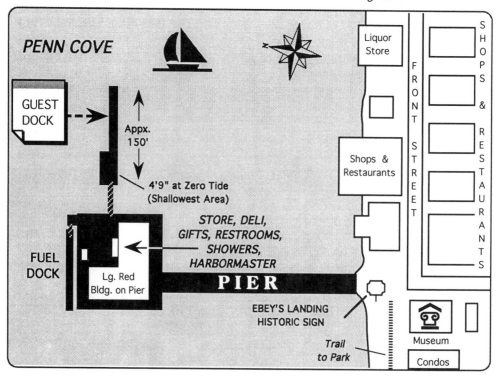

La Conner

NAME OF MARINA: *LA CONNER CITY FLOATS*   RADIO: None
ADDRESS: City of La Conner   La Conner   WA 98257
TELEPHONE: 360-466-3933   MGR: Randy Young

SHORT DESCRIPTION & LOCATION:

48°23.50' - 122°30.20' Located midway on the Swinomish Channel which connects Skagit Bay (south) and Padilla Bay (north). The city floats in this historic and scenic town offer moorage in three locations right at the base of many tourist activities.

GUEST BOAT CAPACITY: ....Appx. 6-8 boats	GUEST DOCK: 40' (Max size-45')
SEASON: ....All year	GUEST SLIPS: ....6 - 40' berths
RESERVATION POLICY:.......................None	WATER: ....None
AMT W/ELECTRICITY: ....None	AMPS: ....None
FUEL DOCK: ....Close by	PUMP OUT STATION ....None
MARINE REPAIRS: ....Close by	HAUL OUT: ....Close by
TOILETS: ....Close by	BOAT RAMP:.....................Close by
HOT SHOWERS: ....None	LAUNDRY: ....Close by
RESTAURANT: ....Close by	LOUNGE: ....Close by
PICNIC AREA: ....None	POOL:...None
PLAY AREA: ....None	BBQ: ....None
BASIC STORE: ....Close by	GOLF: ....Close by
ELECTRICITY: ....None	OTHER: Tourist oriented town with specialty shops, restaurants, marine stores, & art galleries.
DAILY RATE: 5 Hrs. or less - $5.00 30' & under ....$8.00 over 30' **Overnight** - $12.00 30' & under ....$16.00 over 30'	

CAUTION! This chartlet not intended for use in navigation.

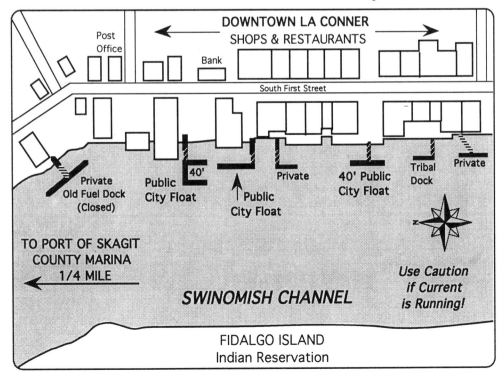

La Conner

NAME OF MARINA: *THE LA CONNER MARINA*   **RADIO:** VHF Ch. 68

ADDRESS: P.O. Box 456   La Conner   WA 98257

TELEPHONE: 360-466-3118   **MGR:** Eric Edlund

SHORT DESCRIPTION & LOCATION:

48°23.70' - 122°30.30' Located midway on the Swinomish Channel which connects Skagit Bay (south) and Padilla Bay (north). This marina in this historic and scenic town offers moorage in two boat basins on two guest docks as well as vacated tenant's slips.

GUEST BOAT CAPACITY: ....Appx. 50-75 boats	GUEST DOCK: 600' (2) plus slips
SEASON: ....All year	GUEST SLIPS: ....Varies
RESERVATION POLICY: ....None	WATER: ....Yes
AMT W/ELECTRICITY: ....All	AMPS: ....30 A
FUEL DOCK: ....Gas & Diesel	PUMP OUT STATION ....Yes
MARINE REPAIRS: ....On premises	HAUL OUT: ....Travel-Lift
TOILETS: ....Yes	BOAT RAMP: ....Close by
HOT SHOWERS: ....Yes	LAUNDRY: ....Yes
RESTAURANT: ....Yes	LOUNGE: ....Close by
PICNIC AREA: ....Yes	POOL: ....None
PLAY AREA: ....None	BBQ: ....Yes
BASIC STORE: ....Yes	GOLF: ....Close by
ELECTRICITY: ....$ 2.00 per day	OTHER: Pump-out station,
DAILY RATE: ....Appx. .40¢ per foot	tourist oriented town
	with specialty shops,
	restaurants, marine
	stores, & art galleries.

NAME OF YACHT CLUB: *SWINOMISH YACHT CLUB*

CLUB ADDRESS: P.O. Box 602, La Conner, WA 98257

CLUB TELEPHONE: 360-466-4902   **PERSON IN CHARGE:** Reciprocal Chair.

LOCATION & SPECIAL NOTES

The reciprocal dock is located on "E" Dock in the Port's south boat basin & offers appx. 175'. All visitors must register dockside at the M/V Poco Loco or with a SYC. representative. Please show current membership card. No boats over 50 feet.

RECIPROCAL BOAT CAPACITY: Appx 4 boats	RECIPROCAL DOCK: Appx. 175'
RECIPROCAL SEASON:................................All year	RECIPROCAL SLIPS: Dock only
RESERVATION POLICY: ....None	WATER: ....Yes
TOILETS: ....At Marina	AMT W/ELECTRICITY: ....All
HOT SHOWERS: ....At Marina	AMPS: ....30 A
RESTAURANT: ....Close by	LOUNGE: ....Close by
DAILY RATE: ....Electricity - $2.00 per day	OTHER: ....Same as marina listing
48 hrs. max stay, 1st 24 hrs. N/C	

NOTE: THIS IS PRIVATE MOORAGE _ONLY_ AVAILABLE TO MEMBERS OF RECIPROCAL YACHT CLUBS! YOUR CLUB _MUST_ HAVE RECIPROCAL PRIVILEGES AND YOU MUST FLY YOUR BURGEE!

CAUTION! This chartlet not intended for use in navigation.

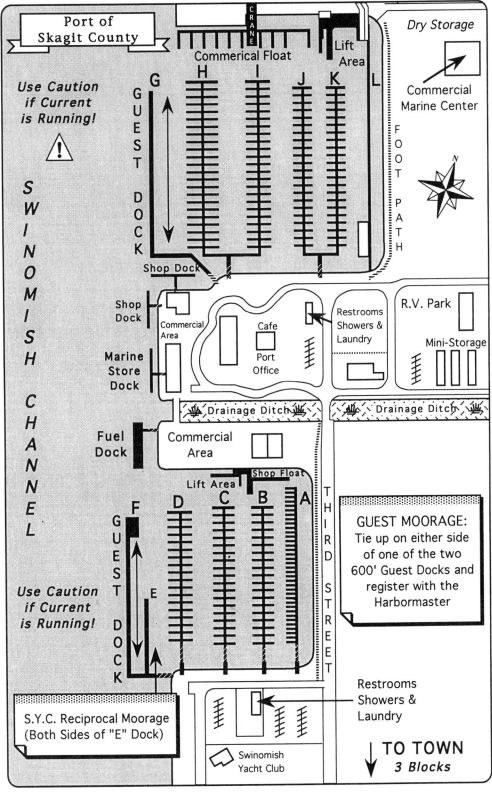

Port of Skagit County

Use Caution if Current is Running!

SWINOMISH CHANNEL

Commerical Float

CRANE

Lift Area

Dry Storage

Commercial Marine Center

FOOT PATH

N

G
H
I
J
K
L

GUEST DOCK

Shop Dock

Shop Dock

Commercial Area

Cafe

Port Office

Restrooms Showers & Laundry

R.V. Park

Mini-Storage

Marine Store Dock

Drainage Ditch

Drainage Ditch

Fuel Dock

Commercial Area

Shop Float

Lift Area

F
D
C
B
A

E

GUEST DOCK

THIRD STREET

Use Caution if Current is Running!

GUEST MOORAGE:
Tie up on either side of one of the two 600' Guest Docks and register with the Harbormaster

S.Y.C. Reciprocal Moorage (Both Sides of "E" Dock)

Swinomish Yacht Club

Restrooms Showers & Laundry

↓ TO TOWN
3 Blocks

NOTES

Langley

NAME OF MARINA: *LANGLEY SMALL BOAT HARBOR* **RADIO:** None
ADDRESS: Langley City Hall, Box 366 Langley, WA 98260
TELEPHONE: 360-321-4246 **MGR:** Ben Reams, Harbormaster

SHORT DESCRIPTION & LOCATION:

48°02.30' - 122°24.15' Located on east side of Whidbey Island on Saratoga Passage about one mile north of Sandy Point. Small marina is walking distance to picturesque little town full of tourist oriented amenities. Rafting is mandatory on outside docks.

GUEST BOAT CAPACITY:	Appx. 35 boats	GUEST DOCK:	54 ft. plus slips
SEASON:	All year	GUEST SLIPS:	Appx. 30
RESERVATION POLICY:	None	WATER:	Yes
AMT W/ELECTRICITY:	Appx. 18	AMPS:	20-30 A
FUEL DOCK:	Close by	PUMP OUT STATION	None
MARINE REPAIRS:	Close by	HAUL OUT:	Small Lift
TOILETS:	Yes	BOAT RAMP:	Yes
HOT SHOWERS:	Yes	LAUNDRY:	Close by
RESTAURANT:	Close by	LOUNGE:	Close by
PICNIC AREA:	Yes	POOL:	None
PLAY AREA:	Yes	BBQ:	Yes
BASIC STORE:	Close by	GOLF:	Close by
ELECTRICITY:	$ 2.00 per day	OTHER:	Fishing pier, nice
DAILY RATE:	Appx. .40¢ per foot		restaurants, groceries,

•NOTE: In winter about 50% of space is rented for permanent moorage. Summer - all guest.

OTHER: Fishing pier, nice restaurants, groceries, shops, antiques, and many services. Marina motto: "We are never full........."

CAUTION! This chartlet not intended for use in navigation.

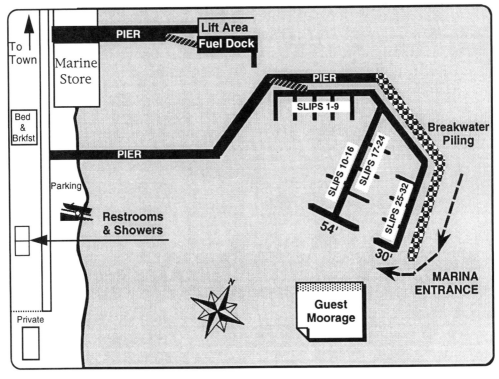

Oak Harbor

NAME OF MARINA: *OAK HARBOR MARINA*   **RADIO:** VHF Ch. 16

ADDRESS: 3075 300 Ave. West   Oak Harbor   WA 98277

TELEPHONE: 360-679-2628   **MGR:** Dave Williams

SHORT DESCRIPTION & LOCATION:

48°17.10' - 122°38.10' Marina is located at the head of Oak Harbor Bay which is situated at the northern end of Saratoga passage on east side of Whidbey Island. The facilities are modern and friendly and within a 3/4 mile walk from Town of Oak Harbor.

GUEST BOAT CAPACITY: ....Appx. 80 boats	GUEST DOCK: ....800' plus slips
SEASON: ....All year	GUEST SLIPS: 34
RESERVATION POLICY: ....Groups only	WATER: ....Yes
AMT W/ELECTRICITY: ....All	AMPS: ....30 A
FUEL DOCK: ....Gas, Dsl, & LP	PUMP OUT STATION ....Yes
MARINE REPAIRS: ....Close by	HAUL OUT: ....Close by
TOILETS: ....Yes	BOAT RAMP: ....Yes
HOT SHOWERS: ....Yes	LAUNDRY: ....None
RESTAURANT: ....Close by	LOUNGE: ....Close by
PICNIC AREA: ....Yes	POOL: ....None
PLAY AREA: ....Yes	BBQ: ....Yes
BASIC STORE: ....Appx. 2 miles away	GOLF: ....Close by
ELECTRICITY: ....Included in moorage	OTHER: Shopping nearby,
DAILY RATE: ....Appx. .50¢ per foot	volleyball, horseshoes,
	close to marine
	chandlery & Navy
	Exchange/ Com'sry.

NAME OF YACHT CLUB: *OAK HARBOR YACHT CLUB*   Ⓑ

CLUB ADDRESS: P.O. Box 121, Oak Harbor, WA 98277

CLUB TELEPHONE: 360-675-1314   **PERSON IN CHARGE:**   Club Manager

LOCATION & SPECIAL NOTES

OHYC provides 4 slips on the end of "F" Dock in the Oak Hbr. Marina on a first come basis. Upon arrival, check in with the Harbormaster. The club is open Wed. thru Sun. night. Restaurant service is generally available on weekends, please check at club for dining schedule.

RECIPROCAL BOAT CAPACITY:...............4 Boats	RECIPROCAL DOCK: .....Slips only
RECIPROCAL SEASON:................................All year	RECIPROCAL SLIPS: 4
RESERVATION POLICY: ....None	WATER: ....Yes
TOILETS: ....At Marina	AMT W/ELECTRICITY: ....All
HOT SHOWERS: ....At Marina	AMPS: ....30 A
RESTAURANT: ....Close by	LOUNGE: ....Close by
DAILY RATE: ....$2.00 per night for electricity	OTHER: ....Same as marina listing
...................................**48 Hour Limit**	

NOTE: *THIS IS PRIVATE MOORAGE **ONLY** AVAILABLE TO MEMBERS OF RECIPROCAL YACHT CLUBS! YOUR CLUB **MUST** HAVE RECIPROCAL PRIVILEGES AND YOU MUST FLY YOUR BURGEE!*

Oak Harbor

CAUTION! This chartlet not intended for use in navigation.

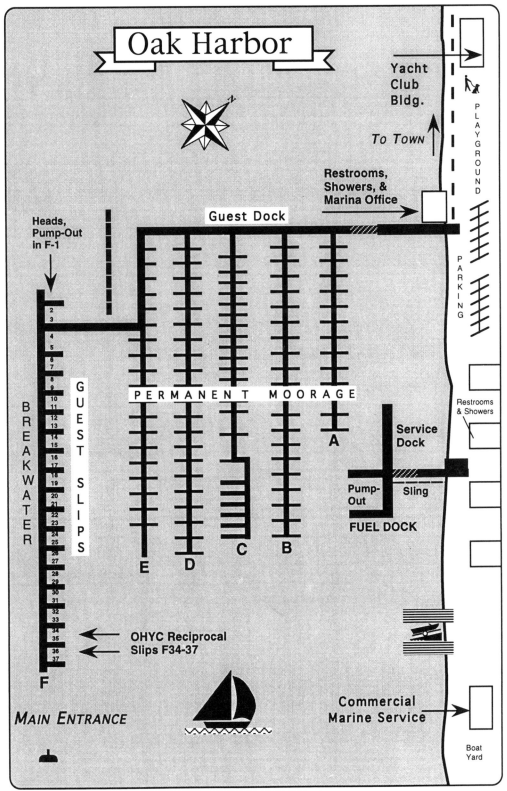

Oak Harbor

Yacht Club Bldg.

PLAYGROUND

To Town

Restrooms, Showers, & Marina Office

PARKING

Heads, Pump-Out in F-1

Guest Dock

PERMANENT MOORAGE

BREAKWATER

GUEST SLIPS

2
3
4
5
6
7
8
9
10
11
12
13
14
15
16
17
18
19
20
21
22
23
24
25
26
27
28
29
30
31
32
33
34
35
36
37

A

Service Dock

Restrooms & Showers

Pump-Out

Sling

FUEL DOCK

E   D   C   B

OHYC Reciprocal Slips F34-37

F

MAIN ENTRANCE

Commercial Marine Service

Boat Yard

"The Burgee Book" is the perfect gift for fellow boaters. Please copy this page and use this handy order blank. Telephone Orders Accepted! 1-800-445-8270 Ask for "The Burgee Book"

ORDER FORM

Ordered by (Name & Complete Address):		
First Name	Last Name	
Street or P.O. Box		
City	State	Zip
Telephone:		

Ship to: (Fill out only if different than "ordered by")		
First Name	Last Name	
Street or P.O. Box		
City	State	Zip

Item Description	Quantity	Unit Price	Total Price
The Burgee - Second Edition		22.95	
		Merchandise Total	
		WA. Sales Tax $1.90 per book	
		U.S. Shipping & Handling ($3.00 first book, $1.00 ea. additional)	
		Canadian Shipping & Handling-Priority (US $5.00 first book, $1.00 ea. additional)	
		TOTAL	

Payment by: ☐ Visa ☐ Mastercard

Card number: ☐ Check or Money Order enclosed

Expiration date:

Signature

Please mail, fax, or phone order to:

Pierside Publishing
23911 Newell Ln. N.E.
Kingston, WA 98346
Tel: (360) 297-2935
Fax: (360) 297-3505

Thank You!

Telephone Orders Accepted!
1-800-445-8270 Ask for "The Burgee Book"

C H A P T E R

5

SAN JUAN ISLANDS
&
NORTHERN WASHINGTON

Anacortes

NAME OF MARINA:	*CAP SANTE BOAT HAVEN*	RADIO: VHF Ch. 66A
ADDRESS:	P.O. Box 297	Anacortes, WA 98221
TELEPHONE:	360-293-0694	MGR: Dale Fowler

SHORT DESCRIPTION & LOCATION:

48°30.60' - 122°36.20' Located in Fidalgo Bay by Cap Sante Head, this modern and spacious marina is close to any marine service a boater could want. The town is one of the boating capitals of the N.W. and offers many attractions for visitors.

GUEST BOAT CAPACITY:	Appx. 150 boats	GUEST DOCK:	170 ft. plus slips
SEASON:	All year	GUEST SLIPS:	Varies
RESERVATION POLICY:	Accepts	WATER:	Yes
AMT W/ELECTRICITY:	All	AMPS:	20-30 A
FUEL DOCK:	Gas, Dsl, & LP	PUMP OUT STATION	Yes
MARINE REPAIRS:	On premises	HAUL OUT:	Travel-Lift
TOILETS:	Yes	BOAT RAMP:	Close by
HOT SHOWERS:	Yes	LAUNDRY:	Yes
RESTAURANT:	Yes	LOUNGE:	Close by
PICNIC AREA:	Yes	POOL:	Close by
PLAY AREA:	Close by	BBQ:	Close by at Rotary Park
BASIC STORE:	Yes	GOLF:	Close by
ELECTRICITY:	$ 2.50 per day	OTHER:	Customs port-of-entry, close to many shops, art galleries, historic steam railroad. free public transit in county.
DAILY RATE:	Appx. .55¢ per foot		

CAUTION! This chartlet not intended for use in navigation.

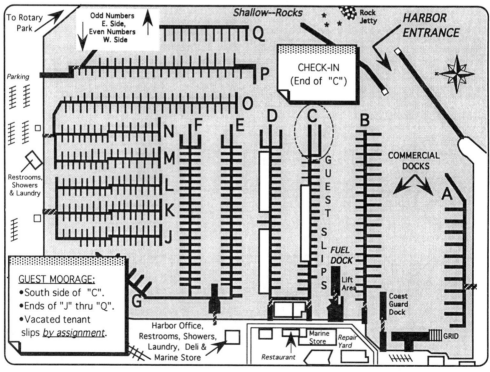

Anacortes

NAME OF YACHT CLUB: *ANACORTES YACHT CLUB*

ADDRESS: 504 7th Street   Anacortes,   WA   98221

TELEPHONE: 360-293-2202   **PERSON IN CHARGE:** Recip. Chairman

SHORT DESCRIPTION & LOCATION:

48°30.60' - 122°36.20' AYC offers reciprocal moorage at **Cap Sante** Boat Haven. Moorage is located on "D" dock & will accomodate 3 yachts up to 45 ft. Please register w/marina staff upon arrival. Usage is limited to 1 night per week per boat. The clubhouse is open most Fri. & Sat. nights during summer and located at N.E. end of marina.

RECIPROCAL BOAT CAPACITY Appx. 3 boats	**RECIPROCAL DOCK:** Slips only
SEASON: ....All year	**RECIPROCAL SLIPS:** Appx. 2-3
RESERVATION POLICY:...................None	**WATER:** ....Yes
TOILETS: ....At Marina	**AMT W/ELECTRICITY:** ....All
HOT SHOWERS: ....At Marina	**AMPS:** ....30 A
RESTAURANT:..............................Close by	**LOUNGE:** ....Close by
DAILY RATE: ....No Charge POWER CHARGE $2.50/DAY	**OTHER:** Services same as marina listing for Cap Sante Boat Haven on Page 152.

<u>NOTE:</u> THIS IS PRIVATE MOORAGE AND ONLY AVAILABLE TO MEMBERS OF RECIPROCAL YACHT CLUBS. YOUR CLUB <u>MUST</u> HAVE RECIPROCAL PRIVILEGES AND YOU MUST FLY YOUR BURGEE.

CAUTION! This chartlet not intended for use in navigation.

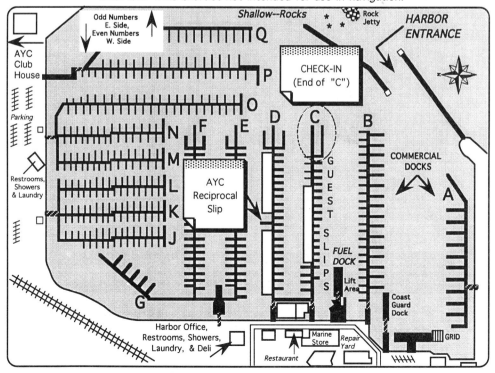

Anacortes

NAME OF MARINA: *SKYLINE MARINA*   RADIO: VHF Ch. 16
ADDRESS: 2011 Skyline Way   Anacortes,   WA 98221
TELEPHONE: 360-293-5134   MGR: Alex Britton

SHORT DESCRIPTION & LOCATION:

48°29.40' - 122°40.60' Located near Fidalgo Head in Flounder Bay at the N end of Burrows Bay about 1/2 mile by land W of ferry terminal. This well protected large boat basin is situated in a marine oriented and residential area appx. 3 miles W of Anacortes.

GUEST BOAT CAPACITY: ....Varies	GUEST DOCK: None designated
SEASON: ....All year	GUEST SLIPS: ....Varies
RESERVATION POLICY: ....Accepts	WATER: ....Yes
AMT W/ELECTRICITY: ....All	AMPS: ....30 A
FUEL DOCK: ....Gas, Dsl, & LP	PUMP OUT STATION ....Yes
MARINE REPAIRS: ....On premises	HAUL OUT: ....Travel-Lift
TOILETS: ....Yes	BOAT RAMP: ....Sling only
HOT SHOWERS: ....Yes	LAUNDRY: ....Yes
RESTAURANT: ....Close by	LOUNGE: ....Close by
PICNIC AREA: ....Yes	POOL: ....None
PLAY AREA: ....None	BBQ: ....None
BASIC STORE: ....Close by	GOLF: ....Close by
ELECTRICITY: ....$3.00 per day	OTHER: Customs port-of-entry,
DAILY RATE: ....Appx. .60¢ per foot	pump-out, charters &

Note: Guest moorage is available by renting open slips of permanent marina tenants.

OTHER: brokerage, chandlery.

NAME OF YACHT CLUB: *FLOUNDER BAY YACHT CLUB*   Ⓑ
CLUB ADDRESS: 2400 Skyline Way, Anacortes, WA 98221
CLUB TELEPHONE: 360-293-7288   PERSON IN CHARGE: Dockmaster

LOCATION & SPECIAL NOTES

The club dock, located in front of the Club building, is used for visitor check in only. The building is between "D" and "E" Docks. Follow the simple instructions given in the club building <u>laundry room</u> to be assigned a member's vacant slip. Usually ample slips are open.

RECIPROCAL BOAT CAPACITY:..................Varies	RECIPROCAL DOCK: ....Slips only
RECIPROCAL SEASON:................................All year	RECIPROCAL SLIPS: ....Varies
RESERVATION POLICY: ....None	WATER: ....Yes
TOILETS: ....Yes	AMT W/ELECTRICITY: ....All
HOT SHOWERS: ....Yes	AMPS: ....30 A
RESTAURANT: ....Close by	LOUNGE: ....Close by
DAILY RATE: First day of each visit is free. Ea. add'l day is $5.00 - 5 days max yr.	OTHER: ....Same as marina listing. <u>POWER $2.00 PER DAY</u>

NOTE: THIS IS PRIVATE MOORAGE <u>ONLY</u> AVAILABLE TO MEMBERS OF RECIPROCAL YACHT CLUBS! YOUR CLUB <u>MUST</u> HAVE RECIPROCAL PRIVILEGES AND YOU MUST FLY YOUR BURGEE!

Anacortes

CAUTION! This chartlet not intended for use in navigation.

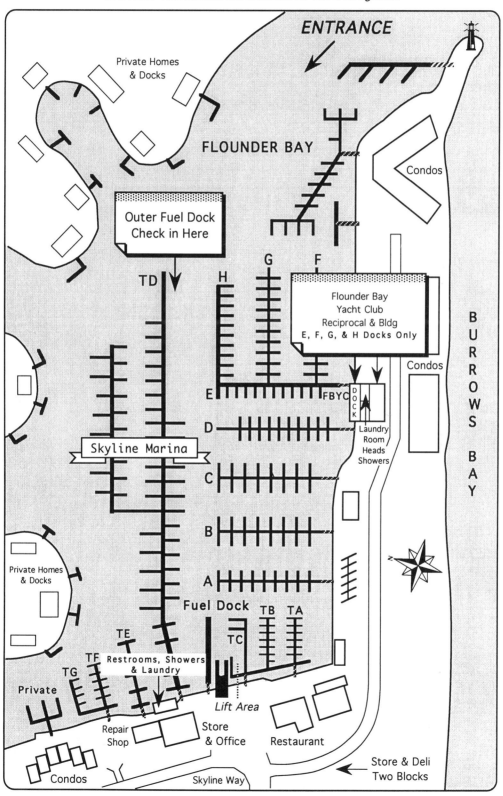

ENTRANCE

Private Homes & Docks

FLOUNDER BAY

Condos

Outer Fuel Dock
Check in Here

TD

G

F

H

Flounder Bay
Yacht Club
Reciprocal & Bldg
E, F, G, & H Docks Only

Condos

E

FBYC

DOCK

Laundry
Room
Heads
Showers

Condos

Skyline Marina

D

C

B

A

Private Homes
& Docks

Fuel Dock

TB   TA

TE

TC

TF

Restrooms, Showers
& Laundry

TG

Private

Lift Area

Repair
Shop

Store
& Office

Restaurant

Store & Deli
Two Blocks

Condos

Skyline Way

BURROWS BAY

N

Bellingham

NAME OF MARINA: *SQUALICUM HARBOR-Port of Bellingham* RADIO: VHF Ch. 16

ADDRESS: #2 Squalicum Mall   Bellingham   WA 98227

TELEPHONE: 360-676-2500   MGR: John Sibold

SHORT DESCRIPTION & LOCATION:

47°45.20' - 122°30.40' Bellingham is at the head of Bellingham Bay on the E shore
& the large marina is adjacent to & SE of the Squalicum Creek Waterway. Two moorage
basins are well protected by breakwaters & offer many marine-oriented services close by.

GUEST BOAT CAPACITY: ....Appx. 50 boats	GUEST DOCK: ...375 ft. plus slips
SEASON: ....All year	GUEST SLIPS: ....Appx. 20
RESERVATION POLICY: ....None	WATER: ....Yes
AMT W/ELECTRICITY: ....All	AMPS: ....20-30 A
FUEL DOCK: ....Gas, Dsl, & LP	PUMP OUT STATION ....Yes
MARINE REPAIRS: ....On premises	HAUL OUT: ....Travel-Lift
TOILETS: ....Yes	BOAT RAMP: ....Yes
HOT SHOWERS: ....Yes	LAUNDRY: ....Yes
RESTAURANT: ....Close by	LOUNGE: ....Close by
PICNIC AREA: ....Yes	POOL: ....None
PLAY AREA: ....Yes	BBQ: ....None
BASIC STORE: ....Close by	GOLF: ....Close by
ELECTRICITY: ....Included in moorage	OTHER: Customs port-of-entry,
DAILY RATE: ....25¢ per foot	Pump-out, shopping
....................................FIRST DAY FREE	mall, chandlery, public
	transit, tourist
	attractions, theaters.

NAME OF YACHT CLUB: *BELLINGHAM YACHT CLUB*   **B**

CLUB ADDRESS: 2625 Harbor Loop, Bellingham, WA 98225

CLUB TELEPHONE: 360-733-7390   PERSON IN CHARGE: Commodore

LOCATION & SPECIAL NOTES

Although the BYC does not have guest moorage, the Port of Bellingham has made over
300' of moorage space available on a first come basis. Reciprocal club members are invited
to visit the club's beautiful lounge for refreshments & snacks. Please also check at club
house for current schedule of club restaurant service.

RECIPROCAL BOAT CAPACITY: Appx 8 boats	RECIPROCAL DOCK: Appx. 300'
RECIPROCAL SEASON:................................All year	RECIPROCAL SLIPS: Dock only
RESERVATION POLICY: ....Groups only	WATER: ....Yes
TOILETS: ....Yes	AMT W/ELECTRICITY: ....All
HOT SHOWERS: ....Yes	AMPS: ....20-30 A
RESTAURANT: ....Yes	LOUNGE: ....Yes
DAILY RATE: ....25¢ per foot	OTHER: ....Same as marina listing
....................................FIRST DAY FREE	

**NOTE: THIS IS PRIVATE MOORAGE ONLY AVAILABLE TO MEMBERS OF RECIPROCAL YACHT
CLUBS! YOUR CLUB MUST HAVE RECIPROCAL PRIVILEGES AND YOU MUST FLY YOUR BURGEE!**

Bellingham

CAUTION! This chartlet not intended for use in navigation.

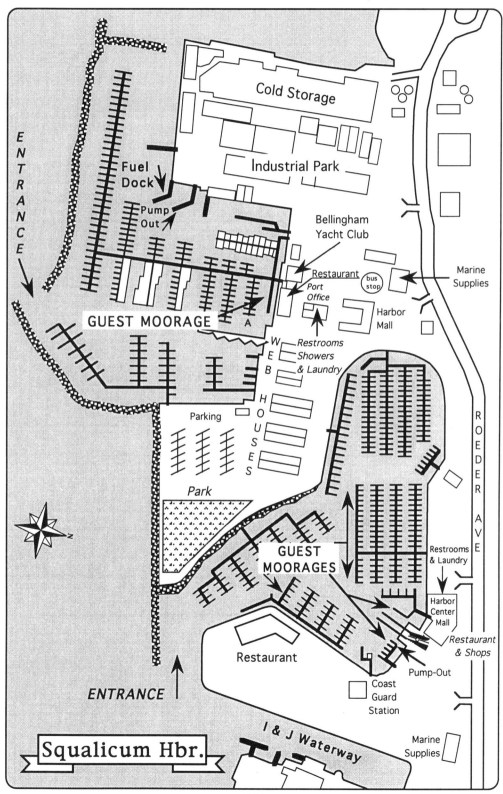

Cold Storage

Industrial Park

ENTRANCE

Fuel Dock

Pump Out

Bellingham Yacht Club

Restaurant

Port Office

bus stop

Marine Supplies

GUEST MOORAGE

A

Harbor Mall

W E B H O U S E S

Restrooms Showers & Laundry

Parking

Park

ROEDER AVE

GUEST MOORAGES

Restrooms & Laundry

Harbor Center Mall

Restaurant & Shops

Pump-Out

ENTRANCE

Restaurant

Coast Guard Station

Marine Supplies

Squalicum Hbr.

I & J Waterway

Blaine

NAME OF MARINA: *BLAINE HARBOR - Port of Bellingham* RADIO: VHF Ch.66/16

ADDRESS: P.O. Box 1245 Blaine, WA 98231

TELEPHONE: 360-332-8037 MGR: Alan Birdsall

SHORT DESCRIPTION & LOCATION:

48°59.50' - 122°45.90' Located near the entrance to Drayton Harbor on the N. shore of Blaine. The large & well equipped small-boat basin is a active fishing center and offers many marine-oriented & commercial businesses close by at Drayton Harbor Mall.

GUEST BOAT CAPACITY: ....Appx. 20-30 boats	GUEST DOCK: ....175' plus slips
SEASON: ....All year	GUEST SLIPS: 14
RESERVATION POLICY: ....None	WATER: ....Yes
AMT W/ELECTRICITY: ....Main guest dock only	AMPS: ....20 A
FUEL DOCK: ....Gas & Diesel	PUMP OUT STATION ....Yes
MARINE REPAIRS: ....On premises	HAUL OUT: ....Travel-Lift
TOILETS: ....Yes	BOAT RAMP: ....Yes
HOT SHOWERS: ....Yes	LAUNDRY: ....Close by
RESTAURANT: ....Close by	LOUNGE: ....Close by
PICNIC AREA: ....Yes	POOL: ....None
PLAY AREA: ....None	BBQ: ....Yes
BASIC STORE: ....Close by	GOLF: ....Close by
ELECTRICITY: ....Included in moorage	OTHER: Customs port-of-entry,
DAILY RATE: ....25¢ per foot	Pump-out, charter
....................................FIRST DAY FREE	fishing, close to city,
	many service facilities.

NAME OF YACHT CLUB: *INTERNATIONAL YACHT CLUB*

CLUB ADDRESS: 1469 George Street, White Rock, B.C. V4B A43

CLUB TELEPHONE: 604-535-4699 PERSON IN CHARGE: Commodore

LOCATION & SPECIAL NOTES

IYC of B.C. & Blaine offer reciprocal moorage in the Blaine Harbor Marina on the guest dock (appx. 190 ft.) on a first-come basis. Upon entering the marina proceed to the guest dock below the marina office and register your reciprocal with IYC with the harbor master.

RECIPROCAL BOAT CAPACITY: Appx. 6 Boats	RECIPROCAL DOCK: Appx. 175'
RECIPROCAL SEASON:................All year	RECIPROCAL SLIPS: Dock only
RESERVATION POLICY: ....None	WATER: ....Yes
TOILETS: ....At Marina	AMT W/ELECTRICITY: ....All
HOT SHOWERS: ....At Marina	AMPS: ....20 A
RESTAURANT: ....Close by	LOUNGE: ....Close by
DAILY RATE: ....25¢ per foot	OTHER: ......Same as marina listing
....................................FIRST DAY FREE	

NOTE: *THIS IS PRIVATE MOORAGE ONLY AVAILABLE TO MEMBERS OF RECIPROCAL YACHT CLUBS! YOUR CLUB MUST HAVE RECIPROCAL PRIVILEGES AND YOU MUST FLY YOUR BURGEE!*

Blaine

CAUTION! This chartlet not intended for use in navigation.

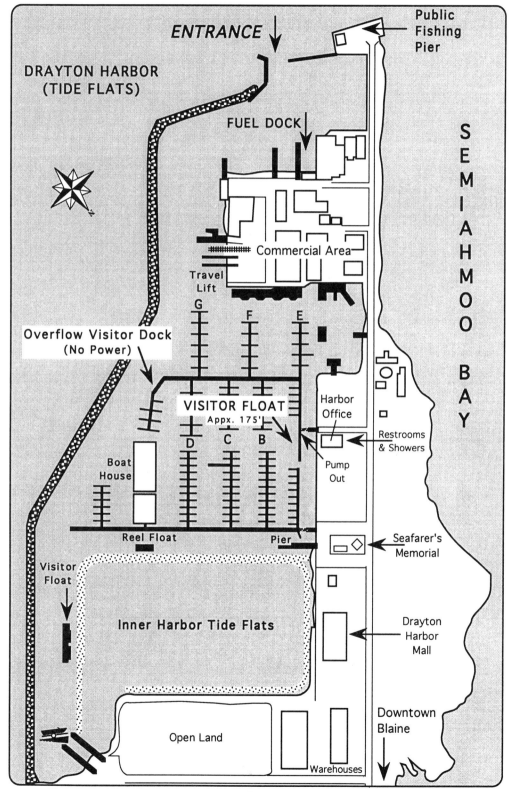

ENTRANCE

Public Fishing Pier

DRAYTON HARBOR
(TIDE FLATS)

FUEL DOCK

S E M I A H M O O   B A Y

Commercial Area

Travel Lift

G   F   E

Overflow Visitor Dock
(No Power)

VISITOR FLOAT
Appx. 175'

Harbor Office

Restrooms & Showers

D   C   B

Boat House

Pump Out

Reel Float

Pier

Seafarer's Memorial

Visitor Float

Inner Harbor Tide Flats

Drayton Harbor Mall

Open Land

Downtown Blaine

Warehouses

Blaine

NAME OF MARINA: **SEMIAHMOO MARINA** RADIO: VHF Ch. 68

ADDRESS: 9550 Semiahmoo Pkwy. Blaine, WA 98230

TELEPHONE: 360-371-5700 MGR: Dale Jensen

SHORT DESCRIPTION & LOCATION:

48°59.60' - 122°46.17' Located across from Blaine on the S. side of the entrance to Drayton Harbor on the N. end of the sand spit that forms the S.W. side of the harbor. The modern & well maintained marina offers all the amenities of a first-class resort.

GUEST BOAT CAPACITY: ....Ample	GUEST DOCK: ....Slips only
SEASON: ....All year	GUEST SLIPS: ....Varies
RESERVATION POLICY: ....Accepts	WATER: ....Yes
AMT W/ELECTRICITY: ....All	AMPS: ....30 A
FUEL DOCK: ....Gas & Diesel	PUMP OUT STATION ....Yes
MARINE REPAIRS: ....On premises	HAUL OUT: ....Travel-Lift
TOILETS: ....Yes	BOAT RAMP: ....None
HOT SHOWERS: ....Yes	LAUNDRY: ....Yes
RESTAURANT: ....Yes	LOUNGE: ....Yes
PICNIC AREA: ....Yes	POOL: ....Yes
PLAY AREA: ....None	BBQ: ....None
BASIC STORE: ....Yes	GOLF: ....Yes
ELECTRICITY: ....Included in moorage	OTHER: Award winning golf
DAILY RATE: ....60¢ per foot	course, health club,
	hiking & cycling trails,
	boutique, fishing tackle,
	park area nearby.

NAME OF YACHT CLUB: **SEMIAHMOO YACHT CLUB** **B**

CLUB ADDRESS: 9540 Semiahmoo Parkway #117, Blaine, WA 98230

CLUB TELEPHONE: 360-332-2101 PERSON IN CHARGE: Port Captain

LOCATION & SPECIAL NOTES

The club is located beside the Inn at Semaihmoo Resort. SYC asks you moor at the fuel dock and register at the Marina Managers office. Moorage is offered to members of reciprocal clubs in good standing for 1 night per boat & a maximum of 3 boats per night.

RECIPROCAL BOAT CAPACITY:...............3 Boats	RECIPROCAL DOCK: ....None
RECIPROCAL SEASON:...................................All year	RECIPROCAL SLIPS: 3
RESERVATION POLICY: ....None	WATER: ....Yes
TOILETS: ....At Marina	AMT W/ELECTRICITY: ....All
HOT SHOWERS: ....At Marina	AMPS: ....30 A
RESTAURANT: ....Close by	LOUNGE: ....Close by
DAILY RATE: No charge for 1 night per boat and a maximum of 3 boats.	OTHER: Mooring buoy in back of bay (rafting required)

NOTE: THIS IS PRIVATE MOORAGE *ONLY* AVAILABLE TO MEMBERS OF RECIPROCAL YACHT CLUBS! YOUR CLUB *MUST* HAVE RECIPROCAL PRIVILEGES AND YOU MUST FLY YOUR BURGEE!

CAUTION! This chartlet not intended for use in navigation.

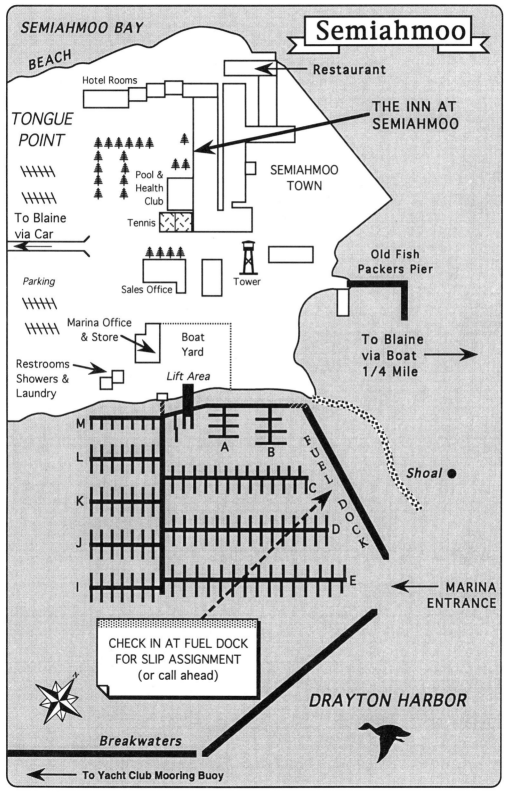

SEMIAHMOO BAY

BEACH

Semiahmoo

Restaurant

Hotel Rooms

TONGUE POINT

THE INN AT SEMIAHMOO

Pool & Health Club

SEMIAHMOO TOWN

To Blaine via Car

Tennis

Old Fish Packers Pier

Parking

Tower

To Blaine via Boat 1/4 Mile

Sales Office

Marina Office & Store

Boat Yard

Restrooms Showers & Laundry

Lift Area

Shoal ●

M

L

A   B

FUEL DOCK

K

C

J

D

I

E

MARINA ENTRANCE

CHECK IN AT FUEL DOCK FOR SLIP ASSIGNMENT (or call ahead)

DRAYTON HARBOR

Breakwaters

To Yacht Club Mooring Buoy

Blakely Island

NAME OF MARINA: *BLAKELY ISLAND MARINA*   RADIO: None

ADDRESS: Blakely Island,   WA 98222

TELEPHONE: 360-375-6121   MGR: Barbara & Duffy Nightingale

SHORT DESCRIPTION & LOCATION:

48°35.20' - 122°48.80' Located on north end of Blakely Island just off west end of Peavine Pass. This is a pristine and well maintained full service marina in a picturesque and quiet setting. The Island is completely private.

GUEST BOAT CAPACITY: ....Appx. 60 boats	GUEST DOCK: ....80' plus slips
SEASON: ....All year	GUEST SLIPS: ....Appx. 60
RESERVATION POLICY: ....Accepts	WATER: ....Yes
AMT W/ELECTRICITY: ....All	AMPS: ....30-50 A
FUEL DOCK: ....Gas & Diesel	PUMP OUT STATION ....None
MARINE REPAIRS: ....None	HAUL OUT: ....None
TOILETS: ....Yes	BOAT RAMP: ....Yes
HOT SHOWERS: ....Yes	LAUNDRY: ....Yes
RESTAURANT: ....None	LOUNGE: ....None
PICNIC AREA: ....Yes	POOL: ....None
PLAY AREA: ....Proposed	BBQ: ....Yes
BASIC STORE: ....Yes	GOLF: ....None
ELECTRICITY: ....Included in moorage	OTHER: Great covered BBQ
DAILY RATE: ....Appx. .65¢ per foot	pavilion & picnic area. Well stocked store with clothing, tackle, & gifts.

CAUTION! This chartlet not intended for use in navigation.

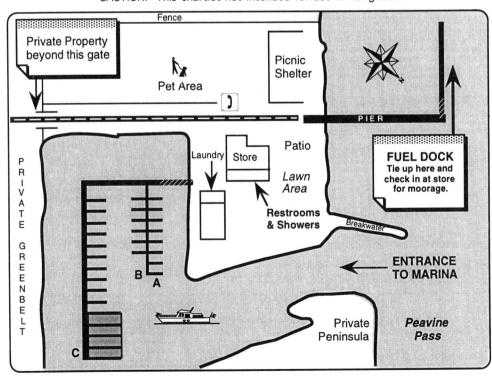

Doe Island

NAME OF PARK: *DOE ISLAND STATE MARINE PARK*
ADDRESS: Star Rt. Box 177   Olga WA   98279
TELEPHONE: 360-376-2073   MGR: Dave Castor

SHORT DESCRIPTION & LOCATION:

48°38.00' - 122°47.10' Six acre island park located off S.E. shore of Orcas Island midway between Deer and Lawrence Points. Dock on inward side of island. Trails and primitive camp sites located on island. No facilities. Adjacent mooring buoys are private.

GUEST BOAT CAPACITY: ....Appx. 2-4 boats

SEASON: ....Closed winter

AMT W/ELECTRICITY: ....None

TOILETS: ....Vault toilet

HOT SHOWERS: ....None

PICNIC AREA: ....Yes

PLAY AREA: ....None

BASIC STORE: ....None

DAILY RATE: Boats under 26 ft...........$8.00/night
Boats 26 ft. & Over.....$11.00/night
Subject to Change in 1997

GUEST DOCK: ....Appx. 30 ft.

MOORING BUOYS: ....**None**

WATER: ....None

PAY PHONES: ....None

BOAT RAMP: ....None

PICNIC SHELTER: ....None

BBQ: ....None

PUMP OUT STATION: ......None

OTHER: Fishing, crabbing, camping, & beachcombing. Note: Adjacent mooring buoys are privately owned.

CAUTION! This chartlet not intended for use in navigation.

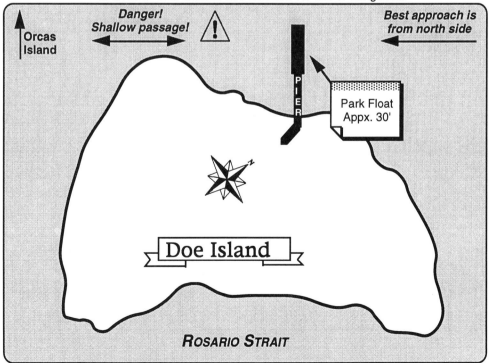

James Island

NAME OF PARK: *JAMES ISLAND STATE MARINE PARK*

ADDRESS: 6158 Lighthouse Rd.   Friday Harbor, WA   98250

TELEPHONE: 360-378-2044   MGR: Chris Guidotti

SHORT DESCRIPTION & LOCATION:

48°30.80' - 122°46.50'   Located in Rosario Strait close off Decatur Head on the east end of Decatur Island, just south of Thatcher Pass. This 114 acre naturally beautiful island park offers moorage, buoys, hiking trails, gravel beaches, and campsites.

GUEST BOAT CAPACITY: ....Appx. 4 boats

GUEST DOCK: ....Appx. 64 ft.

SEASON: ....All year

MOORING BUOYS: 5

AMT W/ELECTRICITY: ....None

WATER: ....None

TOILETS: ....Vault & pit toilets

PAY PHONES: ....None

HOT SHOWERS: ....None

BOAT RAMP: ....None

PICNIC AREA: ....Yes

PICNIC SHELTER: ....Yes

PLAY AREA: ....None

BBQ: ....None

BASIC STORE: ....None

PUMP OUT STATION: ......None

DAILY RATE: Mooring Buoys.................$5.00/night
Boats under 26 ft...........$8.00/night
Boats 26 ft. & Over.....$11.00/night
Campsites.........................$5.00/night

OTHER: ....Rafting permitted up to 4 boats, network of wildlife trails, and beachcombing.

Subject to Change in 1997

CAUTION! This chartlet not intended for use in navigation.

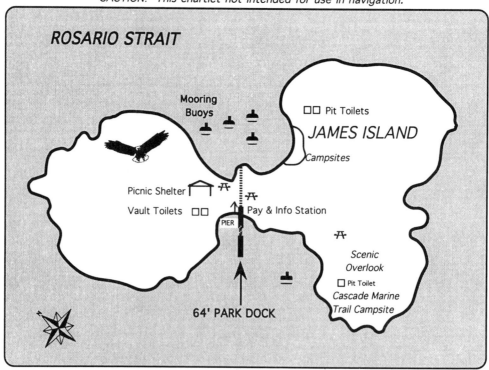

Jones Island

NAME OF PARK: **JONES ISLAND STATE MARINE PARK**

ADDRESS: 6158 Lighthouse Rd.   Friday Harbor, WA   98250

TELEPHONE: 360-378-2044   MGR: Dave Castor

SHORT DESCRIPTION & LOCATION:

48°37.30' - 123°02.80' Located 3/4 mile off the S.W. end of Orcas Is. in Spring Passage. This popular island marine park is only accessible by boat. Beauty and wildlife abound on the island. Mooring buoys can also be found on the island's south side.

GUEST BOAT CAPACITY: ....Appx. 8 boats

SEASON: ....Closed winter

AMT W/ELECTRICITY: ....None

TOILETS: ....Composting, vault, & pit toilets

HOT SHOWERS: ....None

PICNIC AREA: ....Yes

PLAY AREA: ....Yes

BASIC STORE: ....None

DAILY RATE: Mooring Buoys.................$5.00/night
Boats under 26 ft..........$8.00/night
Boats 26 ft. & Over.....$11.00/night
Campsites.......................$5.00/night
Subject to Change in 1997

GUEST DOCK: ....Appx. 135 ft.

MOORING BUOYS: 7

WATER: ....Yes

PAY PHONES: ....None

BOAT RAMP: ....None

PICNIC SHELTER: ....Yes

BBQ: ....None

PUMP OUT STATION: ......None

OTHER: 4 mooring buoys on N. side and 3 on S. side, campsites, group camping area, wildlife reserve, hiking trails.

CAUTION! This chartlet not intended for use in navigation.

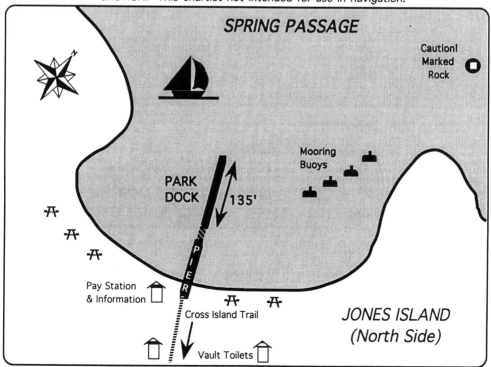

Lopez Island

NAME OF MARINA: *ISLANDER LOPEZ MARINA RESORT*   RADIO: VHF Ch. 78

ADDRESS: P.O. Box 459 Fish. Bay Rd.   Lopez Island   WA   98261

TELEPHONE: 360-468-3383   **MGR:**   Walt Schoonover

SHORT DESCRIPTION & LOCATION:

48°31.00' - 122°54.80' Family oriented marina & hotel resort located in Fisherman Bay 1 mile south of Lopez Village on W. side of Lopez Is. The dock has recently been rebuilt and the facility is close to marine services. Hotel accommodations available.

GUEST BOAT CAPACITY: ....Appx. 35 boats	GUEST DOCK: ....120' plus slips
SEASON: ....All year	GUEST SLIPS: ....Appx. 34
RESERVATION POLICY: ....Recommended	WATER: ....Yes
AMT W/ELECTRICITY: ....All	AMPS: ....30-50 A
FUEL DOCK: ....Gas & Diesel	PUMP OUT STATION ....None
MARINE REPAIRS: ....Close by	HAUL OUT: ....Close by
TOILETS: ....Yes	BOAT RAMP: ....Close by
HOT SHOWERS: ....Yes	LAUNDRY: ....Yes
RESTAURANT: ....Yes	LOUNGE: ....Yes
PICNIC AREA: ....Yes	POOL: ....Yes - Seasonal
PLAY AREA: ....Yes	BBQ: ....Yes
BASIC STORE: ....Yes	GOLF: ....Close by
ELECTRICITY: ....Included in moorage	OTHER: Good dinghy bay, fishing,
DAILY RATE: ....Appx. .80¢ per foot	crabbing. volleyball, horseshoes, bike & kayak rentals, hot tub, meeting & banquet facilities.

CAUTION! This chartlet not intended for use in navigation.

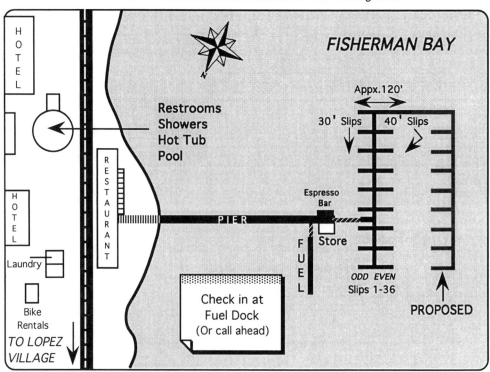

Lopez Island

NAME OF MARINA: *ISLANDS MARINE CENTER* **RADIO:** VHF 69/CB9

ADDRESS: Fisherman Bay Road Lopez Island WA 98261

TELEPHONE: 360-468-3377 **MGR:** Ron & Jennifer Meng

SHORT DESCRIPTION & LOCATION:

48°31.10' - 122°54.80' Modern & complete marina facility w/chandlery & auto parts store located in Fisherman Bay on W side of Lopez Is. 1/2 mile south of Lopez Village. Walking distance to bike rentals, shops, & restaurants. Full marine repair service center.

GUEST BOAT CAPACITY: ....Appx. 50 boats	GUEST DOCK: Apx. 1200' overall
SEASON: ....All year	GUEST SLIPS: ....Docks only
RESERVATION POLICY: ....Accepts	WATER: ....Yes
AMT W/ELECTRICITY: ....All	AMPS: ....30 A
FUEL DOCK: ....Close by	PUMP OUT STATION ....Yes
MARINE REPAIRS: ....On premises	HAUL OUT: ....Travel-Lift
TOILETS: ....Yes	BOAT RAMP: ....Yes
HOT SHOWERS: ....Yes	LAUNDRY: ....Close by
RESTAURANT: ....Close by	LOUNGE: ....Close by
PICNIC AREA: ....Yes	POOL: ....None
PLAY AREA: ....Close by	BBQ: ....Yes
BASIC STORE: ....Yes	GOLF: ....Close by
ELECTRICITY: ....$ 3.00 per day	OTHER: Emergency marine repairs 7 days a week. Good dinghy area, fishing & crabbing. Float plane service to Seattle area.
DAILY RATE: ....Appx. .60¢ per foot	

CAUTION! This chartlet not intended for use in navigation.

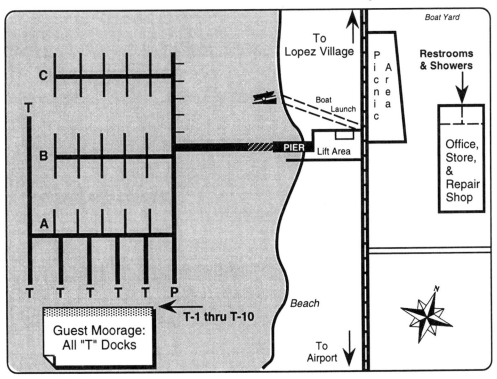

Matia Island

NAME OF PARK: **MATIA ISLAND STATE MARINE PARK**

ADDRESS: Star Rt. Box 177   Olga, WA   98279

TELEPHONE: 360-378-2044   **MGR:** Dave Castor

SHORT DESCRIPTION & LOCATION:

48°44.90' - 122°50.50' Matia Island is located at the base of the Strait of Georgia about 3 mi. N. of the middle of Orcas Island. This 145 acre sandstone island park primarily a bird sanctuary. The dock & mooring buoys are in Rolfe Cove on the W. side of island.

GUEST BOAT CAPACITY: ....Appx. 4-6 boats

SEASON: ....Closed winter

AMT W/ELECTRICITY: ....None

TOILETS: ....Composting toilet

HOT SHOWERS: ....None

PICNIC AREA: ....Yes

PLAY AREA: ....Yes

BASIC STORE: ....None

DAILY RATE: Mooring Buoys.................$5.00/night
Boats under 26 ft..........$8.00/night
Boats 26 ft. & Over.....$11.00/night
Subject to Change in 1997

GUEST DOCK: ....Appx. 64 ft.

MOORING BUOYS: 2

WATER: ....None

PAY PHONES: ....None

BOAT RAMP: ....None

PICNIC SHELTER: ....None

BBQ: ....Yes

PUMP OUT STATION: ......None

OTHER: Hiking Trails, wildlife, good anchorage, fishing and beachcombing.

CAUTION! This chartlet not intended for use in navigation.

Islet

Shallow!

ROLFE COVE

Entrance

Appx. 64'

PIER

Composting Toilet

Park Float

Pay Station

Mooring Buoys

MATIA ISLAND

N

Orcas Island

NAME OF MARINA:	*DEER HARBOR MARINA*	**RADIO:** VHF Ch. 16
ADDRESS:	P.O. Box 200 Deer Harbor	WA 98243
TELEPHONE:	360-376-4420 **MGR: Owners:** Casales	

SHORT DESCRIPTION & LOCATION:

48°37.20' - 123°00.20' Small harbor on west side of Orcas Island between Pole Pass and Steep Point. Family oriented marina resort located on east side of harbor in typically beautiful San Juan Island setting.

GUEST BOAT CAPACITY: ....Appx. 80 boats	GUEST DOCK: ....Slips only
SEASON: ....All year	GUEST SLIPS: 65
RESERVATION POLICY: ....Accepts	WATER: ....At gas dock
AMT W/ELECTRICITY: ....Appx. 90%	AMPS: ....20 A
FUEL DOCK: ....Gas & Diesel	PUMP OUT STATION ....None
MARINE REPAIRS: ....Close by	HAUL OUT: ....Close by
TOILETS: ....Yes	BOAT RAMP: ....Close by
HOT SHOWERS: ....Yes	LAUNDRY: ....None
RESTAURANT: ....Yes	LOUNGE: ....None
PICNIC AREA: ....Yes	POOL: ....Yes
PLAY AREA: ....Yes	BBQ: ....Yes
BASIC STORE: ....Yes	GOLF: ....12 miles away
ELECTRICITY: ....Included in moorage fee	OTHER: Hot tub, Great dinghy
DAILY RATE: ....0-19'=$16.00	area, fishing, crabbing,
Add $4.00 20'-25'=$18.00	Post Office, gift shop,
on holidays 26' & above=	heated pool, massage.
.50¢--.80¢ per ft.	

CAUTION! This chartlet not intended for use in navigation.

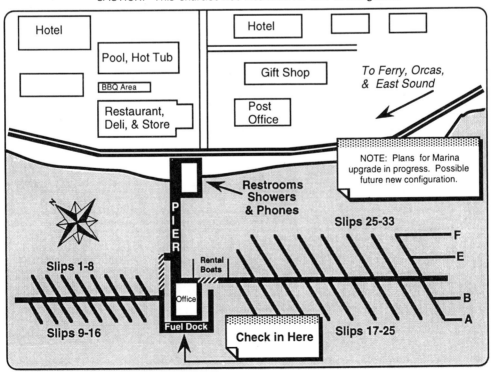

Orcas Island

NAME OF MARINA: *OLGA COMMUNITY FLOAT*   RADIO: None

ADDRESS: Olga Community Club   Olga,   WA 98279

TELEPHONE: MGR: Dockmaster

SHORT DESCRIPTION & LOCATION:

48°37.00' - 122°50.20' Olga is located on Orcas Island on the S.E. shore of East Sound. The guest float is maintained w/community labor and moorage fees. The quiet moorage is adjacent to the Village of Olga and is a pleasant walk to Orcas Island Artworks.

GUEST BOAT CAPACITY: ....Appx. 6-8 boats	GUEST DOCK: ....90 ft.
SEASON: ....May thru September	GUEST SLIPS: ....Dock only
RESERVATION POLICY:.................................None	WATER: ....Yes
AMT W/ELECTRICITY: ....None	AMPS: ....None
FUEL DOCK: ....None	PUMP OUT STATION ....None
MARINE REPAIRS: ....None	HAUL OUT: ....None
TOILETS: ....Yes	BOAT RAMP:.........................None
HOT SHOWERS: ....None	LAUNDRY: ....None
RESTAURANT: ....Close by	LOUNGE: ....None
PICNIC AREA: ....Yes	POOL:..None
PLAY AREA: ....None	BBQ: ....None
BASIC STORE: ....Summer only	GOLF:..None
ELECTRICITY: ....None	OTHER: Please side tie dinghy,
DAILY RATE: ....Appx. .25¢ per foot	all mooring buoys are private, well stocked store open in summer.

CAUTION! This chartlet not intended for use in navigation.

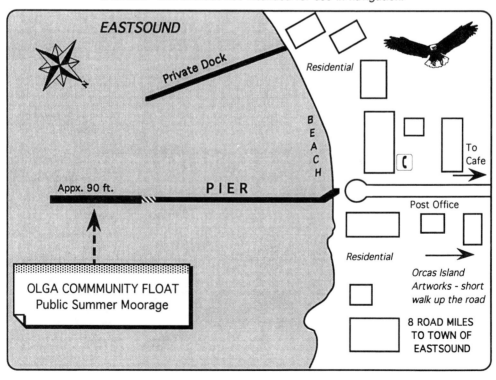

Orcas Island

NAME OF YACHT CLUB: ORCAS ISLAND YACHT CLUB

ADDRESS: P.O. Box 686   Eastsound   WA   98245

TELEPHONE: **PERSON IN CHARGE:** Commodore

SHORT DESCRIPTION & LOCATION:

48°37.80' -122°57.50' OIYC has a small "T" float located about 2 blocks north of West Sound Marina in the N.E. corner of West Sound for use by reciprocal yacht club members in good standing. Dock is situated in a pristine & quiet neighborhood location.

RECIPROCAL BOAT CAPACITY............Appx. 6-8	**RECIPROCAL DOCK:** Appx. 250'
SEASON: ....All year	**RECIPROCAL SLIPS:** Dock only
RESERVATION POLICY:....................None	**WATER:** ....No
TOILETS: ....None	**AMT W/ELECTRICITY:** ....None
HOT SHOWERS: ....None	**AMPS:** ....None
RESTAURANT:................................None	**LOUNGE:** ....None
DAILY RATE: ....No Charge	**OTHER:** ....West Sound Marina is close by offering many services for boaters

NOTE: THIS IS PRIVATE MOORAGE AND ONLY AVAILABLE TO MEMBERS OF RECIPROCAL YACHT CLUBS. YOUR CLUB MUST HAVE RECIPROCAL PRIVILEGES AND YOU MUST FLY YOUR BURGEE.

CAUTION! This chartlet not intended for use in navigation.

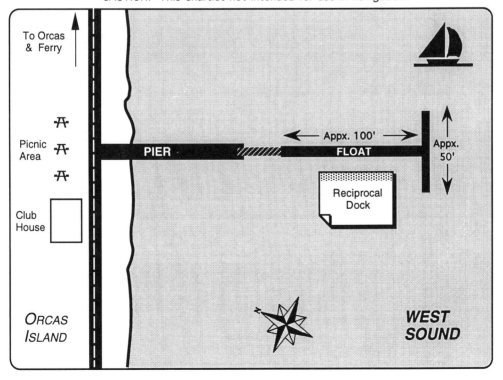

Orcas Island

NAME OF MARINA: *ROSARIO RESORT*   **RADIO:** None

ADDRESS: One Rosario Way   Eastsound   WA   98245

TELEPHONE: 800-562-8820   **MGR:** John Messinger

SHORT DESCRIPTION & LOCATION:

48°38.80' - 122°52.20' Located on Orcas Island on east side of East Sound at base of Cascade Bay. World famous resort in park like setting with historic and multiple amenities for boaters. **Reservations are a must in the summer.**

GUEST BOAT CAPACITY: ....Appx. 30 boats	GUEST DOCK: ....100' plus slips
SEASON: ....All year	GUEST SLIPS: ....Appx. 30
RESERVATION POLICY: ....Recommended	WATER: ....Yes
AMT W/ELECTRICITY: ....All	AMPS: ....30 A
FUEL DOCK: ....Gas & Diesel	PUMP OUT STATION ....None
MARINE REPAIRS: ....None	HAUL OUT: ....None
TOILETS: ....Yes	BOAT RAMP: ....Yes
HOT SHOWERS: ....Yes	LAUNDRY: ....Yes
RESTAURANT: ....Yes	LOUNGE: ....Yes
PICNIC AREA: ....Yes	POOL: ....Yes
PLAY AREA: ....Yes	BBQ: ....None
BASIC STORE: ....Seasonal	GOLF: ....Close by
ELECTRICITY: ....Included in moorage	OTHER: 35 Mooring buoys.
DAILY RATE: ....Appx. $1 per foot/day	Summer Jitney service

DAILY RATE: ....Appx. $1 per foot/day

Note: A landing fee of $20.00/day which includes use of all resort facilities & jitney service <u>is required to come ashore on resort property</u> whether tied to resort buoy or anchored.

OTHER: 35 Mooring buoys. Summer Jitney service to shore, recreational equipment, spa, tennis, shops, car rentals.

CAUTION! This chartlet not intended for use in navigation.

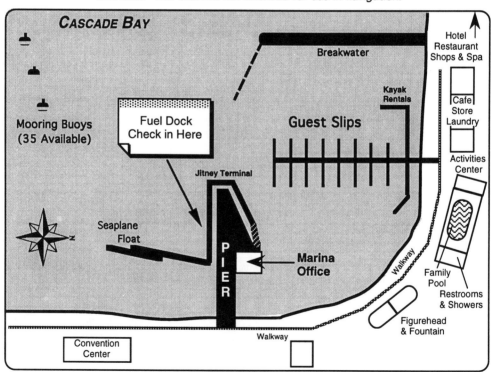

Orcas Island

NAME OF MARINA:	*WEST SOUND MARINA INC.* RADIO: VHF Ch.16
ADDRESS:	P.O. Box 19 Orcas WA 98280
TELEPHONE:	360-376-2314 MGR: Mike Wareham

SHORT DESCRIPTION & LOCATION:

48°37.80' - 122°57.40' Quiet local marina located in a picturesque cove on N.W. corner of West Sound. Marina sits in the lee of Picnic Island. Many marine services available.

GUEST BOAT CAPACITY:	Appx. 8-10 boats	GUEST DOCK:	Appx. 250 ft.
SEASON:	All year	GUEST SLIPS:	Dock only
RESERVATION POLICY:	Accepts	WATER:	Yes
AMT W/ELECTRICITY:	4 Outlets	AMPS:	20 A
FUEL DOCK:	Gas, Dsl, & LP	PUMP OUT STATION	Yes
MARINE REPAIRS:	On premises	HAUL OUT:	30 Ton Travel-Haul
TOILETS:	Yes	BOAT RAMP:	None
HOT SHOWERS:	Yes	LAUNDRY:	None
RESTAURANT:	None	LOUNGE:	Non
PICNIC AREA:	None	POOL:	None
PLAY AREA:	None	BBQ:	None
BASIC STORE:	Yes	GOLF:	Close by
ELECTRICITY:	$ 2.00 per day	OTHER:	Full marine chandlery, fishing supplies.
DAILY RATE:	Appx. .50¢ per foot		

CAUTION! This chartlet not intended for use in navigation.

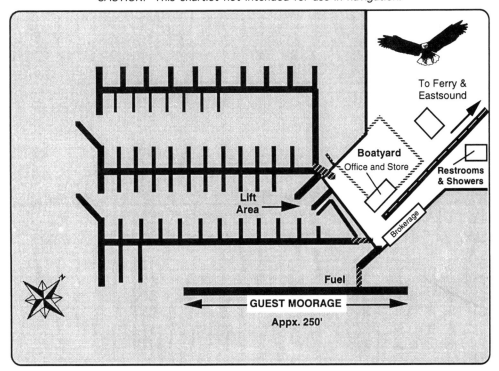

Point Roberts

NAME OF MARINA: *POINT ROBERTS MARINA*   RADIO: None
ADDRESS: 713 Simundson Dr.   Point Roberts,   WA 98281
TELEPHONE: 360-945-2255   MGR: Bruce Gustafson
SHORT DESCRIPTION & LOCATION:

48°58.30' - 123°03.60'   Located at the S.W. end of a peninsula that is an unconnected portion of the USA on the W. shore of Boundary Bay. The tear dropped shaped boat basin & marina offer a pleasant quiet setting with complete marine services.

GUEST BOAT CAPACITY: ....Appx, 60-80 boats	GUEST DOCK:.........120' plus slips
SEASON: ....All year	GUEST SLIPS:..........30 large slips
RESERVATION POLICY:.....................Not needed	WATER: ....Yes
AMT W/ELECTRICITY: ....All	AMPS: ....30-50 A
FUEL DOCK: ....Gas, Dsl, & LP	PUMP OUT STATION ....Yes
MARINE REPAIRS: ....On premises	HAUL OUT: ....Travel-Lift
TOILETS: ....Yes	BOAT RAMP: ....Monorail
HOT SHOWERS: ....Yes	LAUNDRY: ....Yes
RESTAURANT: ....Yes	LOUNGE: ....Close by
PICNIC AREA: ....Yes	POOL:....................................None
PLAY AREA: ....Yes	BBQ: ....Close by
BASIC STORE: ....Yes	GOLF: ....Close by
ELECTRICITY: ....Included in moorage	OTHER: Customs port-of-entry,
DAILY RATE: ....Appx. .50¢ per foot	Pump-out, provisions,
	close to Lighthouse
	Marine Park with nature
	& wildlife walks.

CAUTION! This chartlet not intended for use in navigation.

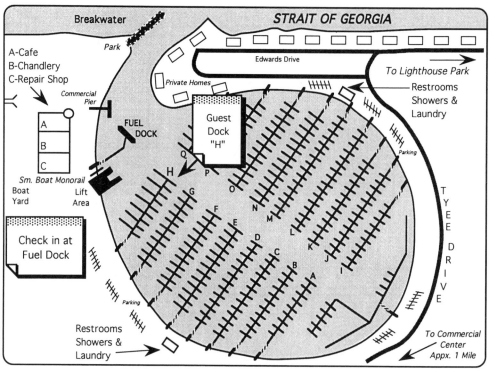

Point Roberts

NAME OF YACHT CLUB: *POINT ROBERTS YACHT CLUB*

ADDRESS: P.O. Box 1009   Point Roberts,   WA   98281

TELEPHONE: PERSON IN CHARGE: Commodore

SHORT DESCRIPTION & LOCATION:

P.R.Y.C. offers 2 days reciprocal moorage per year at the **Point Roberts Marina** guest dock ("H" Dock). Upon arrival check in with the dock master & show current membership card to be assigned moorage. Moorage is limited to 2 reciprocal boats per day. A gate key may be obtained from the dock master with a deposit.

RECIPROCAL BOAT CAPACITY Appx. 2 boats

SEASON: ....All year

RESERVATION POLICY:...............................None

TOILETS: ....At Point Roberts Marina

HOT SHOWERS: ....At Point Roberts Marina

RESTAURANT:...Close by

DAILY RATE: ...Electricity charge - $3.00/ day
Moorage - No charge for 2 days
per year per reciprocal boater.

RECIPROCAL DOCK: At marina

RECIPROCAL SLIPS: At marina

WATER: ....Yes

AMT W/ELECTRICITY: ....All

AMPS: ....30-50 A

LOUNGE: ....Close by

OTHER: Services same as
Point Roberts Marina
listing on Page 174

<u>NOTE:</u> THIS IS PRIVATE MOORAGE AND ONLY AVAILABLE TO MEMBERS OF RECIPROCAL YACHT CLUBS. YOUR CLUB <u>MUST</u> HAVE RECIPROCAL PRIVILEGES AND YOU MUST FLY YOUR BURGEE.

CAUTION! This chartlet not intended for use in navigation.

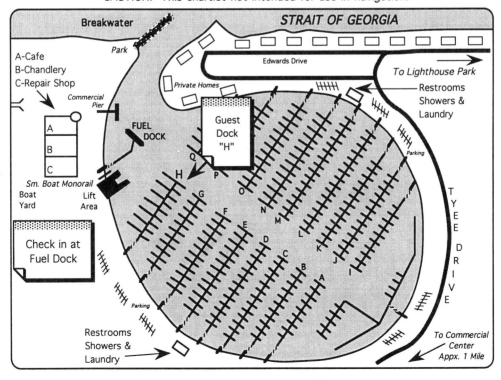

San Juan Island

NAME OF MARINA: *PORT OF FRIDAY HARBOR MARINA*   RADIO: VHF Ch. 66A

ADDRESS: P.O. Box 889   Friday Harbor   WA   98250

TELEPHONE: 360-378-2688   MGR: Tami Hayes/Ed Barrett

SHORT DESCRIPTION & LOCATION:

48°32.40' - 123°00.80' Located on east side in about the middle of San Juan Island in a scenic harbor. Largest & busiest marina in the Islands. Services abound for boaters at the marina and in town.   U.S. Customs dock manned in the summer.

GUEST BOAT CAPACITY: ....Appx. 150 boats	GUEST DOCK: 800 ft. plus slips
SEASON: ....All year	GUEST SLIPS: ....Appx. 85
RESERVATION POLICY: Yes- .65¢ ft. surcharge	WATER: ....Yes
AMT W/ELECTRICITY: ....All	AMPS: ....30 A
FUEL DOCK: ....Close by	PUMP OUT STATION ....Yes
MARINE REPAIRS: ....Close by	HAUL OUT: ....Close by
TOILETS: ....Yes	BOAT RAMP: ....Close by
HOT SHOWERS: ....Yes	LAUNDRY: ....Close by
RESTAURANT: ....Close by	LOUNGE: ....Close by
PICNIC AREA: ....Yes	POOL: ....None
PLAY AREA: ....Yes	BBQ: ....None
BASIC STORE: ....Close by	GOLF: ....Close by
ELECTRICITY: ....$ 3.00 per day	OTHER: Museums, shopping, air
DAILY RATE: ....Appx. .45¢ per foot-Winter	& water transportation
..........Appx. .55¢ per foot-Summer	to mainland, Annual Jazz
	Festival in July.

NOTES

_____

_____

_____

_____

_____

_____

_____

_____

_____

_____

_____

San Juan Island

CAUTION! This chartlet not intended for use in navigation.

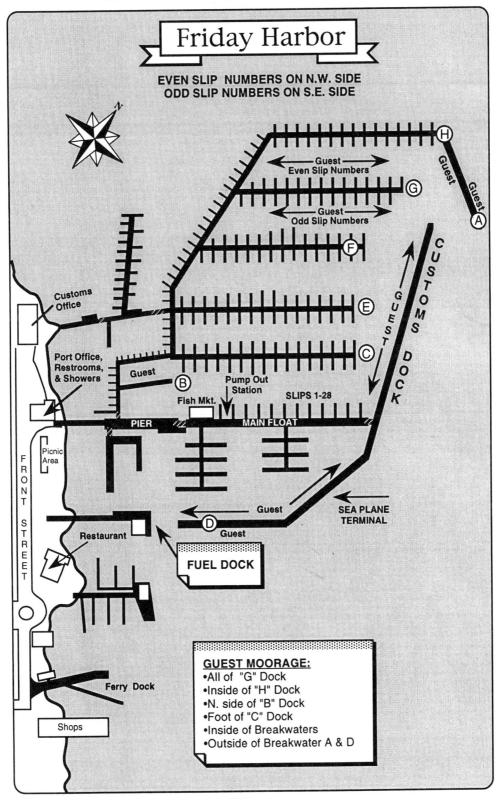

Friday Harbor

EVEN SLIP NUMBERS ON N.W. SIDE
ODD SLIP NUMBERS ON S.E. SIDE

N

Guest Even Slip Numbers

Guest Odd Slip Numbers

H

G

F

E

C

Guest

A

CUSTOMS DOCK

GUEST

Customs Office

Port Office, Restrooms, & Showers

Guest

B

Fish Mkt.

Pump Out Station

SLIPS 1-28

PIER

MAIN FLOAT

Picnic Area

F R O N T   S T R E E T

SEA PLANE TERMINAL

Guest

D

Guest

Restaurant

FUEL DOCK

Ferry Dock

Shops

GUEST MOORAGE:
• All of "G" Dock
• Inside of "H" Dock
• N. side of "B" Dock
• Foot of "C" Dock
• Inside of Breakwaters
• Outside of Breakwater A & D

San Juan Island

NAME OF MARINA: *ROCHE HARBOR RESORT* **RADIO:** VHF Ch. 78
ADDRESS: P.O. Box 4001 Roche Harbor WA 98250
TELEPHONE: 1-800-451-8910 **MGR:** Kevin Carlton

SHORT DESCRIPTION & LOCATION:

48°36.60' - 123°09.10' Historic premier marina resort with extensive moorage facilities and vacation amenities located on north end of San Juan Island approximately 10 miles north of Friday Harbor. U.S. Customs Port-of-Entry.

GUEST BOAT CAPACITY: ....Appx. 120 boats	**GUEST DOCK:** 110 ft. plus slips
SEASON: ....All year	**GUEST SLIPS:** 46
RESERVATION POLICY: ....Accepts	**WATER:** ....Yes
AMT W/ELECTRICITY: ....All	**AMPS:** ....30-50 A
FUEL DOCK: ....Gas, Dsl, & LP	**PUMP OUT STATION** ....None
MARINE REPAIRS: ....Yes	**HAUL OUT:** ....None
TOILETS: ....Yes	**BOAT RAMP:** ....Yes
HOT SHOWERS: ....Yes	**LAUNDRY:** ....Yes
RESTAURANT: ....Yes	**LOUNGE:** ....Yes
PICNIC AREA: ....Yes	**POOL:** ....Yes
PLAY AREA: ....Yes	**BBQ:** ....Yes
BASIC STORE: ....Yes	**GOLF:** ....Close by
ELECTRICITY: ....Included in moorage	**OTHER:** 45 Mooring buoys,
DAILY RATE: ....Appx. .90¢ per foot	tennis, airport, float
Mooring Buoys $15.00 for boats	plane service, shops,
under 35 ft./$20.00 over 35 ft.	USPO, **traditional**
	evening colors.

CAUTION! This chartlet not intended for use in navigation.

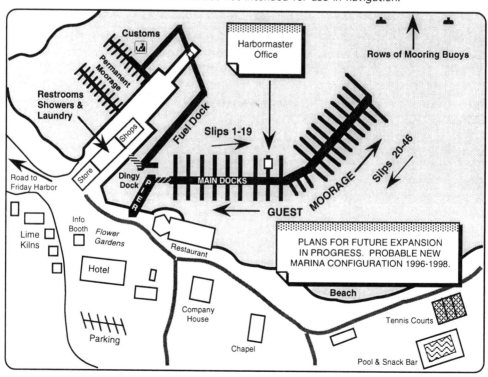

San Juan Island

NAME OF MARINA: *SNUG HARBOR MARINA RESORT*   RADIO: ....None

ADDRESS: 2371 Mitchell Bay Rd.   Friday Harbor,   WA   98250

TELEPHONE: 360-378-4762   MGR: Richard Barnes

SHORT DESCRIPTION & LOCATION:

48°34.30' - 123°09.90' Charming and rustic marina fishing resort located In peaceful Mitchell Bay on northeast corner of San Juan Island. *Note: Recommended 4-5 ft. working draft maximum at zero tide upon entering Miitchell Bay.*

GUEST BOAT CAPACITY: ....Appx.30-40 boats

SEASON: ....All year

RESERVATION POLICY:............................Accepts

AMT W/ELECTRICITY: 90%

FUEL DOCK: ....Gas & LP

MARINE REPAIRS: ....On premises

TOILETS: ....Yes

HOT SHOWERS: ..Space available in guest rooms

RESTAURANT: ....None

PICNIC AREA: ....None

PLAY AREA: ....Yes

BASIC STORE: ....Yes

ELECTRICITY: ....$ 2.00 per day

DAILY RATE: ....Summer Rate - .75¢ per foot
...........Winter Rate - .45¢ per foot

GUEST DOCK: 70 ft. plus slips

GUEST SLIPS:...........Appx. 30-40

WATER: ....Three hoses on dock

AMPS: ....15-20 A

PUMP OUT STATION ....None

HAUL OUT: ....None

BOAT RAMP:...............................Yes

LAUNDRY: ....Yes

LOUNGE: ....None

POOL:......................Pond swimming

BBQ: ....Yes

GOLF:...None

OTHER: Great dinghy area in Bay. Crabbing, fishing, whale watching. Kayak, skiff & boat rentals. Crab & fish gear rentals.

CAUTION! This chartlet not intended for use in navigation.

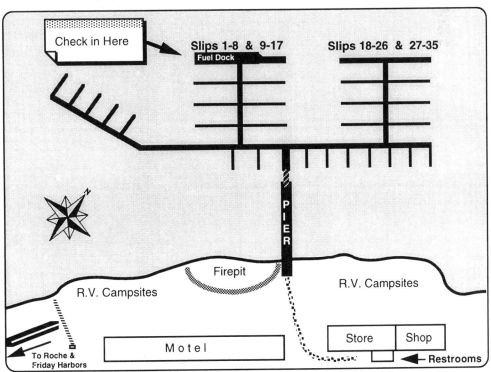

Shaw Island

NAME OF MARINA: *LITTLE PORTION STORE*   RADIO: None

ADDRESS: Box 455   Shaw Island   WA   98268

TELEPHONE: 360-468-2288   MGR: Sister Dorothy Hood

SHORT DESCRIPTION & LOCATION:

48°35.10' - 122°35.70' Sm. marina located on N.E. corner of Blind Bay on north side of Shaw Is. next to ferry landing. The store and dock are operated by Franciscan Sisters who also act as State Ferry agents. <u>No big boats allowed overnight - maximum size 25 ft.</u>

GUEST BOAT CAPACITY:	Appx. 2-3 boats	GUEST DOCK: ....Appx. 30 ft.
SEASON:	All year	GUEST SLIPS: ....None
RESERVATION POLICY:	Accepts	WATER: ....None
AMT W/ELECTRICITY:	None	AMPS: ....None
FUEL DOCK:	None	PUMP OUT STATION ....None
MARINE REPAIRS:	None	HAUL OUT: ....None
TOILETS:	Yes	BOAT RAMP: ....None
HOT SHOWERS:	None	LAUNDRY: ....None
RESTAURANT:	None	LOUNGE: ....None
PICNIC AREA:	None	POOL: ....None
PLAY AREA:	None	BBQ: ....None
BASIC STORE:	Yes	GOLF: ....None
ELECTRICITY:	None	OTHER: USPO, chapel, well stock-
DAILY RATE:	Appx. .35¢ per foot	ed store, county park, campground & museum 2.5 miles away, bicycling, & marine park adjacent.

CAUTION! This chartlet not intended for use in navigation.

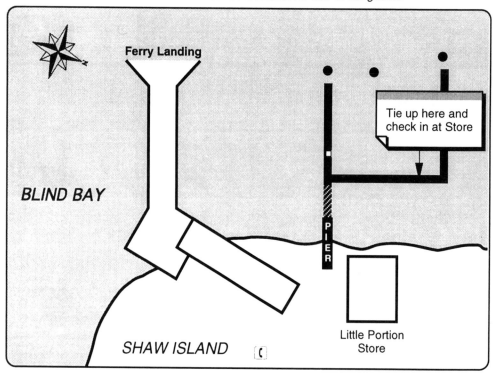

Ferry Landing

Tie up here and check in at Store

BLIND BAY

PIER

Little Portion Store

SHAW ISLAND

Stuart Island

NAME OF PARK: *REID HARBOR & PREVOST HARBOR MARINE PARKS*

ADDRESS: 6158 Lighthouse Rd.   Friday Harbor, WA   98250

TELEPHONE: 360-378-2044   **MGR:** Chris Guidotti

SHORT DESCRIPTION & LOCATION:

48°41.60'-123°12' (**Appx**) Stuart Island is the most N.W. island in the San Juans and hosts 2 marine parks with floats, buoys, and good anchorages. Reid Harbor is only 3 mi. N. of Roche Harbor while Prevost Harbor is about 5 mi. S. of Bedwell Harbour, Canada.

GUEST BOAT CAPACITY: ....Appx. 50 boats

SEASON: ....All year

AMT W/ELECTRICITY: ....None

TOILETS: ....Yes

HOT SHOWERS: ....None

PICNIC AREA: ....Yes

PLAY AREA: ....None

BASIC STORE: ....None

DAILY RATE: Mooring Buoys.................$5.00/night
Boats under 26 ft...........$8.00/night
Boats 26 ft. & Over.....$11.00/night
Campsites........................$5.00/night
Subject to Change in 1997

GUEST DOCK: Reid: 110'/Pr: 126'

MOORING BUOYS: Reid: 15/Pr: 7

WATER: ....Fresh water in park

PAY PHONES: ....None

BOAT RAMP: ....None

PICNIC SHELTER: ....None

BBQ: ....Yes

PUMP OUT STATION: ....Yes

OTHER: Extensive network of trails, 18 campsites, wildlife, clams, oysters nearby, fishing, and great family boating.

CAUTION! This chartlet not intended for use in navigation.

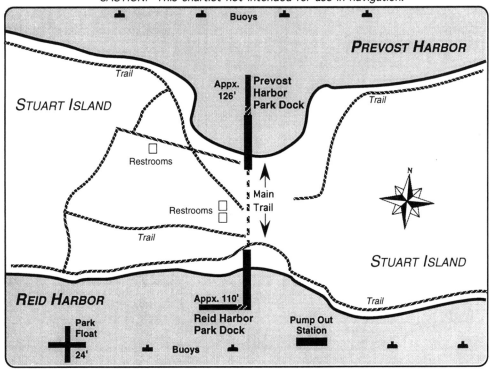

Sucia Island

NAME OF PARK: *SUCIA ISLAND STATE MARINE PARK*

ADDRESS: Star Rt. Box 177   Olga, WA   98279

TELEPHONE: 360-376-2073   **MGR:** Dave Castor

SHORT DESCRIPTION & LOCATION:

48°45.05' - 123°54.10' Sucia is located at the base of the Strait of Georgia 2.5 mi. N. of mid Orcas Is. The park is 562 acres and comprised of 11 islands. Several bays have park facilities and buoys, but Fossil Bay on the SW side has 2 docks and the most buoys.

GUEST BOAT CAPACITY: ....,..Appx. 20-25 boats

SEASON: ....All year

AMT W/ELECTRICITY: ....None

TOILETS: ....Composting toilets

HOT SHOWERS: ....None

PICNIC AREA: ....Yes

PLAY AREA: ....Yes

BASIC STORE: ....None

DAILY RATE: Mooring Buoys.................$5.00/night
Boats under 26 ft...........$8.00/night
Boats 26 ft. & Over.....$11.00/night
Campsites.........................$5.00/night
Subject to Change in 1997

GUEST DOCK: 2 lg. docks-160 ft.

MOORING BUOYS: 48

WATER: ....Summer only

PAY PHONES: ....None

BOAT RAMP: ....None

PICNIC SHELTER: ....Yes

BBQ: ....Yes

PUMP OUT STATION: ......None

OTHER: 10 Miles of hiking trails, fossil digging, clams, oysters, crabbing, 55 campsites, and 2 group camping areas.

CAUTION! This chartlet not intended for use in navigation.

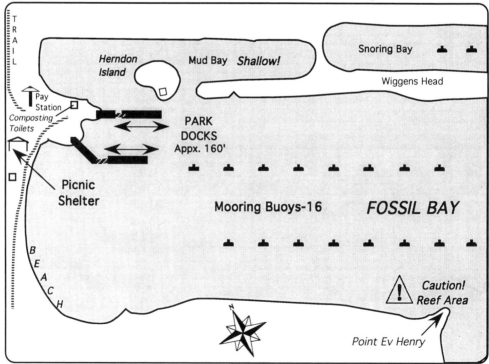

C H A P T E R

6

GULF ISLANDS CANADA

Gabriola Island

NAME OF MARINA: *DEGNEN BAY GOVERNMENT FLOAT*   RADIO: None
ADDRESS: RR #2 SHC 27 C30   Gabriola Island, B.C.   Canada V0R 1X0
TELEPHONE: 604-247-9753   MGR: Brenda Upton
SHORT DESCRIPTION & LOCATION:
49°08.40' - 123°42.65' The public floats are located at the head of Degnen Bay on the N. side of Gabriola Passage on S. side of Gabriola Island. The floats are about 1 1/2 miles from both Silva Bay and Drumbeg Park by road. The Bay offers great anchorage.

GUEST BOAT CAPACITY:	Appx. 6-10 boats	GUEST DOCK:	Appx. 200 ft.
SEASON:	All year	GUEST SLIPS:	None
RESERVATION POLICY:	None	WATER:	None
AMT W/ELECTRICITY:	All	AMPS:	15-20 A
FUEL DOCK:	None	PUMP OUT STATION	None
MARINE REPAIRS:	None	HAUL OUT:	None
TOILETS:	None	BOAT RAMP:	None
HOT SHOWERS:	None	LAUNDRY:	None
RESTAURANT:	None	LOUNGE:	None
PICNIC AREA:	None	POOL:	None
PLAY AREA:	None	BBQ:	None
BASIC STORE:	None	GOLF:	None
ELECTRICITY:	$2.68 per day	OTHER:	Tidal grid, crane, taxi service & phone. A killer whale petroglyph is near head of the bay.
DAILY RATE:	Appx. .40¢ per foot		

CAUTION! This chartlet not intended for use in navigation.

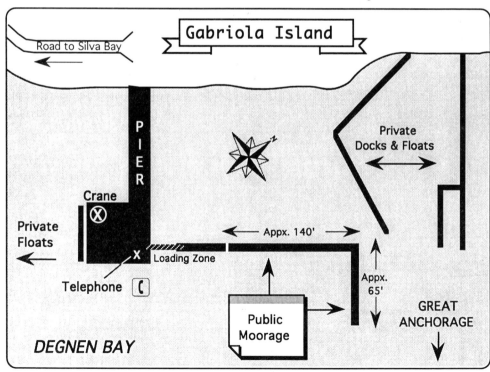

Gabriola Island

NAME OF MARINA: *PAGE'S MARINA (at Silva Bay)* RADIO: None

ADDRESS: RR 2 Coast Rd. Site 30 Gabriola, B.C. Canada VOR 1XO

TELEPHONE: 604-247-8931 MGR: Ted & Phyllis Reeve

SHORT DESCRIPTION & LOCATION:

49°09.00' - 123°42.20' Silva Bay is a fairly well protected harbour on the SE end of Gabriola Is. inside of the Flattop Isl. group. Page's is the southerly marina of the 3 in the harbour. Open slips are rented to guest boaters. Local large scale charts are needed.

GUEST BOAT CAPACITY: ....Appx. 10 boats	GUEST DOCK: ....Varies
SEASON: ....All year	GUEST SLIPS: ....Varies
RESERVATION POLICY: ....Accepts	WATER: ....Limited
AMT W/ELECTRICITY: ....All	AMPS: ....15 A
FUEL DOCK: ....Gas & Diesel	PUMP OUT STATION ....None
MARINE REPAIRS: ....Close by	HAUL OUT: ....None
TOILETS: ....Yes	BOAT RAMP: ....None
HOT SHOWERS: ....Yes	LAUNDRY: ....Yes
RESTAURANT: ....Seasonal snack bar	LOUNGE: ....None
PICNIC AREA: ....Close by	POOL: ....None
PLAY AREA: ....None	BBQ: ....Yes
BASIC STORE: ....Close by	GOLF: ....Close by
ELECTRICITY: ....$2.50 per day	OTHER: Cottage rentals, marine
DAILY RATE: ....Appx. .50¢ per foot	chandlery, taxi service,
	diving supplies & air,
	close to Drumbeg Park.

CAUTION! This chartlet not intended for use in navigation.

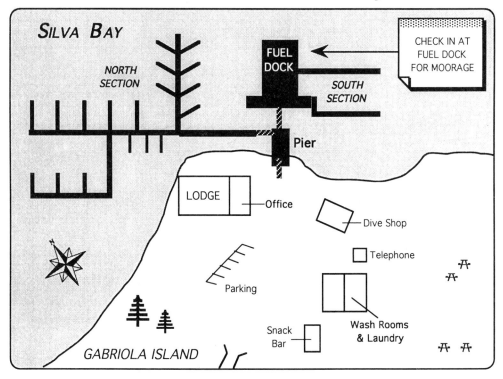

Gabriola Island

NAME OF MARINA: *SILVA BAY BOATEL*   RADIO: None

ADDRESS: RR #2, Site 33 - C2   Gabriola, B.C.   Canada VOR 1X0

TELEPHONE: 604-247-9351   MGR: Audrey & Leo Leloup

SHORT DESCRIPTION & LOCATION:

49°09.00' - 123°42.20' Silva Bay is located on the S.E. end of Gabriola Island inside of the Flattop Is. group. This is smallest marina of the 3 in the harbour & situated at the far N.W. side. Floats shallow at low tide - **4.5 ft. maximum draft allowed at dock**.

GUEST BOAT CAPACITY: ....Appx. 10-12 boats	GUEST DOCK: ....Varies
SEASON: ....All year	GUEST SLIPS: ....Dock only
RESERVATION POLICY:.............................Accepts	WATER: ....Limited
AMT W/ELECTRICITY: ....All	AMPS: ....15 A
FUEL DOCK: ....None	PUMP OUT STATION ....None
MARINE REPAIRS: ....Close by	HAUL OUT: ....None
TOILETS: ....Yes	BOAT RAMP: ....None
HOT SHOWERS: ....In guest rooms if vacant	LAUNDRY: ....Yes
RESTAURANT: ....Close by	LOUNGE: ....Close by
PICNIC AREA: ....Yes	POOL: ....None
PLAY AREA: ....Yes	BBQ: ....None
BASIC STORE: ....Yes	GOLF: ....Close by
ELECTRICITY: ....$5.00 per day	OTHER: Motel accomodations,
DAILY RATE: ....Appx. .50¢ per foot	scuba diving, taxi service (Tel. 247-9348), groceries, propane, fishing & marine supplies.

CAUTION! This chartlet not intended for use in navigation.

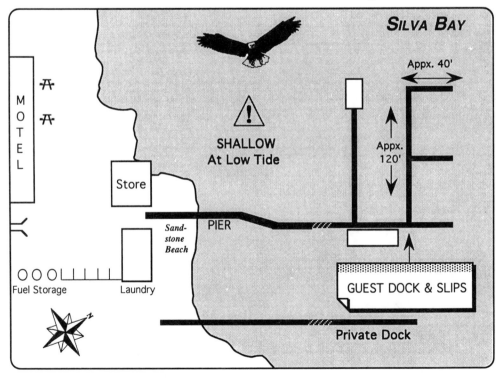

Gabriola Island

NAME OF MARINA: *SILVA BAY RESORT & MARINA*   RADIO: VHF Ch.68

ADDRESS: R.R. 2, Site 31, C-2   Gabriola,   B.C. V0R 1X0

TELEPHONE: 604-247-8662   MGR: Mark Sager

SHORT DESCRIPTION & LOCATION:

49°09.00' - 123°42.20' Silva Bay is a harbour located on the S.E. end of Gabriola Is. inside of the Flattop Island group. The marina, under new management, is the largest of the 3 marinas in the harbor & situated in the middle. <u>Good large scale charts are needed.</u>

GUEST BOAT CAPACITY: ....Appx. 40 boats	GUEST DOCK: ....80' plus slips
SEASON: ....All year	GUEST SLIPS: ....Appx. 35
RESERVATION POLICY: ....Accepts	WATER: ....Yes - At fuel dock
AMT W/ELECTRICITY: ....All	AMPS: ....15-30 A
FUEL DOCK: ....Gas, Dsl, & LP	PUMP OUT STATION ....None
MARINE REPAIRS: ....On premises	HAUL OUT: ....Rail & Travel-Lift
TOILETS: ....Yes	BOAT RAMP: ....None
HOT SHOWERS: ....Yes	LAUNDRY: ....Yes
RESTAURANT: ....Yes	LOUNGE: ....Yes
PICNIC AREA: ....Yes	POOL: ....Yes
PLAY AREA: ....None	BBQ: ....Yes
BASIC STORE: ....Yes	GOLF: ....Close by
ELECTRICITY: ....$3.00 per day	OTHER: General store and
DAILY RATE: ....Appx. .65 cents per foot	chandlery, shipyard, gift
	shop, fishing charters,
	tennis courts, and kids
	only dining room.

CAUTION! This chartlet not intended for use in navigation.

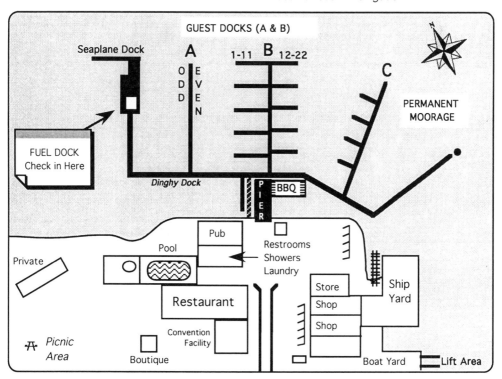

Galiano Island

NAME OF MARINA: *MONTAGUE HARBOUR MARINA*   **RADIO:** VHF Ch. 68
ADDRESS: RR 1 Montague Road   Galiano, B.C.., Canada VON 1PO
TELEPHONE: 604-539-5733   **MGR:** Bob Walker

SHORT DESCRIPTION & LOCATION:

48°53.50' - 123°23.40' Convenient location situated in picturesque and protected Montague Harbour on S.E. side of Galiano Island. Adjacent to (alt.) B.C. Ferry Terminal and close to Provincial Park, the marina offers services, including bus service to Pub.

GUEST BOAT CAPACITY: ....Appx. 25 boats	GUEST DOCK: ....70 Ft. slips
SEASON: ....May thru Oct. 15 - closed winter	GUEST SLIPS: ....12 large slips
RESERVATION POLICY: ....Encouraged	WATER: ....Yes - limited
AMT W/ELECTRICITY: ....All	AMPS: ....15-30 A
FUEL DOCK: ....Gas & Diesel	PUMP OUT STATION ....None
MARINE REPAIRS: ...."On Call"	HAUL OUT: ....None
TOILETS: ....Yes	BOAT RAMP: ....Close by
HOT SHOWERS: ....None	LAUNDRY: ....None
RESTAURANT: ....(French) close by-resv. required	LOUNGE: ....Close by
PICNIC AREA: ....Yes - On Deck	POOL: ....None
PLAY AREA: ....None	BBQ: ....None
BASIC STORE: ....Yes	GOLF: ...Close by-shuttle available
ELECTRICITY: ...$3.00 day-15 Amp/$5.00-30 amp	OTHER: Well stocked grocery
DAILY RATE: ....Appx. .55¢ per foot	store, fresh produce,
Note: Sturdie's Bay ferry terminal	gifts, bookshop, charts,
handles Island traffic. Montague	speciality coffee shop.
terminal only used as an alternate.	**NO TRASH DROP.**

CAUTION! This chartlet not intended for use in navigation.

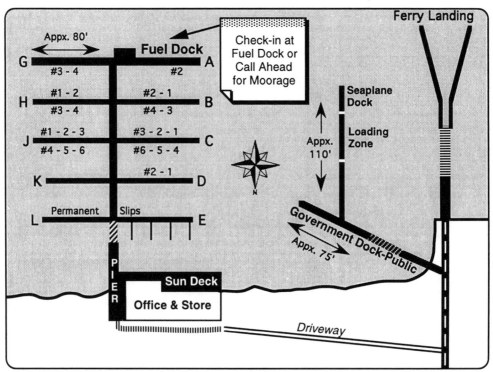

Mayne Island

NAME OF MARINA: *HORTON BAY GOVERNMENT WHARF*   **RADIO:** None

ADDRESS: Mayne Island, B.C.   Canada

TELEPHONE: 604-539-5425   **MGR:**

SHORT DESCRIPTION & LOCATION:

48°49.60' - 123°14.70' This busy & often full Gov't Float is situated on the SE side of Horton Bay on the SE side of Mayne Island. Floats are protected in the quiet & peaceful bay but the approach is hazardous and good charts & current tables are a must.

GUEST BOAT CAPACITY: ....Appx 6-10 boats	GUEST DOCK: ....Appx. 175 ft.
SEASON: ....All year	GUEST SLIPS: ....Dock only
RESERVATION POLICY: ....None	WATER: ....None
AMT W/ELECTRICITY: ....None	AMPS: ....None
FUEL DOCK: ....None	PUMP OUT STATION ....None
MARINE REPAIRS: ....None	HAUL OUT: ....None
TOILETS: ....None	BOAT RAMP: ....None
HOT SHOWERS: ....None	LAUNDRY: ....None
RESTAURANT: ....None	LOUNGE: ....None
PICNIC AREA: ....None	POOL: ....None
PLAY AREA: ....None	BBQ: ....None
BASIC STORE: ....None	GOLF: ....None
ELECTRICITY: ....None	OTHER: Good anchorage in bay if
DAILY RATE: ....Appx .45¢ per foot	docks full, taxi service available (Tel: 539-3439) to island services.

CAUTION! This chartlet not intended for use in navigation.

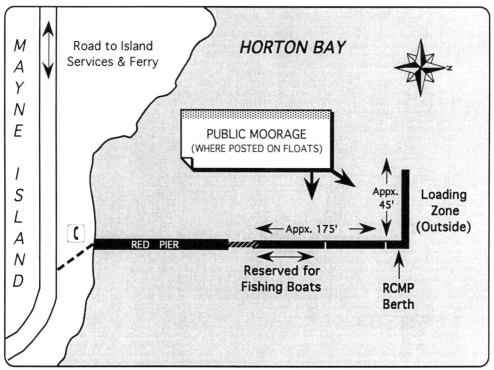

North Pender Is.

NAME OF MARINA:	*HOPE BAY GOVERNMENT WHARF* **RADIO:** None
ADDRESS:	4301 Bedwell Hbr. Rd. Pender Island, B.C. Canada V0N 2M0
TELEPHONE:	604-629-3423 **MGR:** Carol & Kees Van der valk

SHORT DESCRIPTION & LOCATION:

48°48.20' - 123°16.40' Fairly large gov't dock situated in pretty Hope Bay on E. side of N. Pender Is. behind Fane Island. Overnight moorage possible but can be open to light to mod. swells. The store & art gallery make good landmarks with their red & green roofs.

GUEST BOAT CAPACITY:	Appx 9-12 boats	**GUEST DOCK:**	170' + 1 slip
SEASON:	All year	**GUEST SLIPS:**	1 lg. 65' slip
RESERVATION POLICY:	None	**WATER:**	None
AMT W/ELECTRICITY:	None	**AMPS:**	None
FUEL DOCK:	None	**PUMP OUT STATION**	None
MARINE REPAIRS:	Close by	**HAUL OUT:**	None
TOILETS:	None	**BOAT RAMP:**	None
HOT SHOWERS:	None	**LAUNDRY:**	None
RESTAURANT:	Close by	**LOUNGE:**	None
PICNIC AREA:	Yes	**POOL:**	None
PLAY AREA:	None	**BBQ:**	None
BASIC STORE:	Yes	**GOLF:**	Close by
ELECTRICITY:	None	**OTHER:**	Telephone, artists' galleries, historic Hope Bay Store, espresso & cappuccino, taxi service.
DAILY RATE:	Appx. 45¢ per foot		

CAUTION! This chartlet not intended for use in navigation.

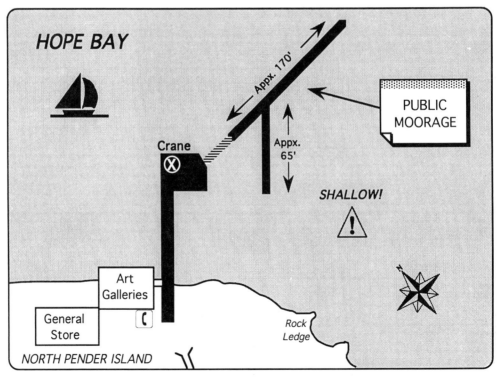

North Pender Is.

NAME OF MARINA: *OTTER BAY MARINA* **RADIO:** VHF Ch. 68

ADDRESS: RR 1 Pender Island, B.C. Canada VON 2M0

TELEPHONE: 604-629-3579 **MGR:** Chuck & Kay Spence

SHORT DESCRIPTION & LOCATION:

48°48.00' - 123°19.50' Located in Hyashi Cove in Otter Bay on N.W. side of North Pender Island. The recently upgraded marina has new floats & is well protected w/a rock breakwater covered by a beautiful deck w/ flags flying which make a great landmark.

GUEST BOAT CAPACITY: ....Appx 40+ boats	**GUEST DOCK:** ....300 ft. plus slips
SEASON: ....All year	**GUEST SLIPS:** 20
RESERVATION POLICY: ....Accepts	**WATER:** ....Yes
AMT W/ELECTRICITY: ....All	**AMPS:** ....15-30 A
FUEL DOCK: ....None	**PUMP OUT STATION** ....None
MARINE REPAIRS: ....Close by	**HAUL OUT:** ....None
TOILETS: ....Yes	**BOAT RAMP:** ....Yes
HOT SHOWERS: ....Yes	**LAUNDRY:** ....Yes
RESTAURANT: Close by-shuttle service available	**LOUNGE:** ....Close by
PICNIC AREA: ....Yes	**POOL:** ....Yes
PLAY AREA: ....Yes	**BBQ:** ....Yes
BASIC STORE: ....Yes	**GOLF:** ....Close by
ELECTRICITY: ....$ 3.00-15 Amp/$5.00-30 Amp	**OTHER:** Family & group oriented,
DAILY RATE: ....Appx .60-.70¢ per foot	function area gazebo,
	close to ferry, fishing
	supplies, kayak and
	bicycle rentals, espresso.

CAUTION! This chartlet not intended for use in navigation.

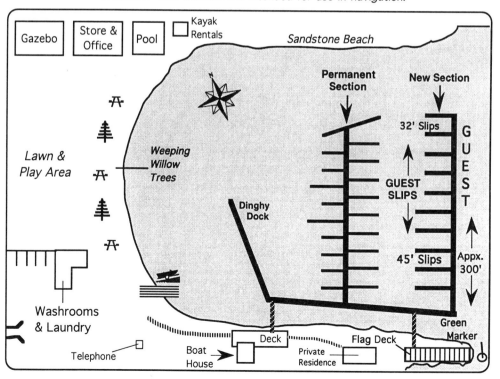

North Pender Is.

NAME OF MARINA: *PORT BROWNING MARINA RESORT* **RADIO:** VHF Ch. 68

ADDRESS: General Delivery North Pender Is., B.C., Can. V0N 2M0

TELEPHONE: 604-629-3493 **MGR:** Leila Pattersall

SHORT DESCRIPTION & LOCATION:

48°46.60' - 123°16.30' Situated on east side of North Pender Island at head of Port Browning. Country atmosphere with lots to do for entire family. Walking distance to shopping centre w/groceries, liquor store, gift shops, and gas station.

GUEST BOAT CAPACITY:	Appx. 110 boats	**GUEST DOCK:**	140' plus slips
SEASON:	All year	**GUEST SLIPS:**	46 large slips
RESERVATION POLICY:	Accepts	**WATER:**	Limited
AMT W/ELECTRICITY:	All	**AMPS:**	15 A
FUEL DOCK:	None	**PUMP OUT STATION**	None
MARINE REPAIRS:	Close by	**HAUL OUT:**	None
TOILETS:	Yes	**BOAT RAMP:**	Close by
HOT SHOWERS:	Yes	**LAUNDRY:**	Yes
RESTAURANT:	Yes	**LOUNGE:**	Yes
PICNIC AREA:	Yes	**POOL:**	Yes
PLAY AREA:	Yes	**BBQ:**	Yes
BASIC STORE:	Yes	**GOLF:**	Close by
ELECTRICITY:	$ 2.00 per day	**OTHER:**	Cold beer & wine store, campground, tennis, cabins, gift shop, swimming, eagle watching.
DAILY RATE:	Up to 34' = $10.00 Over 35' = $15.00		

Subject to change in 1996-7

CAUTION! This chartlet not intended for use in navigation.

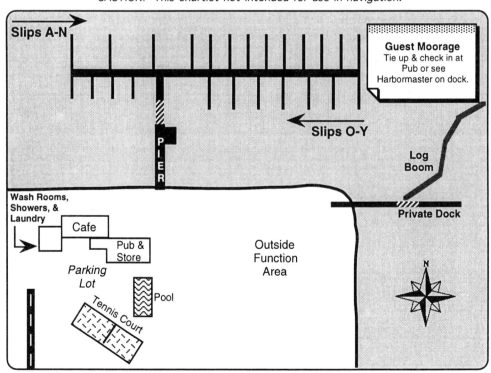

North Pender Is.

NAME OF MARINA: *PORT WASHINGTON GOV'T WHARF* RADIO: None

ADDRESS: Transport Canada Dock   N. Pender Is., B.C.   Canada V0N 2M0

TELEPHONE: MGR: Unknown

SHORT DESCRIPTION & LOCATION:

48°48.6' - 123°19.2 Located in the quiet & peaceful small settlement of Port Washington in Grimmer Bay on N.W. side of North Pender Island. The Gov't float is good for short stopovers, but open to swells and could be uncomfortable for overnight stays.

GUEST BOAT CAPACITY:	Appx 5-7 boats	GUEST DOCK:	100 ft.
SEASON:	All year	GUEST SLIPS:	Dock only
RESERVATION POLICY:	None	WATER:	None
AMT W/ELECTRICITY:	None	AMPS:	None
FUEL DOCK:	None	PUMP OUT STATION	None
MARINE REPAIRS:	None	HAUL OUT:	None
TOILETS:	None	BOAT RAMP:	None
HOT SHOWERS:	None	LAUNDRY:	None
RESTAURANT:	Close by	LOUNGE:	Close by
PICNIC AREA:	None	POOL:	None
PLAY AREA:	None	BBQ:	None
BASIC STORE:	Store closed at time of survey	GOLF:	Close by
ELECTRICITY:	None	OTHER:	Clothing store at head of pier, appx. 6 mi. from Port Browning shopping centre.
DAILY RATE:	Appx. .50¢ per foot		

CAUTION! This chartlet not intended for use in navigation.

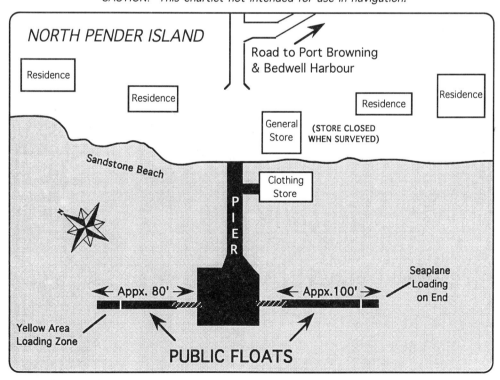

Salt Spring Is.

NAME OF MARINA: **FULFORD MARINA**   RADIO: VHF Ch. 68

ADDRESS: 2810 Fulford-Ganges Rd.   Salt Spring Is., B.C.   Canada V8K 1Z2

TELEPHONE: 604-653-9600   MGR: Jason Manchester

SHORT DESCRIPTION & LOCATION:

48°46.20' - 123°27.00'   Located near head of Fulford Harbour on south end of Salt Spring Island, this modern marina is situated on beautifully landscaped grounds. Quaint Fulford Village with shops, B.C. Ferry Terminal, pub and park is a ten minute walk south.

GUEST BOAT CAPACITY: ....Appx. 50 boats	GUEST DOCK: ....500' plus slips
SEASON: ....All year	GUEST SLIPS: 44
RESERVATION POLICY:..........................Accepts	WATER: ....Yes
AMT W/ELECTRICITY: ....All	AMPS: ....20-30 A
FUEL DOCK: ....Gas & Diesel	PUMP OUT STATION ....None
MARINE REPAIRS: ....Close by	HAUL OUT: ....None
TOILETS: ....Yes	BOAT RAMP:...........................None
HOT SHOWERS: ....Yes	LAUNDRY: ....None
RESTAURANT: ....Close by	LOUNGE: ....Close by
PICNIC AREA: ....Yes	POOL:.......................................None
PLAY AREA: ....Yes	BBQ: ....Yes
BASIC STORE: ....Yes	GOLF: ....15 K away
ELECTRICITY: ....$3.00 per day	OTHER: Groceries, deli, fresh
DAILY RATE: ....Appx. .60¢ per foot	meats & produce, pizza,
	gifts, books, marine
	supplies, business
	centre, gazebos, tennis.

CAUTION! This chartlet not intended for use in navigation.

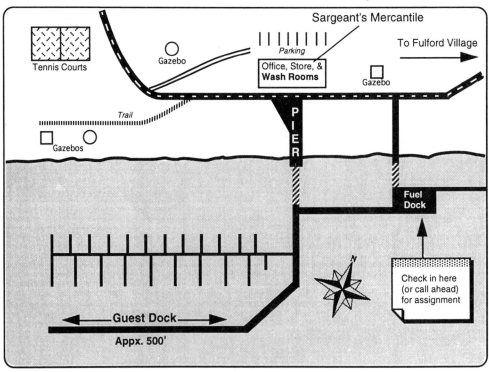

Salt Spring Is.

NAME OF MARINA: *GANGES GOV'T BOAT BASIN - South* RADIO: VHF Ch. 69

ADDRESS: 127 Fulford-Ganges Rd Saltspring Island, B.C. Canada V8K 2T9

TELEPHONE: 604-537-5711　　　MGR: Bob Morrisette

SHORT DESCRIPTION & LOCATION:

48°51.1' - 123°29.7' Moorage is located at the Gov't boat basin behind the breakwater just S. of Grace Peninsula adjacent to town of Ganges. This marina serves both commercial & recreational vessels and has designated areas for each. Rafting is required.

GUEST BOAT CAPACITY: Appx. 60 boats	GUEST DOCK: 3 docks appx. 200'
SEASON: All year	GUEST SLIPS: None
RESERVATION POLICY: None	WATER: Yes
AMT W/ELECTRICITY: All	AMPS: 20 A
FUEL DOCK: Close by	PUMP OUT STATION None
MARINE REPAIRS: Close by	HAUL OUT: None
TOILETS: Yes (in park)	BOAT RAMP: Yes
HOT SHOWERS: Yes (in park)	LAUNDRY: Close by
RESTAURANT: Close by	LOUNGE: Close by
PICNIC AREA: Yes	POOL: None
PLAY AREA: Yes	BBQ: None
BASIC STORE: Close by	GOLF: Close by
ELECTRICITY: $ 2.14 per day	OTHER: Busy but convenient
DAILY RATE: Appx. .40¢ per foot	location. Close to shops and restaurants.

CAUTION! This chartlet not intended for use in navigation.

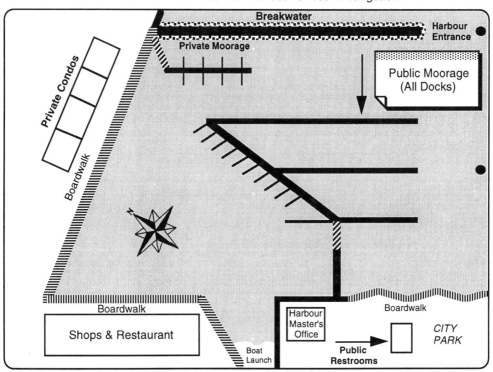

Salt Spring Is.

NAME OF MARINA: *GANGES GOV'T FLOAT- North*   RADIO: VHF Ch. 69

ADDRESS: 127 Fulford-Ganges Rd   Saltspring Island, B.C.   Canada V8K 2T9

TELEPHONE: 604-537-5715   MGR: Bob Morrisette

SHORT DESCRIPTION & LOCATION:

48°51.20' - 123°29.80'   Moorage is located at Government float on north side of Grace Peninsula directly in front of picturesque town of Ganges located at head of Ganges Harbour.

GUEST BOAT CAPACITY: ....Appx . 25 boats	GUEST DOCK: ....3 Ea.80 ft. floats
SEASON: ....All year	GUEST SLIPS: ....None
RESERVATION POLICY: ....None	WATER: ....Yes
AMT W/ELECTRICITY: ....None	AMPS: ....N/A
FUEL DOCK: ....Close by	PUMP OUT STATION ....None
MARINE REPAIRS: ....Close by	HAUL OUT: ....Close by
TOILETS: ....None	BOAT RAMP:......................Close by
HOT SHOWERS: ....Close by	LAUNDRY: ....Close by
RESTAURANT: ....Close by	LOUNGE: ....Close by
PICNIC AREA: ....Yes	POOL:..None
PLAY AREA: ....Close by	BBQ: ....None
BASIC STORE: ....Close by	GOLF: ....Close by
ELECTRICITY: ....None	OTHER: Convenient location for
DAILY RATE: ....Appx. .40¢ per foot	short or overnight stay.
	Close to nice shops and
	restaurants.

CAUTION! This chartlet not intended for use in navigation.

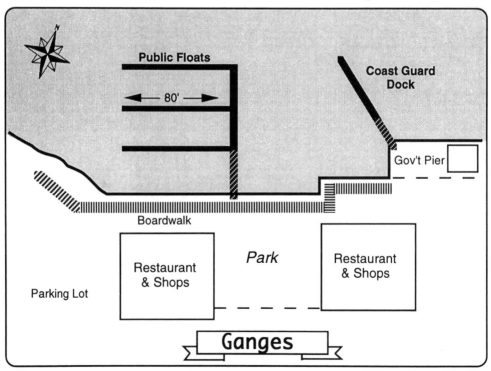

Salt Spring Is.

NAME OF MARINA: *GANGES MARINA* **RADIO:** VHF Ch. 68

ADDRESS: P.O. Box 299 Salt Spring Island, B.C. Canada V8K 2V9

TELEPHONE: 604-537-5242 **MGR:** Suzanne Guiness

SHORT DESCRIPTION & LOCATION:

48°51.30' - 123°29.90' Friendly older marina situated about 3 blocks north of heart of picturesque town of Ganges at head of Ganges Harbour. Walking distance to many tourist oriented activities. First Aid attendant and float plane service on site.

GUEST BOAT CAPACITY: ....Appx. 125 boats

SEASON: ....All year

RESERVATION POLICY: ....Accepts

AMT W/ELECTRICITY: ....Appx. 90%

FUEL DOCK: ....Gas, Dsl, & LP

MARINE REPAIRS: ....Close by

TOILETS: ....Yes

HOT SHOWERS: ....Yes

RESTAURANT: ....Close by

PICNIC AREA: ....Yes (On dock)

PLAY AREA: ....Close by

BASIC STORE: ....Yes

ELECTRICITY: ....Included in moorage

DAILY RATE: ....Appx. .85¢ per foot

Special boater 1/2 day rates.

GUEST DOCK: 180 ft. plus slips

GUEST SLIPS: ....Appx. 55

WATER: ....Yes

AMPS: ....15 & 30 A

PUMP OUT STATION ....None

HAUL OUT: ....None

BOAT RAMP: ....None

LAUNDRY: ....Yes

LOUNGE: ....Close by

POOL: ....None

BBQ: ....None

GOLF: ....Close by

OTHER: Complimentary coffee & muffins each morning! Car rentals, fishing tackle, ice. Close to shops and galleries.

CAUTION! This chartlet not intended for use in navigation.

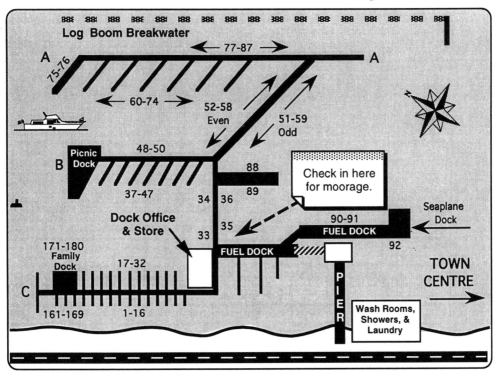

Salt Spring Island

NAME OF MARINA: *SALT SPRING MARINA LTD.*   **RADIO:** VHF Ch. 68

ADDRESS: 124 Upper Ganges Rd. Salt Spring Island, B.C.. Canada V8K 2S2

TELEPHONE: 604-537-5810   **MGR:** Lesley Cheeseman

SHORT DESCRIPTION & LOCATION:

48°51.50' - 123°29.90' Modern & friendly marina located at head of Ganges Harbour approximately 1/3 mile north of center of picturesque town of Ganges. Walking distance to Ganges business center w/complete boater amenities and provisions.

GUEST BOAT CAPACITY:	Appx. 35-40 boats	GUEST DOCK:	380 ft. plus slips
SEASON:	All year	GUEST SLIPS:	Varies-Appx. 30
RESERVATION POLICY:	Accepts	WATER:	Yes
AMT W/ELECTRICITY:	All	AMPS:	30 A
FUEL DOCK:	Close by	PUMP OUT STATION	None
MARINE REPAIRS:	On premises	HAUL OUT:	Up to 35' boats
TOILETS:	Yes	BOAT RAMP:	Yes
HOT SHOWERS:	Yes	LAUNDRY:	Yes
RESTAURANT:	Yes	LOUNGE:	Yes
PICNIC AREA:	Yes	POOL:	None
PLAY AREA:	None	BBQ:	None
BASIC STORE:	Close by	GOLF:	Close by
ELECTRICITY:	$ 3.00 per day	OTHER:	Marine sales and service,
DAILY RATE:	Appx. .60¢ per foot		kayak, scooter & bike
			rentals, scuba shop, fish
Toll Free Tel. #1-800-334-6629			-ing charters, chandlery.

CAUTION! This chartlet not intended for use in navigation.

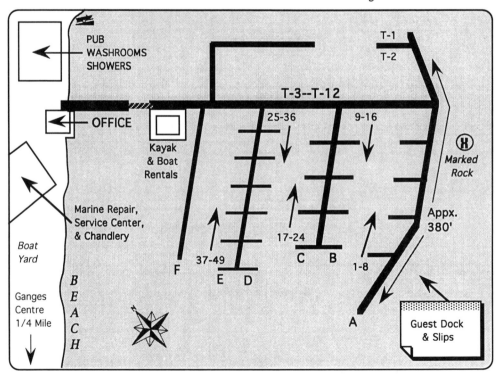

Salt Spring Island

NAME OF MARINA: *MUSGRAVE LANDING GOV'T WHARF* **RADIO:** ....None

ADDRESS: 127 Fulford-Ganges Rd Salt Spring Is., B.C. Canada V8K 2T9

TELEPHONE: 604-537-5711 **MGR:** Salt Spring Harbour Authority

SHORT DESCRIPTION & LOCATION:

48°44.90' - 123°33.95' This is a sm. public float on the S.W. side of Salt Spring Island adjacent to S. entrance of Sansum Narrows. The quiet and peaceful cove is a popular location during the summer months. The facility is park-like & very picturesque.

GUEST BOAT CAPACITY: ....Appx. 8-10 boats

SEASON: ....All year

RESERVATION POLICY:...................None

AMT W/ELECTRICITY: ....None

FUEL DOCK: ....None

MARINE REPAIRS: ....None

TOILETS: ....None

HOT SHOWERS: ....None

RESTAURANT: ....None

PICNIC AREA: ....None

PLAY AREA: ....None

BASIC STORE: ....None

ELECTRICITY: ....None

DAILY RATE: ....Appx. .45¢ per foot

GUEST DOCK: ....Appx. 175 ft.

GUEST SLIPS: ....Dock only

WATER: ....None

AMPS: ....None

PUMP OUT STATION ....None

HAUL OUT: ....None

BOAT RAMP: ....None

LAUNDRY: ....None

LOUNGE: ....None

POOL: ....None

BBQ: ....None

GOLF: ....None

OTHER: Rafting is customary, hiking trails on adjacent logging roads, fishing grounds close by.

CAUTION! This chartlet not intended for use in navigation.

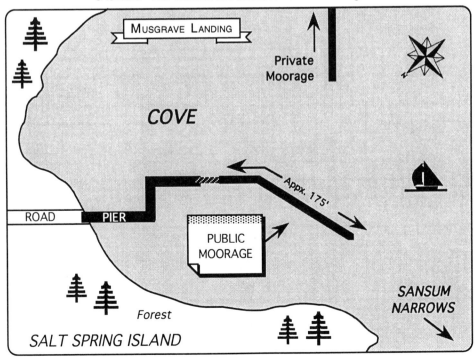

Saturna Island

NAME OF MARINA: *LYALL HARBOUR GOV'T WHARF*   RADIO: None
ADDRESS: 101 East Point Rd.   Saturna Island, B.C.   Canada V0N 2Y0
TELEPHONE: 604-539-2229   MGR: Gloria Manzano

SHORT DESCRIPTION & LOCATION:

48°47.90' - 123°11.00' The public float is located at Saturna Pt. on the NW side of Saturna Is. at the S. entrance of Lyall Hbr. next to the Saturna Ferry Landing. This good little overnight or short stay stopover is handy to groceries, pub, fuel and basic services.

GUEST BOAT CAPACITY: ....Appx. 8-10 boats	GUEST DOCK: ....Appx. 180 ft.
SEASON: ....All year	GUEST SLIPS: ....Dock only
RESERVATION POLICY:...................................None	WATER: ....None
AMT W/ELECTRICITY: ....None	AMPS: ....None
FUEL DOCK: ....Gas & Diesel	PUMP OUT STATION ....None
MARINE REPAIRS: ....Close by	HAUL OUT: ....None
TOILETS: ....Yes	BOAT RAMP:.........................None
HOT SHOWERS: ....None	LAUNDRY: ....None
RESTAURANT: ....Yes	LOUNGE: ....Yes
PICNIC AREA: ....None	POOL:...None
PLAY AREA: ....None	BBQ: ....None
BASIC STORE: ....Yes	GOLF:...None
ELECTRICITY: ....None	OTHER: Liquor store appx. 1.25
DAILY RATE: ....Appx. .45¢ per foot	mile walk, well stocked
	store & pub at head of
	dock. Ferry service off
	island. Rafting allowed.

CAUTION! This chartlet not intended for use in navigation.

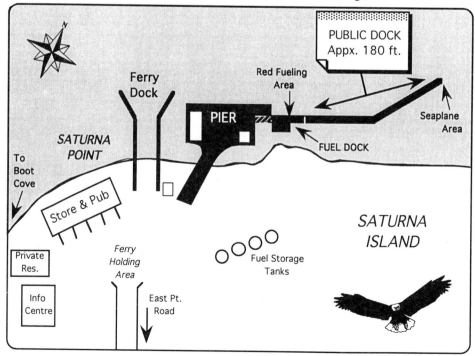

South Pender Is.

NAME OF MARINA:	*BEDWELL HARBOUR MARINA*　RADIO: VHF Ch. 68
ADDRESS:	9801 Spalding Rd RR1, South Pender Island, B.C. VON2MO
TELEPHONE:	604-629-3212　MGR: Brandi Fitzpatrick

SHORT DESCRIPTION & LOCATION:

48°44.80' - 123°13.60' Highly rated beautiful marina resort located on west side of South Pender Island adjacent to Hay Point. Many amenities available for the traveling boater. Major marine customs point-of-entry for Canadian waters.

GUEST BOAT CAPACITY:	Appx 120 boats	GUEST DOCK:	120' plus slips
SEASON:	Open March thru October	GUEST SLIPS:	100
RESERVATION POLICY:	Accepts	WATER:	Yes
AMT W/ELECTRICITY:	All	AMPS:	15 &30 A
FUEL DOCK:	Gas & Diesel	PUMP OUT STATION	None
MARINE REPAIRS:	"On Call"	HAUL OUT:	None
TOILETS:	Yes	BOAT RAMP:	None
HOT SHOWERS:	Yes	LAUNDRY:	Yes
RESTAURANT:	Yes	LOUNGE:	Yes
PICNIC AREA:	Yes	POOL:	Yes
PLAY AREA:	Yes	BBQ:	Yes
BASIC STORE:	Yes	GOLF:	Close by
ELECTRICITY:	$ 3.00 per day	OTHER:	Provincial park nearby, Great bicycling & dinghying areas. Boat & Sea-Doo rentals. Tennis & volleyball courts.
DAILY RATE:	Appx. 85¢ per foot/weekends Appx. 65¢ per foot/weekdays		

CAUTION! This chartlet not intended for use in navigation.

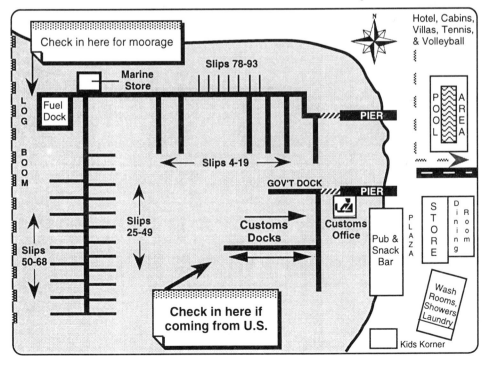

Thetis Island

NAME OF MARINA: *TELEGRAPH HARBOUR MARINA*   RADIO: VHF Ch. 68

ADDRESS: Thetis Is. Post Office   B.C., Canada   V0R 2Y0

TELEPHONE: 604-246-9511   MGR: John and Jan Ohman

SHORT DESCRIPTION & LOCATION:

48°58.90' - 123°40.20'   A friendly marina situated at back of Telegraph Harbour on south end of Thetis Island. Ample and well maintained slips located in a park like setting offering many amenities for groups and kids. Clamming, Oysters, Cod & Salmon close by.

GUEST BOAT CAPACITY: ....Appx. 75 boats	GUEST DOCK: ....3000 ft. total
SEASON: ....All year	GUEST SLIPS: ....Docks only
RESERVATION POLICY:............................Accepts	WATER: ....*Yes
AMT W/ELECTRICITY: ....All	AMPS: ....15-30 A
FUEL DOCK: ....Gas & Diesel	PUMP OUT STATION ....None
MARINE REPAIRS: ....Close by	HAUL OUT: ....None
TOILETS: ....Yes	BOAT RAMP: ....Close by
HOT SHOWERS: ....*Yes	LAUNDRY: ....*Yes
RESTAURANT: ....Cafe	LOUNGE: ....None
PICNIC AREA: ....Yes	POOL: ....None
PLAY AREA: ....Yes	BBQ: ....Yes
BASIC STORE: ....Yes	GOLF: ....In Chemainus
ELECTRICITY: ...$3.00 day-15 Amp/$5.00-30 amp	OTHER: Covered pavilion, charts,
DAILY RATE: ....Appx. .55¢ per foot	home-baked pies, gift
	shop, game area, walk-
	ing distance to ferry.

*Limited to Moored Guests Only

CAUTION! This chartlet not intended for use in navigation.

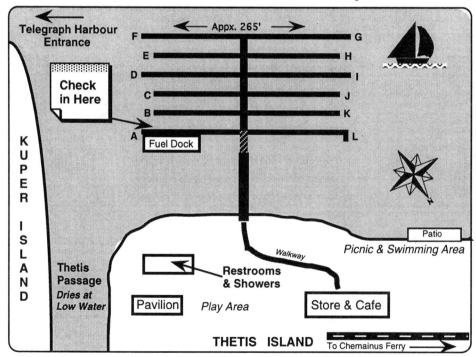

Thetis Island

NAME OF MARINA: *THETIS ISLAND MARINA & PUB*	**RADIO:** VHF Ch. 68
ADDRESS: General Delivery	Thetis Island B.C. VOR 2YO
TELEPHONE: 604-246-3464	**MGR:** Paul & Dawn Deacon

SHORT DESCRIPTION & LOCATION:

48°58.70' - 123°40.10' Located half-way down the entrance of Telegraph Harbour on the port side, this family oriented marina offers many services for the vacationing boater. The marina is just a short walk to the Chemainus ferry.

GUEST BOAT CAPACITY: ....Appx. 60 boats	GUEST DOCK: ....180' plus slips
SEASON: ....All year	GUEST SLIPS: ....12 large slips
RESERVATION POLICY: ....Accepts	WATER: ....Yes
AMT W/ELECTRICITY: ....All	AMPS: ....15-30 A
FUEL DOCK: ....Gas, Dsl, Kerosene & LP	PUMP OUT STATION ....None
MARINE REPAIRS: ....None	HAUL OUT: ....None
TOILETS: ....Yes	BOAT RAMP: ....Close by
HOT SHOWERS: ....Yes	LAUNDRY: ....Yes
RESTAURANT: ....Yes	LOUNGE: ....Yes
PICNIC AREA: ....Yes	POOL: ....None
PLAY AREA: ....Yes	BBQ: ....Yes
BASIC STORE: ....Yes	GOLF: ....Ferry to Chemainus
ELECTRICITY: ....$3.00 15A/$5.00 30 A	OTHER: Post Office, Pub w/satel-
DAILY RATE: ....Appx. .55¢ per foot	lite TV, Saturday farmers
	market in season, clam-
<u>Fax: 604-246-1433</u>	ming & oysters close by.
	Pig roasts a specialty.

CAUTION! This chartlet not intended for use in navigation.

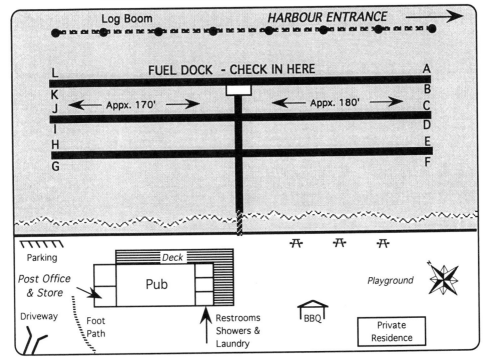

NOTES

C H A P T E R

7

VANCOUVER ISLAND

Brentwood Bay

NAME OF MARINA: ***BRENTWOOD INN RESORT***	RADIO: VHF Ch. 68
ADDRESS: 7172 Brentwood Drive Brentwood Bay, B.C. Canada V0S 1A0	
TELEPHONE: 604-652-2413/3151	MGR: Mike Keepence/Brian Conn

SHORT DESCRIPTION & LOCATION:

48°34.65' - 123°27.90' This is the nearest marina to Butchart Gardens, located at head of Brentwood Bay on E side of Saanich Inlet on Vancouver Is. The marina has guest moorage and on-site amenities plus easy access to greater Victoria services.

GUEST BOAT CAPACITY:	Appx. 10-15 boats	GUEST DOCK:	3 @ Appx. 100 ft.
SEASON:	All year	GUEST SLIPS:	Appx. 10
RESERVATION POLICY:	Accepts	WATER:	Yes
AMT W/ELECTRICITY:	All	AMPS:	15-30 A
FUEL DOCK:	None	PUMP OUT STATION	None
MARINE REPAIRS:	Close by	HAUL OUT:	Close by
TOILETS:	Yes	BOAT RAMP:	Close by
HOT SHOWERS:	Yes	LAUNDRY:	Yes
RESTAURANT:	Yes - 2	LOUNGE:	Yes
PICNIC AREA:	Yes	POOL:	None
PLAY AREA:	None	BBQ:	None
BASIC STORE:	Yes	GOLF:	Close by
ELECTRICITY:	$3.00/15 amp - $5.00/30 amp	OTHER:	Resort motel, fishing gear, licenses, bait, ice, pub, dining room. Beach-house Caribbean style food, taxi & bus service.
DAILY RATE:	Appx. .65¢ per foot		

Motorboat & kayak rentals available

CAUTION! This chartlet not intended for use in navigation.

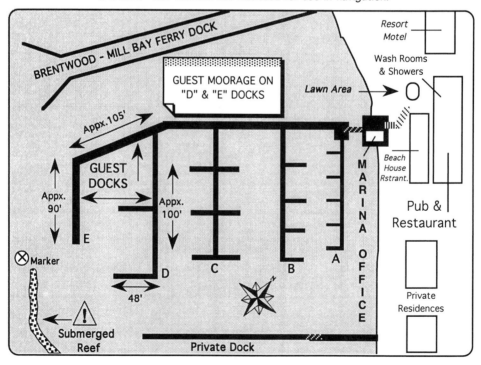

Canoe Cove

NAME OF MARINA:	*CANOE COVE MARINA*	**RADIO:** VHF Ch. 69
ADDRESS:	P.O. Box 2099	Sidney, B.C., Canada V8L 3S6
TELEPHONE:	604-656-5566	**MGR:** John Simson

SHORT DESCRIPTION & LOCATION:

48°41.00' - 123°24.30' Located in beautiful Canoe Bay appx. 2 nautical miles north of Sidney. Full service and do-it-yourself boat yard. Walking distance to Swartz Bay ferry terminal. Guest moorage is available in vacated permanent tenant slips.

GUEST BOAT CAPACITY: Space available basis	**GUEST DOCK:** None-slips only
SEASON: ....All year	**GUEST SLIPS:** Space available
RESERVATION POLICY:...........................Accepts	**WATER:** ....Yes
AMT W/ELECTRICITY: ....All	**AMPS:** ....15-30 A
FUEL DOCK: ....Gas, Dsl, & LP	**PUMP OUT STATION** ....None
MARINE REPAIRS: ....On premises	**HAUL OUT:** Travel-Lift & Ways
TOILETS: ....Yes	**BOAT RAMP:**...........................None
HOT SHOWERS: ....Yes	**LAUNDRY:** ....Yes
RESTAURANT: ....Yes	**LOUNGE:** ....Close by
PICNIC AREA: ....None	**POOL:**.....................................None
PLAY AREA: ....None	**BBQ:** ....None
BASIC STORE: ....None	**GOLF:** ....None
ELECTRICITY: ....Included in moorage	**OTHER:** Marine chandlery & hard-
DAILY RATE: ....$16.00 per day	ware store, complete
	marine repair yard &
<u>Fax: 604-655-7197</u>	shipwright, harbour taxi.
	Customs check in.

CAUTION! This chartlet not intended for use in navigation.

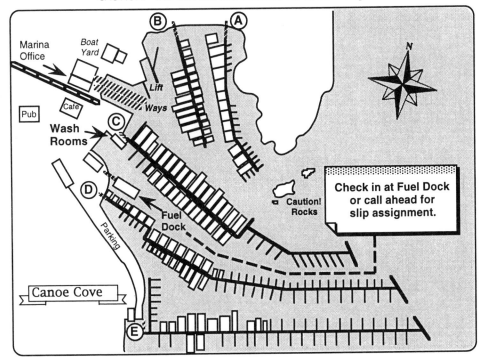

Chemainus

NAME OF MARINA:	*CHEMAINUS WHARF & FLOATS*	RADIO: None
ADDRESS:	Government Wharf Chemainus	B.C. V0R 1K0
TELEPHONE:	604-246-2682	MGR: Ann Hill

SHORT DESCRIPTION & LOCATION:

48°55.50' - 123°42.70' Chemainus is located on the W side of Stuart Channel and is a tourist catering community with many attractions, especially the famous outdoor murals painted on the buildings. The public floats offer moorage adjacent to the ferry

GUEST BOAT CAPACITY:	.......Appx. 20-30 boats	GUEST DOCK: ....130' plus slips
SEASON:	..........All year	GUEST SLIPS: ....8 large slips
RESERVATION POLICY:	..........None	WATER: ....Yes
AMT W/ELECTRICITY:	..........All	AMPS: ....15-20 A
FUEL DOCK:	..........None	PUMP OUT STATION ....None
MARINE REPAIRS:	..........Close by	HAUL OUT: ....Close by
TOILETS:	..........Close by	BOAT RAMP: ....None
HOT SHOWERS:	..........None	LAUNDRY: ....Close by
RESTAURANT:	..........Close by	LOUNGE: ....Close by
PICNIC AREA:	..........Close by	POOL: ....None
PLAY AREA:	..........Close by	BBQ: ....None
BASIC STORE:	..........Close by	GOLF: ....Close by
ELECTRICITY:	..........Appx. $2.50 per day	OTHER: Guided tours of murals, walking & shopping tours, city parks, summer festivals, theater, near hospital & groceries.
DAILY RATE:	..........Appx. .50¢ per foot	

CAUTION! This chartlet not intended for use in navigation.

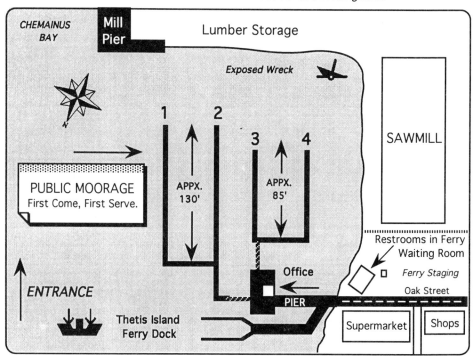

Cowichan Bay

NAME OF MARINA: *COWICHAN BAY SM. CRAFT HARBOUR* RADIO: None

ADDRESS: General Delivery Cowichan Bay B.C. V0R 1N0

TELEPHONE: 604-746-5911 MGR: Carrie Hokanson

SHORT DESCRIPTION & LOCATION:

48°44.50' - 123°37.00' Located at the eastern most end of town, the main public moorage is the Gov't owned marina behind a pile & planked breakwater. Cowichan Bay is a picturesque logging & fishing town famous for Cowichan sweaters.

GUEST BOAT CAPACITY: ....Appx. 35-40 boats	GUEST DOCK: ....200' slips
SEASON: ....Mid-June to Mid-Sept.	GUEST SLIPS: ....8 large slips
RESERVATION POLICY: ....None	WATER: ....Yes
AMT W/ELECTRICITY: ....All	AMPS: ....15-20 A
FUEL DOCK: ....Close by	PUMP OUT STATION ....None
MARINE REPAIRS: ....Close by	HAUL OUT: ....Close by
TOILETS: ....Porta-Potty	BOAT RAMP: ....Close by
HOT SHOWERS: ....Close by	LAUNDRY: ....Close by
RESTAURANT: ....Close by	LOUNGE: ....Close by
PICNIC AREA: ....Close by	POOL: ....Close by
PLAY AREA: ....Close by	BBQ: ....None
BASIC STORE: ....Close by	GOLF: ....Close by
ELECTRICITY: ....$2.00 per day	OTHER: Museum, Wooden Boat
DAILY RATE: ....Appx. .43¢ per foot	Foundation, public eco-

The salmon troll fleet fills the marina from mid-Sept to mid-June but are gone in summer. Summer visitors encouraged.

OTHER: Museum, Wooden Boat Foundation, public eco-station, fish market, chandlery, several good restaurants and pubs.

CAUTION! This chartlet not intended for use in navigation.

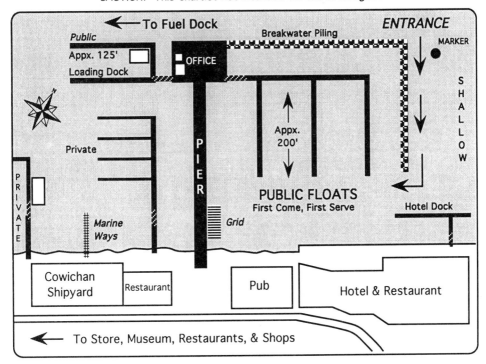

Crofton

NAME OF MARINA: *CROFTON GOVERNMENT DOCK*   RADIO: None

ADDRESS: Fisheries & Oceans   Crofton, B.C.   Canada V0R 1OR

TELEPHONE: 604-246-4512   MGR: Hank Bonsall

SHORT DESCRIPTION & LOCATION:

48°52.00' - 123°38.20' Crofton is located on Van. Is. in Osborne Bay just off Stuart Channel well marked by the huge Crofton Pulp and Paper Mill. The public dock is located behind the breakwater next to the ferry landing. Commercial boats have priority.

GUEST BOAT CAPACITY: ....Appx. 20-25 boats

SEASON: ....All year

RESERVATION POLICY:...........................None

AMT W/ELECTRICITY: ....All

FUEL DOCK: ....None

MARINE REPAIRS: ....None

TOILETS: ....Yes - At Info Centre

HOT SHOWERS: ....Yes - At Info Centre

RESTAURANT: ....Close by

PICNIC AREA: ....Yes

PLAY AREA: ....Yes

BASIC STORE: ....Close by

ELECTRICITY: ....$ 2.50 per day

DAILY RATE: ....Appx. .50¢ per foot

....($1.49/meter)

GUEST DOCK: .Appx. 240 ft. slips

GUEST SLIPS: ....4 large slips

WATER: ....Yes

AMPS: ....15-20 A

PUMP OUT STATION ....None

HAUL OUT: ....None

BOAT RAMP:..............................Yes

LAUNDRY: ....Close by

LOUNGE: ....Close by

POOL:.......................................None

BBQ: ....None

GOLF: ....Close by

OTHER: Walking distance to Town of Crofton offering complete services for the traveling boater.

CAUTION! This chartlet not intended for use in navigation.

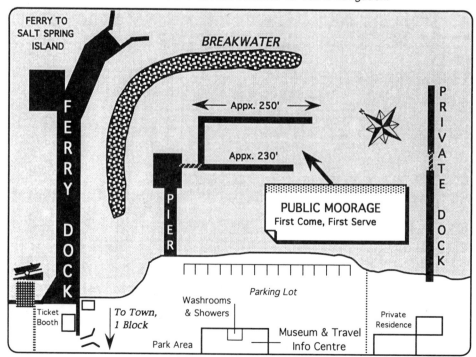

Genoa Bay

NAME OF MARINA: *GENOA BAY MARINA*	**RADIO:** VHF Ch. 68

ADDRESS: R.R. 1, 5100 Genoa Bay   Duncan. B.C., Canada V9L 1M3

TELEPHONE: 604-746-7621   **MGR:** Kay Kirkby

SHORT DESCRIPTION & LOCATION:

48°45.60' - 123°35.60' Marina is protected behind a little peninsula in SW Genoa Bay which opens to the N. end of Cowichan Bay on Vancouver Is. The family oriented facility has a well stocked little store and offers quiet relaxation in the picturesque bay.

GUEST BOAT CAPACITY:	Appx. 30-40 boats	GUEST DOCK:	300 ft. floats
SEASON:	All year	GUEST SLIPS:	3 floats
RESERVATION POLICY:	Accepts	WATER:	Yes
AMT W/ELECTRICITY:	Appx. 50%	AMPS:	15 A
FUEL DOCK:	Close by	PUMP OUT STATION	None
MARINE REPAIRS:	Close by	HAUL OUT:	None
TOILETS:	Yes	BOAT RAMP:	Yes
HOT SHOWERS:	Yes	LAUNDRY:	Yes
RESTAURANT:	Yes	LOUNGE:	Licenced Restaurant
PICNIC AREA:	Yes	POOL:	None
PLAY AREA:	Yes	BBQ:	Yes
BASIC STORE:	Yes	GOLF:	Close by
ELECTRICITY:	$3.00 per day	OTHER:	Crabbing, hiking trails, fishing tackle, fresh baked goods, art gallery, caters to clubs.
DAILY RATE:	Appx. .50¢ per foot		

CAUTION! This chartlet not intended for use in navigation.

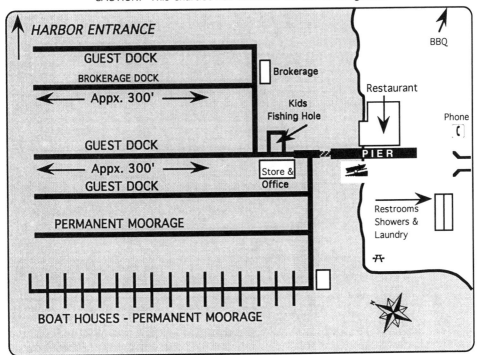

Ladysmith

NAME OF MARINA: *INN OF THE SEA AT YELLOW POINT* RADIO: None
ADDRESS: 3600 Yellow Point Rd.   Ladysmith, B.C.   Canada V0R 2E0
TELEPHONE: 604-245-2211   MGR: Barry & Pam Hooper

SHORT DESCRIPTION & LOCATION:

49°02.30' - 123°44.60' Located at Yellow Pt. on Van. Is. appx. 4 mi. N. of Ladysmith Hbr on Stuart Channel. The modern resort offers moorage and amenities to boaters. The float is partially exposed to weather & swells. Consult chart to avoid reef near entrance.

GUEST BOAT CAPACITY: ....Appx. 5-8 boats	GUEST DOCK: ....100 ft.
SEASON: ....All year	GUEST SLIPS: ....Dock only
RESERVATION POLICY: ....Accepts	WATER: ....Yes
AMT W/ELECTRICITY: ....All	AMPS: ....15 A
FUEL DOCK: ....None	PUMP OUT STATION ....None
MARINE REPAIRS: ....None	HAUL OUT: ....None
TOILETS: ....Yes	BOAT RAMP: ....None
HOT SHOWERS: ....Yes	LAUNDRY: ....Yes
RESTAURANT: ....Yes	LOUNGE: ....Yes
PICNIC AREA: ....Yes	POOL: ....Yes
PLAY AREA: ....Yes	BBQ: ....Yes
BASIC STORE: ....Yes	GOLF: ....Close by
ELECTRICITY: ....Included in moorage	OTHER: Resort hotel, group
DAILY RATE: ....Appx. .75¢ per foot	facilities, swimming, hiking, canoeing, tennis, jacuzzi.

CAUTION! This chartlet not intended for use in navigation.

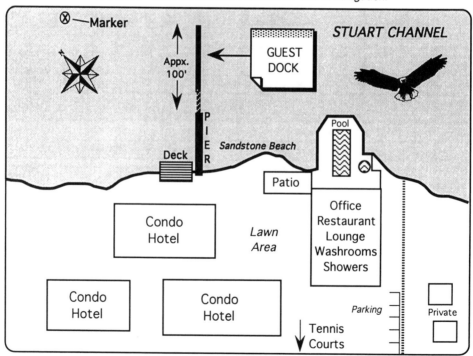

Ladysmith

NAME OF MARINA:	*LADYSMITH SM. CRAFT HARBOUR* RADIO: None
ADDRESS:	Ladysmith Hbr Auth. Box Ladysmith B.C. V0R 2E0
TELEPHONE:	604-245-7511 MGR: Mike Beatty

SHORT DESCRIPTION & LOCATION:

48°59.90' - 123°48.60' The Gov't owned marina is located on SW side of Ladysmith Harbour. Moorage is also available (no water/power) at the Maritime Society floats between Slag Point & the Gov't Floats. Ladysmith offers full services for traveling boats.

GUEST BOAT CAPACITY:	Appx.35-40 boats	GUEST DOCK:	200 ft. slips
SEASON:	All year	GUEST SLIPS:	6 large slips
RESERVATION POLICY:	None	WATER:	Yes
AMT W/ELECTRICITY:	All	AMPS:	15-20 A
FUEL DOCK:	Close by	PUMP OUT STATION	None
MARINE REPAIRS:	Close by	HAUL OUT:	Tidal grid
TOILETS:	Porta-Potty	BOAT RAMP:	Yes
HOT SHOWERS:	None	LAUNDRY:	Close by
RESTAURANT:	Close by	LOUNGE:	Close by
PICNIC AREA:	Close by	POOL:	Close by
PLAY AREA:	Close by	BBQ:	None
BASIC STORE:	Close by	GOLF:	Close by
ELECTRICITY:	$2.00 per day	OTHER:	Museum, shopping
DAILY RATE:	Appx. .50¢ per foot		centre, restaurants &

The salmon troll fleet fills the marina from mid-Sept to mid-June but are gone in summer. Summer visitors encouraged.

OTHER: Museum, shopping centre, restaurants & liquor store are all within walking distance or a short cab ride.

CAUTION! This chartlet not intended for use in navigation.

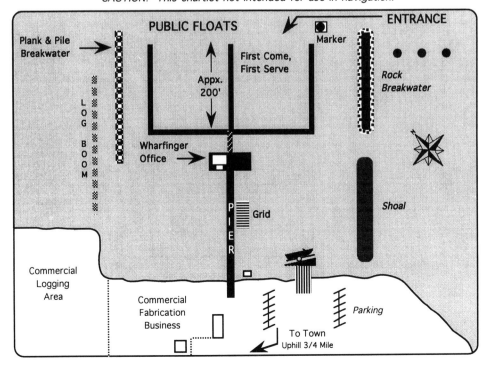

Ladysmith

NAME OF MARINA: **MAÑANA LODGE AND MARINA** RADIO: None

ADDRESS: 4760 Brenton-Page Rd. Ladysmith B.C. V0R 2E0

TELEPHONE: 604-245-2312 MGR: M/M Bangay & M/M Kanelakos

SHORT DESCRIPTION & LOCATION:

49°00.70' - 123°49.30' Located on NE side of Ladysmith Harbour just across from town of Ladysmith at Page Point, this resort marina offers many amenities for boaters. The friendly staff enhances the beautiful Vancouver Island setting.

GUEST BOAT CAPACITY: ....Appx. 20-30 boats

SEASON: ....All year

RESERVATION POLICY: ....Accepts

AMT W/ELECTRICITY: ....All

FUEL DOCK: ....Gas & Diesel

MARINE REPAIRS: ....Close by

TOILETS: ....Yes

HOT SHOWERS: ....Yes

RESTAURANT: ....Yes

PICNIC AREA: ....Yes

PLAY AREA: ....Yes

BASIC STORE: ....Yes

ELECTRICITY: ....$2.50 per day

DAILY RATE: ....Appx. .55¢ per foot

GUEST DOCK: ....280' plus slips

GUEST SLIPS: ....14 large slips

WATER: ....Limited

AMPS: ....15 A

PUMP OUT STATION ....None

HAUL OUT: ....Close by

BOAT RAMP: ....Close by

LAUNDRY: ....Yes

LOUNGE: ....Yes

POOL: ....None

BBQ: ....None

GOLF: ....Close by

OTHER: Bed & breakfast, some rooms w/jacuzzi tubs, car rentals, cabins, gift shop, tackle & bait, boat rentals, cable TV on docks.

CAUTION! This chartlet not intended for use in navigation.

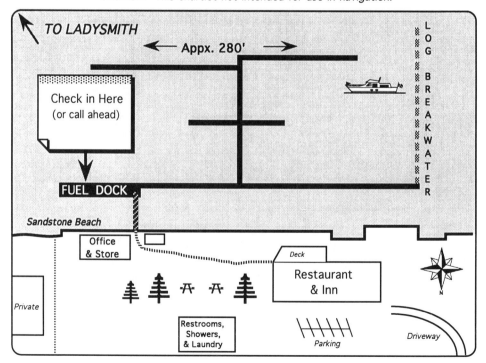

Maple Bay

NAME OF MARINA: *MAPLE BAY MARINA*   RADIO: VHF Ch. 68

ADDRESS: 6145 Genoa Bay Road,   Duncan, B.C., Canada V9L 1M3

TELEPHONE: 604-746-8482   MGR: Bill Neapole & Ted McLeod

SHORT DESCRIPTION & LOCATION:

48°47.80' - 123°36.00'   Full service marina situated in picturesque Birds Eye Cove located at head of Maple Bay near town of Duncan. "B" & "C" Docks are generally used for guest moorage. *Check in at fuel dock for slip assignment or call ahead.*

GUEST BOAT CAPACITY: …………Appx. 85 boats	GUEST DOCK: ………..85' plus slips
SEASON: …………………………………………All year	GUEST SLIPS: …………………………85
RESERVATION POLICY: …………………Accepts	WATER: ……………………………………Yes
AMT W/ELECTRICITY: …………………………………All	AMPS: ………………………………15-20 A
FUEL DOCK: …………………………………Gas, Dsl, & LP	PUMP OUT STATION ………None
MARINE REPAIRS: ………………………Close by	HAUL OUT: ……………………Close by
TOILETS: …………………………………………………Yes	BOAT RAMP: …………………Close by
HOT SHOWERS: ……………………………………Yes	LAUNDRY: …………………………………Yes
RESTAURANT: ……………………………………Yes	LOUNGE: ……………………………………Yes
PICNIC AREA: ……………………………………Yes	POOL: …………………………………None
PLAY AREA: ……………………………………………Yes	BBQ: …………………………………………Yes
BASIC STORE: ……………………………………Yes	GOLF: ………………………………Close by
ELECTRICITY: …………………Included in moorage	OTHER: General store, charts, chandlery, gift shop,hair dressing & esthetician. Close to marine repairs & boat yard.
DAILY RATE: ……………………$20 CDN Flat Rate Includes Power & Tax	

CAUTION! This chartlet not intended for use in navigation.

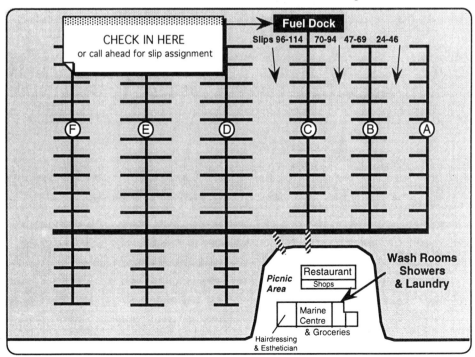

Maple Bay

NAME OF YACHT CLUB: *MAPLE BAY YACHT CLUB*

ADDRESS: P.O. Box 406   Duncan, B.C.   Canada   V9L 3X5

TELEPHONE: 604-746-4521   **PERSON IN CHARGE:** Dockmaster

SHORT DESCRIPTION & LOCATION:

48°48.15' - 123°36.10' The yacht club facility is located in Birds Eye Cove in Maple Bay about 1 mi N of the Maple Bay Marina near the town of Duncan. Tie up on the Guest Float and sign in at Club House. Moorage also allowed on outside of Breakwater Float, but subject to heavy boat wakes at times. No vessels in excess of 60 ft.-Max stay 7 days/year.

RECIPROCAL BOAT CAPACITY.............Appx. 20   RECIPROCAL DOCK:(S) 750 ft.

SEASON: ....All year   RECIPROCAL   SLIPS: Dock only

RESERVATION   POLICY:.......................None   WATER: ....Yes

TOILETS: ....Yes   AMT W/ELECTRICITY: ....All

HOT SHOWERS: ....Yes   AMPS: ....15 A

RESTAURANT:....................................Close by   LOUNGE:...Yes

DAILY RATE: ....No Charge for 24 hours.   OTHER: Boat repairs & fuel close
.............30¢ per foot after 24 hours.   by, MBYC serves dinners
Power - $4.00/day.   on Friday nights.

<u>NOTE:</u> THIS IS PRIVATE MOORAGE AND ONLY AVAILABLE TO MEMBERS OF RECIPROCAL YACHT CLUBS. YOUR CLUB <u>MUST</u> HAVE RECIPROCAL PRIVILEGES AND YOU MUST FLY YOUR BURGEE.

CAUTION! This chartlet not intended for use in navigation.

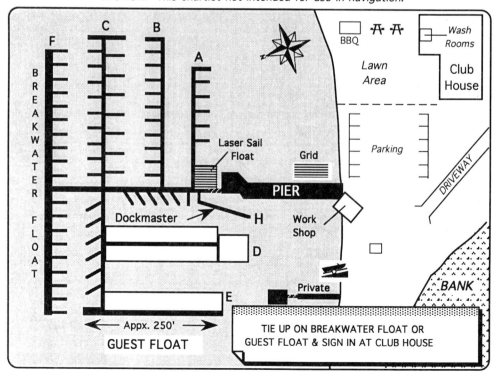

Mill Bay

NAME OF MARINA: *MILL BAY MARINA*   RADIO: CB Ch. 10
ADDRESS: Box 231 Handy Road,   Mill Bay, B..C.   Canada V0R 2P0
TELEPHONE: 604-743-4112   MGR: Fred and Marilyn Laba
SHORT DESCRIPTION & LOCATION:
48°.39.00 - 123°.33.00 Located in Mill Bay on W side of Saanich Inlet on Vancouver Isl. Small friendly marina is within walking distance to a modern & large shopping centre w/ supermarket, liquor store, bank, & shops. 3 Miles N of Brentwood Bay ferry dock.

GUEST BOAT CAPACITY: ....Appx. 20-25 boats	GUEST DOCK: ....2 @ 250 ft.
SEASON: ....All year	GUEST SLIPS: ....Varies
RESERVATION POLICY: ....Accepts	WATER: ....Yes
AMT W/ELECTRICITY: ....All	AMPS: ....20 A
FUEL DOCK: ....Gas & Diesel	PUMP OUT STATION ....None
MARINE REPAIRS: ....None	HAUL OUT: ....None
TOILETS: ....Yes	BOAT RAMP: ....Yes
HOT SHOWERS: ....Yes	LAUNDRY: ....Yes
RESTAURANT: ....Close by	LOUNGE: ....Close by
PICNIC AREA: ....Yes	POOL: ....None
PLAY AREA: ....None	BBQ: ....None
BASIC STORE: ....Yes	GOLF: ....Close by
ELECTRICITY: ....$2.00 per day	OTHER: Bus service to Victoria,
DAILY RATE: ....Appx. .50¢ per foot	marine supplies, boat
($15.00 Minimum)	rentals, charts and
	fishing licenses.

CAUTION! This chartlet not intended for use in navigation.

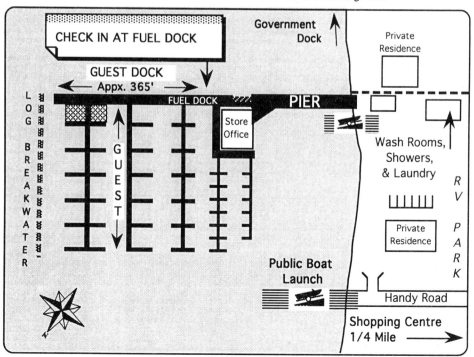

Nanaimo

NAME OF MARINA:	*NANAIMO BOAT BASIN* **RADIO:** VHF Ch. 67
ADDRESS:	P.O. Box 131 Nanaimo B.C. V9R 5K4
TELEPHONE:	604-754-5053 **MGR:** R.A. (Dick) Nickerson

SHORT DESCRIPTION & LOCATION:

49°10.20' - 123°55.90' The protected boat harbour is located adjacent to downtown Nanaimo close to the base of the white round Bastion often used as a landmark. It is the first marina upon entering from the south and the area offers complete marine services.

GUEST BOAT CAPACITY: ....Appx. 250 boats	GUEST DOCK: Total: appx. 9000'
SEASON: ....All year	GUEST SLIPS: ....15 lg. floats
RESERVATION POLICY:.......Ltd.- Tel. 755-1216	WATER: ....Yes
AMT W/ELECTRICITY: ....All	AMPS: ....15-100 A
FUEL DOCK: ....Gas & Diesel	PUMP OUT STATION ....Yes
MARINE REPAIRS: ....Close by	HAUL OUT: ....Close by
TOILETS: ....Yes	BOAT RAMP: ....Close by
HOT SHOWERS: ....Yes	LAUNDRY: ....Yes
RESTAURANT: ....Close by	LOUNGE: ....Close by
PICNIC AREA: ....Yes	POOL: ....Close by
PLAY AREA: ....Close by	BBQ: ....None
BASIC STORE: ....Close by	GOLF: ....Close by
ELECTRICITY: ....$2.10 per day	OTHER: Close to lg. shopping ctr,
DAILY RATE: ....Appx. .65¢ per foot (CDN)	restaurants, pubs, lg. chart
CUSTOMS PORT-OF-ENTRY	store, hardware &
	chandlery, ample trans-
	portation to mainland.

CAUTION! This chartlet not intended for use in navigation.

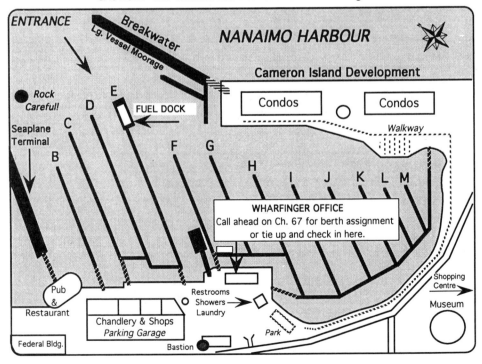

Nanaimo

NAME OF YACHT CLUB: *NANAIMO YACHT CLUB*

ADDRESS: 400 Newcastle Ave. Nanaimo, B.C Canada V9S 4J1

TELEPHONE: 604-754-7011 PERSON IN CHARGE: Geo. Everett

SHORT DESCRIPTION & LOCATION:

49°10.60' - 123°56.35' Located appx. 1 mi. N of city centre at south entrance of Newcastle Island Passage just across the channel from Bate Pt. The club offers 700 ft. of reciprocal moorage on the outside of E, H, & J docks. <u>Maximum boat size is 60 ft.</u>

BUSY IN SUMMER!

RECIPROCAL BOAT CAPACITY.............Appx. 40	RECIPROCAL DOCK: 835' total
SEASON: ....All year	RECIPROCAL SLIPS: Docks only
RESERVATION POLICY:..........................None	WATER: ....Yes
TOILETS: ....Yes	AMT W/ELECTRICITY: ....All
HOT SHOWERS: ....Yes	AMPS: ....15-30 A
RESTAURANT:...................................Close by	LOUNGE:..Yes
DAILY RATE: ....One day free. After one day charge is .50¢ per ft.- Max 5 days. **Power $2.25/day everyday.**	OTHER: Marine services close by. No rafting is allowed. Security gate w/code.

<u>NOTE:</u> THIS IS PRIVATE MOORAGE AND ONLY AVAILABLE TO MEMBERS OF RECIPROCAL YACHT CLUBS. YOUR CLUB <u>MUST</u> HAVE RECIPROCAL PRIVILEGES AND YOU MUST FLY YOUR BURGEE.

CAUTION! This chartlet not intended for use in navigation.

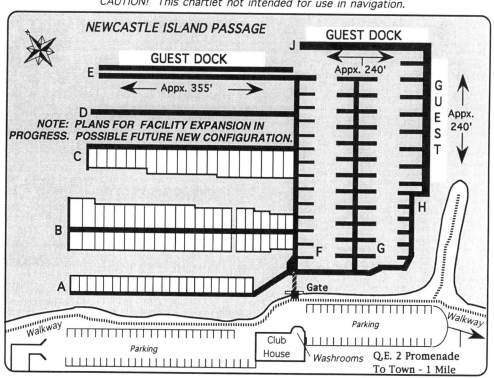

Nanaimo

NAME OF PARK: *NEWCASTLE ISLAND PROVINCIAL MARINE PARK*
ADDRESS: 2930 Trans. Can. Hwy   Victoria B.C.   V9B 5T9
TELEPHONE: 604-754-7893   **MGR:** B.C. Parks

SHORT DESCRIPTION & LOCATION:

49°10.70' - 123°55.70' This 720 acre island park is accessible only by water and is located on the N.E. side of Nanaimo Harbour about 1/2 mile from downtown Nanaimo. The park has a colorful history explained at various park displays.

GUEST BOAT CAPACITY: ....Appx 30-35 boats	**GUEST DOCK:** .....100' long floats
SEASON: ....All year	**MOORING BUOYS:** ....None
AMT W/ELECTRICITY: ....None	**WATER:** ....Yes
TOILETS: ....Yes	**PAY PHONES:** ....Yes
HOT SHOWERS: ....None	**BOAT RAMP:** ....None
PICNIC AREA: ....Yes	**PICNIC SHELTER:** ....Yes
PLAY AREA: ....Yes	**BBQ:** ....None
BASIC STORE: ....None	**PUMP OUT STATION:** ......None
DAILY RATE: ....Appx. .45¢/ft .- $1.50/metre	**OTHER:** Ferry to Nanaimo, park

*NOTE: For more park info
contact B.C.Parks at
604-391-2300 or 754-7893*

OTHER (cont.): interpreter, tent sites, trails, wildlife, snack bar, pavilion, swimming.

CAUTION! This chartlet not intended for use in navigation.

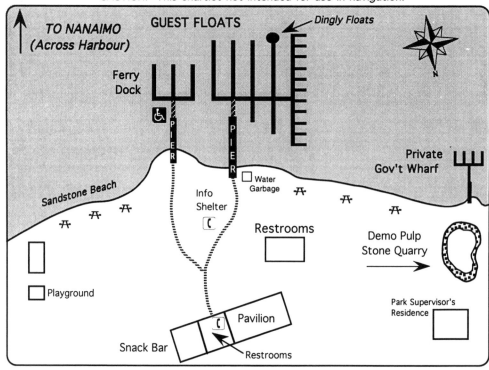

Nanoose Harbour

NAME OF MARINA: *SNAW-NAW-AS CAMPSITE & MARINA* RADIO: CB Ch. 14
ADDRESS: 209 Mallard Way Lantzville, B.C. Canada V0R 2H0
TELEPHONE: 604-390-2616 MGR: Charles Bob

SHORT DESCRIPTION & LOCATION:

49°15.40' - 124°07.70' Located appx. 15 mi. NW of Nanaimo at Fleet Pt. inside of Nanoose Harbour adjacent to Georgia Strait on E coast of Vancouver Is. The quiet marina is situated on tribal property and provides very limited amenities within walking distance.

GUEST BOAT CAPACITY:	Appx. 16-20 boats	GUEST DOCK:	500 ft. plus slips
SEASON:	All year	GUEST SLIPS:	16
RESERVATION POLICY:	Accepts	WATER:	Yes
AMT W/ELECTRICITY:	All	AMPS:	15-30 A
FUEL DOCK:	Gas & Diesel	PUMP OUT STATION	None
MARINE REPAIRS:	Close by	HAUL OUT:	None
TOILETS:	Yes	BOAT RAMP:	Yes
HOT SHOWERS:	Close by	LAUNDRY:	None
RESTAURANT:	Seasonal	LOUNGE:	None
PICNIC AREA:	Yes	POOL:	None
PLAY AREA:	None	BBQ:	None
BASIC STORE:	None	GOLF:	Close by
ELECTRICITY:	$5.00 per day	OTHER:	NO DOGS ALLOWED, campground, very limited services, security gate & lights.
DAILY RATE:	Appx. .45¢ per foot		

CAUTION! This chartlet not intended for use in navigation.

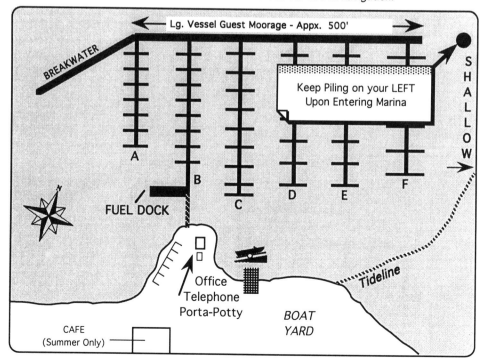

Schooner Cove

NAME OF MARINA: *SCHOONER COVE Resort Hotel & Marina*   **RADIO:** VHF Ch. 73

ADDRESS: Box 12, Schooner House,   Nanoose Bay, B.C.   Canada V0R 2R0

TELEPHONE: 1-800-252-5404   **MGR:** Murray Hamilton

SHORT DESCRIPTION & LOCATION:

49°17.20' - 124°08.00' Located appx. 15 mi. NW of Nanaimo & 2 mi. N of Nanoose Hbr. on Georgia Str. on E coast of Van. Is. just S of Nankivell Pt. This upscale & popular destination resort offers many amenities. GUEST SLIPS ARE MARKED W/ORANGE CLEATS.

GUEST BOAT CAPACITY: ....50 plus boats	**GUEST DOCK:** 120 ft. plus slips
SEASON: ....All year	**GUEST SLIPS:** ....Appx. 20
RESERVATION POLICY: ....Accepts	**WATER:** ....Yes
AMT W/ELECTRICITY: ....All	**AMPS:** ....30-50 A
FUEL DOCK: ....Gas only	**PUMP OUT STATION** ....None
MARINE REPAIRS: ....Close by	**HAUL OUT:** ....Tidal grid
TOILETS: ....Yes	**BOAT RAMP:** ....Yes
HOT SHOWERS: ....Yes	**LAUNDRY:** ....Yes
RESTAURANT: ....Yes	**LOUNGE:** ....Yes
PICNIC AREA: ....Yes	**POOL:**..Yes
PLAY AREA: ....Yes	**BBQ:** ....Yes
BASIC STORE: ....Yes & grocery shuttle daily	**GOLF:** ....Yes
ELECTRICITY: ....$3/15 Amp,, $4/30 A,, $7/50A	**OTHER:** Hotel, exercise room
DAILY RATE: .....Appx. .75¢ per ft. Oct. thru May	hot tub, fishing &
.....Appx. $1 per ft. June thru Sept.	marine supplies, nearby
	horseback riding, hiking,
	tennis, group facilities.

NAME OF YACHT CLUB: *SCHOONER COVE YACHT CLUB*   **B**

CLUB ADDRESS: Box 30, Schooner Cove House, RR #2, Nanoose Bay, B.C. V0R 2R0

CLUB TELEPHONE: 1-800-252-5404   **PERSON IN CHARGE:**   Secretary

LOCATION & SPECIAL NOTES

SCYC offers reciprocal moorage in the general marina to reciprocal clubs in good standing. In summer, availability may be limited by the number of berths vacated by SCYC members. Advance moorage reservations may be made by calling ahead to the marina office.

RECIPROCAL BOAT CAPACITY:.................Varies	**RECIPROCAL DOCK:** ....Varies
RECIPROCAL SEASON:................................All year	**RECIPROCAL SLIPS:** ....Varies
RESERVATION POLICY: ....Recommended	**WATER:** ....Yes
TOILETS: ....At Marina	**AMT W/ELECTRICITY:** ....All
HOT SHOWERS:................................At Marina	**AMPS:** ....30-50 A
RESTAURANT: ....Close by	**LOUNGE:** ....Close by
DAILY RATE: ....No charge for first night.	**OTHER:** PLEASE CHECK IN AT
$1.00 per foot thereafter.	MARINA OFFICE

NOTE: *THIS IS PRIVATE MOORAGE ONLY AVAILABLE TO MEMBERS OF RECIPROCAL YACHT CLUBS! YOUR CLUB MUST HAVE RECIPROCAL PRIVILEGES AND YOU MUST FLY YOUR BURGEE!*

Schooner Cove

CAUTION! This chartlet not intended for use in navigation.

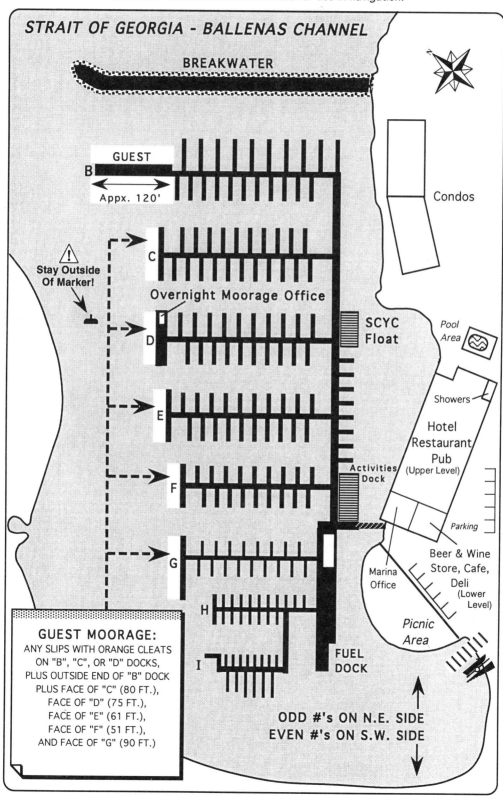

STRAIT OF GEORGIA - BALLENAS CHANNEL

BREAKWATER

Condos

GUEST

B

Appx. 120'

C

Stay Outside Of Marker!

Overnight Moorage Office

D

SCYC Float

Pool Area

Showers

E

Hotel Restaurant Pub (Upper Level)

Activities Dock

F

Parking

G

Beer & Wine Store, Cafe, Deli (Lower Level)

Marina Office

H

Picnic Area

I

FUEL DOCK

GUEST MOORAGE:
ANY SLIPS WITH ORANGE CLEATS
ON "B", "C", OR "D" DOCKS,
PLUS OUTSIDE END OF "B" DOCK
PLUS FACE OF "C" (80 FT.),
FACE OF "D" (75 FT.),
FACE OF "E" (61 FT.),
FACE OF "F" (51 FT.),
AND FACE OF "G" (90 FT.)

ODD #'s ON N.E. SIDE
EVEN #'s ON S.W. SIDE

Sidney

NAME OF YACHT CLUB: *CAPITAL CITY YACHT CLUB*

ADDRESS: 10630 Blue Heron Rd.   Sidney, B.C.   Canada   V8L 5S6

TELEPHONE: 604-656-4512   PERSON IN CHARGE: Director

SHORT DESCRIPTION & LOCATION:

48°40.30' - 123°25.10' Located in Tsehum Hbr, Blue Heron Basin. CCYC provides a 100 ft. Visitor's Dock plus open member slips are available for reciprocals. Tie up temporarily at Visitor's Dock & check list of open slips posted in Kiosk at top of "B" Dock.

RECIPROCAL BOAT CAPACITY .....6-10 (Varies)

RECIPROCAL DOCK: ....100 ft.

SEASON: ....All year

RECIPROCAL SLIPS: ....Varies

RESERVATION POLICY:........................None

WATER: ....Yes

TOILETS: ....Yes

AMT W/ELECTRICITY: ....All

HOT SHOWERS: ....Yes

AMPS: ....15 A

RESTAURANT: ....Close by-Appx. 1 mile

LOUNGE:..None

DAILY RATE: No Charge - 48 hours.
After 48 hrs - $5.00/day.
Power - $2.00/day.

OTHER: <u>Contact any member for gate key.</u> Water taxi to downtown, BBQ pits.

NOTE: THIS IS PRIVATE MOORAGE AND ONLY AVAILABLE TO MEMBERS OF RECIPROCAL YACHT CLUBS. YOUR CLUB MUST HAVE RECIPROCAL PRIVILEGES AND YOU MUST FLY YOUR BURGEE.

CAUTION! This chartlet not intended for use in navigation.

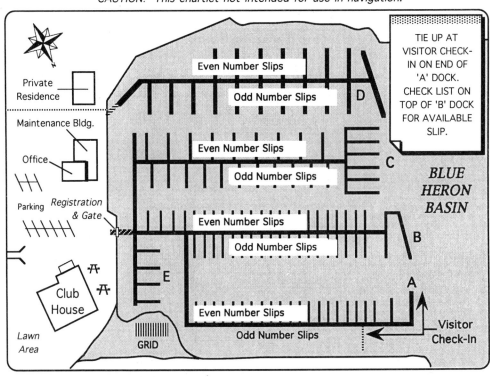

Sidney

NAME OF MARINA: *DEEP COVE MARINA*   RADIO: None

ADDRESS: 10990 Madronna Dr.   Sidney, B.C.   Canada V8L 5R7

TELEPHONE: 604-656-0060   MGR: Noel Currie

SHORT DESCRIPTION & LOCATION:

48°41.10' - 123°28.30' Located in Deep Cove on NW tip of Saanich Peninsula, appx. 5 road miles NW of Sidney. The marina is in a quiet neighborhood and primarily caters to Divers. There is a submerged ship wreck diving attraction adjacent to the marina.

GUEST BOAT CAPACITY:	Appx. 2-4 boats	
SEASON:	All year	
RESERVATION POLICY:	Recommended	
AMT W/ELECTRICITY:	All	
FUEL DOCK:	None	
MARINE REPAIRS:	None	
TOILETS:	Yes	
HOT SHOWERS:	Yes	
RESTAURANT:	Close by	
PICNIC AREA:	None	
PLAY AREA:	None	
BASIC STORE:	Close by	
ELECTRICITY:	Included in moorage	
DAILY RATE:	Appx. .50¢ per foot	

GUEST DOCK: ....None
GUEST SLIPS: ....Varies
WATER: ....Yes
AMPS: ....15 A
PUMP OUT STATION ....None
HAUL OUT: ....None
BOAT RAMP: ....None
LAUNDRY: ....None
LOUNGE: ....Close by
POOL: ....None
BBQ: ....Yes
GOLF: ....Close by
OTHER: Dive shop, air station, hot tub, B&B's close by, ice, Deep Cove Chalet Restaurant close by.

CAUTION! This chartlet not intended for use in navigation.

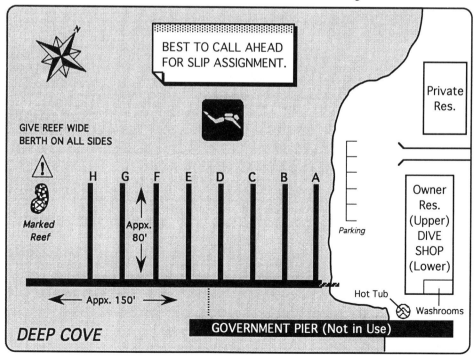

BEST TO CALL AHEAD FOR SLIP ASSIGNMENT.

Private Res.

GIVE REEF WIDE BERTH ON ALL SIDES

Marked Reef

H G F E D C B A

Appx. 80'

Parking

Owner Res. (Upper) DIVE SHOP (Lower)

Appx. 150'

Hot Tub

Washrooms

DEEP COVE

GOVERNMENT PIER (Not in Use)

Sidney

NAME OF MARINA: **PORT SIDNEY MARINA**   RADIO: VHF Ch. 68
ADDRESS: 9835 Seaport Place   Sidney, B.C., Canada V8L 4X3
TELEPHONE: 604-655-3711   MGR: Wayne Pullen
SHORT DESCRIPTION & LOCATION:

48°39.00' - 123°23.55' Located 1 block N. of Sidney city center. Spacious and modern full service tourist oriented marina.. Walking distance to shops, restaurants, and city amenities. Very convenient to Victoria Int'l Airport and ferries to mainland.

GUEST BOAT CAPACITY: ....Appx. 300 boats	GUEST DOCK: ..... 100' plus slips
SEASON: ....All year	GUEST SLIPS: ....Appx. 200
RESERVATION POLICY: ....Accepts	WATER: ....Yes
AMT W/ELECTRICITY: ....All	AMPS: ....30-50 A
FUEL DOCK: ....Close by	PUMP OUT STATION ....Yes
MARINE REPAIRS: ....Close by	HAUL OUT: ....Close by
TOILETS: ....Yes	BOAT RAMP: ....Close by
HOT SHOWERS: ....Yes	LAUNDRY: ....Yes
RESTAURANT: ....Yes	LOUNGE: ....Yes
PICNIC AREA: ....Close by	POOL: ....None
PLAY AREA: ....Close by	BBQ: ....Yes
BASIC STORE: ....Close by	GOLF: ....Close by
ELECTRICITY: ....$ 2-5 per day	OTHER: Customs port-of-entry,
DAILY RATE: ....Appx. .50-.95¢ per foot	cable T.V., pump-out
	station, public
	transportation to
	Vancouver Is. sights.

CAUTION! This chartlet not intended for use in navigation.

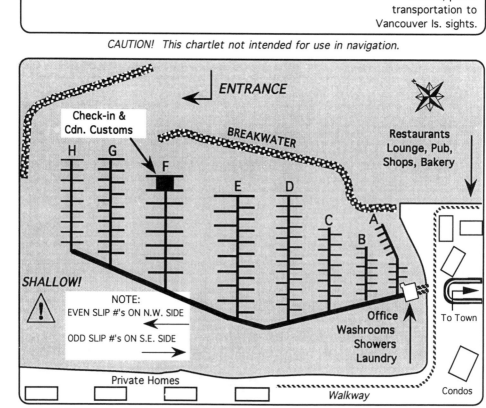

Sidney

NAME OF YACHT CLUB: *SIDNEY NORTH SAANICH YACHT CLUB*

ADDRESS: 10775 McDonld Pk Rd., R.R. 3, Sidney, B.C. Canada V8L 3X9

TELEPHONE: 604-656-4600 **PERSON IN CHARGE:** Recip. Officer.

SHORT DESCRIPTION & LOCATION:

48°40.50'-123°24.98' Located in Tsehum Harbour on the N side of Blue Heron Basin, SNSYC offers reciprocal moorage at N. Saanich Marina on the inside of a big 260 ft. dock. Register upon arrival as per instructions on visitors information posted on the shack on the reciprocal dock. Vacant member slips in marina can also be assigned by foreshoreman.

RECIPROCAL BOAT CAPACITY.......Appx. 10-15 | **RECIPROCAL DOCK:** Appx. 260'

SEASON: ....All year | **RECIPROCAL SLIPS:** ....Varies

RESERVATION POLICY:....................None | **WATER:** ....Yes

TOILETS: ....Yes | **AMT W/ELECTRICITY:** ....All

HOT SHOWERS: ....Yes | **AMPS:** ....15 A

RESTAURANT:......Yes-Open Wed. thru Sun. eves | **LOUNGE:**...Yes

DAILY RATE: Free for 24 hrs. - .40¢ ft. after 24 hours. Power charge $3.00/day ....(Key Deposit $15.00) | **OTHER:** Lounge open Wed-Sun, harbour taxi available to downtown Sidney on call.

NOTE: **THIS IS PRIVATE MOORAGE AND ONLY AVAILABLE TO MEMBERS OF RECIPROCAL YACHT CLUBS. YOUR CLUB MUST HAVE RECIPROCAL PRIVILEGES AND YOU MUST FLY YOUR BURGEE.**

CAUTION! This chartlet not intended for use in navigation.

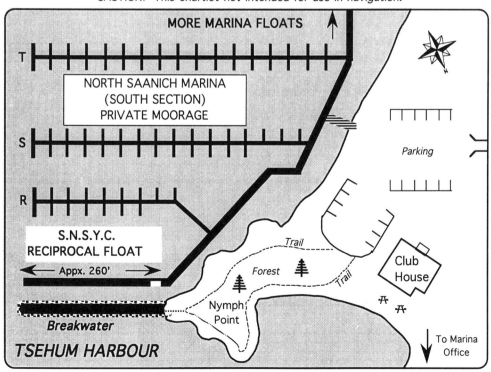

Sidney

NAME OF PARK: *SIDNEY SPIT PROVINCIAL MARINE PARK*
ADDRESS: 2930 Trans-Canada Hwy Victoria B.C. V9B 5T9
TELEPHONE: 604-391-2300 MGR: B.C. Parks

SHORT DESCRIPTION & LOCATION:

48°38.50' - 123°19.90' Located on the NW end of Sidney Island about 2 miles east of Sidney. This 1000 acre marine park offers beautiful sandy beaches and wooded trails with an abundance of birds and wildlife.

GUEST BOAT CAPACITY: ....Appx. 10-15 boats

SEASON: ....May 15 - Oct. 15

AMT W/ELECTRICITY: ....None

TOILETS: ....Pit Toilets

HOT SHOWERS: ....None

PICNIC AREA: ....Yes

PLAY AREA: ....Yes

BASIC STORE: ....None

DAILY RATE: ....Appx. .45¢/ft .- $1.50/metre
.....................Buoys - $6.00 per night
.............Campsites - $9.50 per night

GUEST DOCK: ....Appx. 275 ft.

MOORING BUOYS: 33

WATER: ....Yes

PAY PHONES: ....None

BOAT RAMP: ....None

PICNIC SHELTER: ....Yes

BBQ: ....Yes

PUMP OUT STATION: ......None

OTHER: Great swimming beach, campsites, hiking trails, bird watching, Saturday amphitheater programs.

CAUTION! This chartlet not intended for use in navigation.

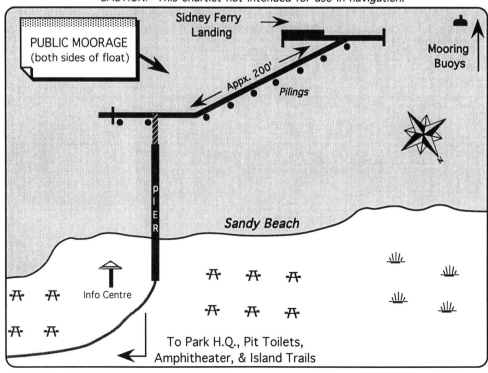

Sidney

NAME OF MARINA:	*TSEHUM HARBOUR GOV'T WHARF* RADIO: None
ADDRESS:	P.O. Box 2252 Sidney, B.C. Canada V8L 3S8
TELEPHONE:	604-363-6466 MGR: John Pye

SHORT DESCRIPTION & LOCATION:

48°40.1' - 123°24.35' This large gov't wharf is located in All Bay within Tsehum Harbour adjacent to Van Isle Marina.. The docks are almost exclusively used for commercial fishing boats except for July thru mid Sept when pleasure boats are allowed.

GUEST BOAT CAPACITY:	Appx. 10-20 boats	GUEST DOCK:	Appx. 260 ft.
SEASON:	Pleasure Boats - July thru mid Sept.	GUEST SLIPS:	Dock only
RESERVATION POLICY:	None	WATER:	Yes
AMT W/ELECTRICITY:	All	AMPS:	15 A
FUEL DOCK:	Close by	PUMP OUT STATION	None
MARINE REPAIRS:	Close by	HAUL OUT:	Close by
TOILETS:	Yes	BOAT RAMP:	Close by
HOT SHOWERS:	Close by	LAUNDRY:	Close by
RESTAURANT:	Close by	LOUNGE:	Close by
PICNIC AREA:	Yes	POOL:	None
PLAY AREA:	Close by	BBQ:	None
BASIC STORE:	Close by	GOLF:	Close by
ELECTRICITY:	$ 2.50 per day	OTHER:	Next to marinas, restaurants, chandlery, shipyard and marine services.
DAILY RATE:	Appx. .50¢ per foot		

CAUTION! This chartlet not intended for use in navigation.

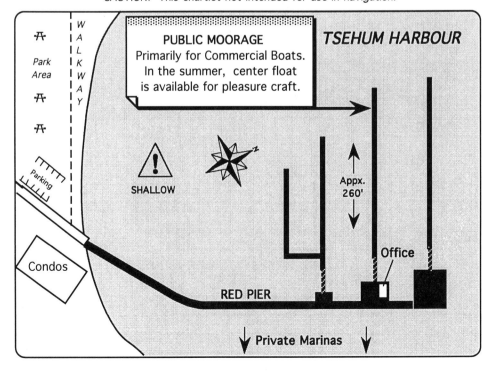

Sidney

NAME OF MARINA: *VAN ISLE MARINA*	**RADIO:** VHF Ch. 68
ADDRESS: 2320 Harbour Rd. Sidney, B.C.	Canada V8L 3P6
TELEPHONE: 604-656-1138	**MGR:** Mark Dickinson

SHORT DESCRIPTION & LOCATION:

48°40.18' - 123°24.30' Located in Tsehum Harbour appx 1 1/4 mi. N of Sidney. This is the first marina on the port side upon entering the harbour & offers complete repair & shipyard services. Guest moorage consists of open slips primarily on "D" dock.

GUEST BOAT CAPACITY: ....Appx. 75 boats	**GUEST DOCK:** ....Slips only
SEASON: ....All year	**GUEST SLIPS:** ....Varies
RESERVATION POLICY: ....Accepts	**WATER:** ....Yes
AMT W/ELECTRICITY: ....All	**AMPS:** 15-30-50A
FUEL DOCK: ....Gas & Diesel	**PUMP OUT STATION** ....Yes
MARINE REPAIRS: ....On premises	**HAUL OUT:** ....Yes
TOILETS: ....Yes	**BOAT RAMP:** ....Yes
HOT SHOWERS: ....Yes	**LAUNDRY:** ....Yes
RESTAURANT: ....Yes	**LOUNGE:** ....Yes
PICNIC AREA: ....None	**POOL:** ....None
PLAY AREA: ....None	**BBQ:** ....None
BASIC STORE: ....Close by	**GOLF:** ....Close by
ELECTRICITY: ....$ 3.00 per day	**OTHER:** Customs port-of-entry,
DAILY RATE: ....Appx. .60-.70¢ per foot	fishing-marine supplies,
	close to shopping &
	services in Sidney, taxi &
	bus service available.

CAUTION! This chartlet not intended for use in navigation.

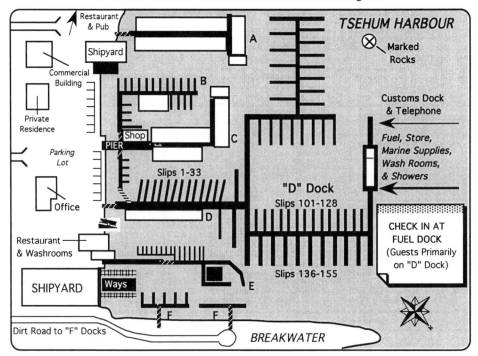

Victoria

NAME OF YACHT CLUB: *CANADIAN FORCES SAILING ASSOCIATION*

ADDRESS: 1001 Maple Bank Road   Victoria, B.C.   Canada   V9A 4M2

TELEPHONE: 604-385-8873/2646   PERSON IN CHARGE: Foreshore Chair.

SHORT DESCRIPTION & LOCATION: 604-384-5758

48°25.60' - 123°25.90' The CFSA moorage facilities are located in Esquimalt Hbr. (E side) in Constance Cove (NW side) just N of Naval Dockyards. Appx. 20 minutes "sailing time" W of Victoria Waterfront, reciprocal privileges are offered in their quiet setting. Best to call ahead on telephone or VHF Ch. 16 for information. Customs Port-of-Entry.

RECIPROCAL BOAT CAPACITY............Appx. 2-4	RECIPROCAL DOCK: ....70 ft.
SEASON: ....All year	RECIPROCAL SLIPS: ....Varies
RESERVATION POLICY:................Call in advance	WATER: ....Yes
TOILETS: ....Yes	AMT W/ELECTRICITY: ....All
HOT SHOWERS: ....Yes	AMPS: ....15 A
RESTAURANT: ....None	LOUNGE:......Yes - Wed. thru Sun.
DAILY RATE: 3 Days free, extensions $5/day subject to moorage availability. Power $2/day.	OTHER: Restaurants, groceries, & liquor store 1-1/2 mi. from club. Taxi /bus OK

NOTE: THIS IS PRIVATE MOORAGE AND ONLY AVAILABLE TO MEMBERS OF RECIPROCAL YACHT CLUBS. YOUR CLUB MUST HAVE RECIPROCAL PRIVILEGES AND YOU MUST FLY YOUR BURGEE.

CAUTION! This chartlet not intended for use in navigation.

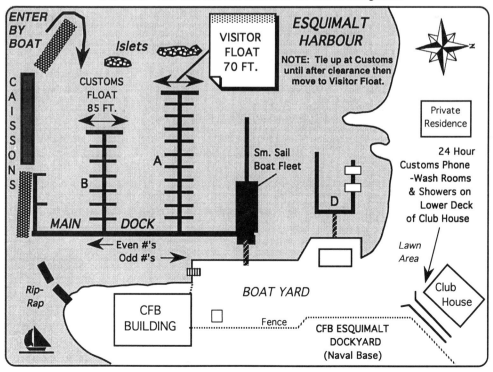

Victoria

NAME OF MARINA: *CAUSEWAY FLOATS* - *City of Victoria*   **RADIO:** VHF Ch 73
ADDRESS: 1002A Wharf Street   Victoria   B.C.   V8W 1T4
TELEPHONE: 604-363-3273   **MGR:**   Cathrine Featherby

SHORT DESCRIPTION & LOCATION:

48°25.80' - 123°22.30' Located in the heart of the Inner Harbour directly in front of the historic and beautiful Empress Hotel and adjacent to the B.C. Parliament Buildings. This location offers the best vantage point for viewing the night lights of Victoria.

GUEST BOAT CAPACITY: ....Appx. 40-50 boats	GUEST DOCK: ....Large 90' slips
SEASON: ....All year	GUEST SLIPS: ....7 large slips
RESERVATION POLICY: ....None	WATER: ....Yes
AMT W/ELECTRICITY: ....Appx. 50%	AMPS: ....20 A
FUEL DOCK: ....Close by	PUMP OUT STATION ....None
MARINE REPAIRS: ....Close by	HAUL OUT: ....Close by
TOILETS: ....On Causeway	BOAT RAMP: ....Close by
HOT SHOWERS: ....On Causeway-Seasonal	LAUNDRY: ....Seasonal
RESTAURANT: ....Close by	LOUNGE: ....Close by
PICNIC AREA: ....Close by	POOL: ....Close by
PLAY AREA: ....Close by	BBQ: ....None
BASIC STORE: ....Close by	GOLF: ....Close by
ELECTRICITY: ....$1.10 per day	OTHER: Customs Port-of-Entry,

DAILY RATE: Appx.. 75¢ per foot <u>LOA</u>-*LIMIT 2 DAYS IN SUMMER WHEN FULL.* ....NOTE: RAFTING IS MANDATORY UPON REQUEST.

fine museums, several sightseeing tours, shopping & night life, planes & ferries to mainland.

NAME OF MARINA: *WHARF ST. FLOATS* - *Transport Canada* **RADIO:** VHF Ch 73
ADDRESS: 1002A Wharf Street   Victoria   B.C.   V8W 1T4
TELEPHONE: 604-363-3273   **MGR:**   Cathrine Featherby

SHORT DESCRIPTION & LOCATION:

48°26.40' - 123°22.30'   Located about 2 blocks north of the Empress Floats next door to the Customs Dock. This location is also very convenient to the many amenities of beautiful Victoria.. **RAFTING IS MANDATORY UPON REQUEST.**

GUEST BOAT CAPACITY:............Appx. 100 boats	GUEST DOCK: 375 ft. plus slips
SEASON: ....All year	GUEST SLIPS: ....Appx. 100
RESERVATION POLICY: ....None	WATER: ....Yes
AMT W/ELECTRICITY: ....All	AMPS: ....20-50 Amp
FUEL DOCK: ....Close by	PUMP OUT STATION ....None
MARINE REPAIRS: ....Close by	HAUL OUT: ....Close by
TOILETS: ....On Causeway	BOAT RAMP: ....Close by
HOT SHOWERS: ....On Causeway-Seasonal	LAUNDRY: ....Close by
RESTAURANT: ....Close by	LOUNGE: ....Close by
PICNIC AREA: ....None	POOL: ....Close by
PLAY AREA: ....None	BBQ: ....None
BASIC STORE: ....Close by	GOLF: ....Close by
ELECTRICITY: $1.60 20A/$2.75 30A/$4.85 50A	OTHER: Customs Port-of-Entry,

DAILY RATE: Appx.. 30¢ per foot <u>LOA</u>-*LIMIT 3 DAYS IN SUMMER WHEN FULL.* NOTE: The Port of Victoria has a policy **not** to turn vessels away.

fine museums, several sightseeing tours, shopping & night life, planes & ferries to mainland.

Victoria

CAUTION! This chartlet not intended for use in navigation.

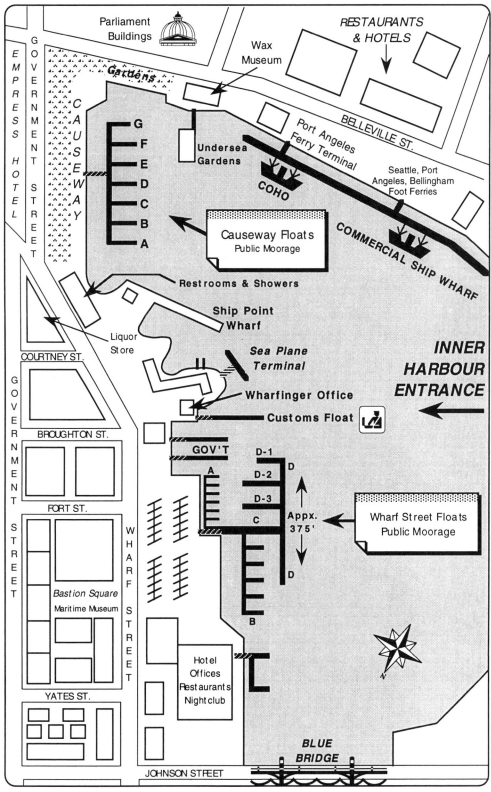

Parliament Buildings

Wax Museum

RESTAURANTS & HOTELS

Gardens

CAUSEWAY

EMPRESS HOTEL

GOVERNMENT STREET

G
F
E
D
C
B
A

Undersea Gardens

Port Angeles Ferry Terminal

BELLEVILLE ST.

COHO

Seattle, Port Angeles, Bellingham Foot Ferries

COMMERCIAL SHIP WHARF

Causeway Floats
Public Moorage

Restrooms & Showers

Ship Point Wharf

Liquor Store

COURTNEY ST.

GOVERNMENT STREET

BROUGHTON ST.

FORT ST.

Bastion Square
Maritime Museum

WHARF STREET

YATES ST.

Sea Plane Terminal

Wharfinger Office

Customs Float

INNER HARBOUR ENTRANCE

GOV'T

A

D-1
D-2
D-3
C

D

D

Appx. 375'

Wharf Street Floats
Public Moorage

B

Hotel
Offices
Restaurants
Nightclub

N

BLUE BRIDGE

JOHNSON STREET

Victoria

NAME OF MARINA: *GOLDSTREAM BOATHOUSE*   RADIO: CB Ch. 13

ADDRESS: RR6 3540 Trans-Can Hwy   Victoria, B.C.   Canada V9B 5T9

TELEPHONE: 604-478-4407   MGR: Mark Aitken & Doug Spence

SHORT DESCRIPTION & LOCATION:

48°30.40' - 123°33.00' Quiet & quaint marina in fjord like setting located at the head (S. end) of Saanich Inlet on E side in Finlayson Arm. Consult chart and provide caution for shoal waters adjacent to marina.. Guest moorage is on main wharf.

GUEST BOAT CAPACITY: ....Appx. 4-6 boats	GUEST DOCK: ....Appx. 200 ft.
SEASON: ....All year	GUEST SLIPS: ....Varies
RESERVATION POLICY:...........................Accepts	WATER: ....Yes
AMT W/ELECTRICITY: ....All	AMPS: ....15 A
FUEL DOCK: ....Gas only	PUMP OUT STATION ....None
MARINE REPAIRS: ....On premises	HAUL OUT: ....Yes
TOILETS: ....Yes	BOAT RAMP:................................Yes
HOT SHOWERS: ....None	LAUNDRY: ....None
RESTAURANT: ....Close by	LOUNGE: ....None
PICNIC AREA: ....Yes	POOL:..None
PLAY AREA: ....None	BBQ: ....None
BASIC STORE: ....Yes	GOLF: ....Close by
ELECTRICITY: ....$1.00 per day	OTHER: Marine & fishing supplies,
DAILY RATE: ....Appx. .25¢ per foot	Park closeby, bus & taxi to
	downtown Victoria

CAUTION! This chartlet not intended for use in navigation.

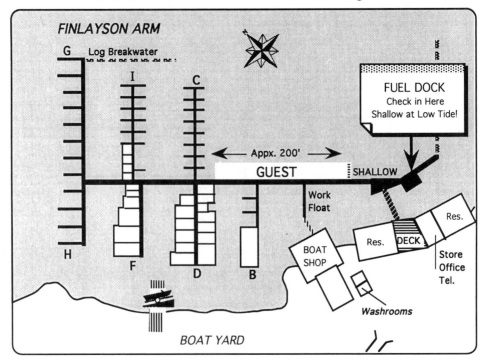

Victoria

NAME OF MARINA: *OAK BAY MARINA*	**RADIO:** VHF Ch. 68
ADDRESS: 1327 Beach Drive	Victoria, B.C. Canada V8S 2N4
TELEPHONE: 604-598-3369	**MGR:** Todd Jakubowski

SHORT DESCRIPTION & LOCATION:

48°26.60' - 123°18.00' Located between Gonzales & Cattle Pts. in Oak Bay on SE tip of Van. Is., The recently renovated upscale marina is appx 3 road mi. from downtown Victoria. The marina has resident seals which can be fed and enjoyed by adults & kids.

GUEST BOAT CAPACITY: ....Appx. 20-25 boats	GUEST DOCK:....260 ft. plus slips
SEASON: ....All year	GUEST SLIPS:.......................Varies
RESERVATION POLICY:...................................None	WATER: ....Yes
AMT W/ELECTRICITY: ....All	AMPS: ....15-30 A
FUEL DOCK: ....Gas & Diesel	PUMP OUT STATION ....None
MARINE REPAIRS: ....On premises	HAUL OUT: ....Rail
TOILETS: ....Yes	BOAT RAMP:...........................Yes
HOT SHOWERS: ....Yes	LAUNDRY: ....Yes
RESTAURANT:..Yes	LOUNGE: ....Yes
PICNIC AREA: ....Yes	POOL:...............................Close by
PLAY AREA: ....None	BBQ: ....None
BASIC STORE: ....Yes	GOLF:.......................Close by
ELECTRICITY: ....$1.00 per day	OTHER: Seal watching, arts & gift
DAILY RATE: ....Appx. $1.00 per foot	store, deli, groceries,
<u>**CUSTOMS PORT-OF-ENTRY**</u>	marine chandlery, cafe,
	shopping centre nearby,
	bus service to city cntr.

CAUTION! This chartlet not intended for use in navigation.

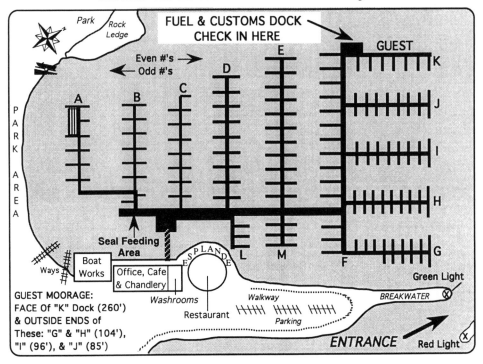

Victoria

NAME OF YACHT CLUB: *ROYAL VICTORIA YACHT CLUB*

ADDRESS: 3475 Ripon Rd.   Victoria, B.C.,, Canada   V8R 6HI

TELEPHONE: 604-592-3433   **PERSON IN CHARGE:** Michelle Lavoie

SHORT DESCRIPTION & LOCATION:

48°27.90' - 123°17.36' RVYC is located about 10 water miles (4 land miles) from downtown Victoria in Cadboro Bay in N.W. corner of Oak Bay. Quiet location close to shopping and public transp. to downtown Victoria.. **Check in at foreshore office.**

RECIPROCAL BOAT CAPACITY .....Appx 6 boats

RECIPROCAL DOCK: Appx. 60 ft.

SEASON: ....All year

RECIPROCAL SLIPS: .....Varies**

RESERVATION POLICY:....................None

WATER: ....Yes

TOILETS: ....Yes

AMT W/ELECTRICITY: ....Limited

HOT SHOWERS: ....Yes

AMPS: ....110 Only

RESTAURANT: ....Close by

LOUNGE:......................................Yes

DAILY RATE: ....No charge for 48 hours.
........After 48 hours - .30¢ per foot.

OTHER: Customs port-of-entry, **Random slips available if vacated by members.

NOTE: THIS IS PRIVATE MOORAGE AND ONLY AVAILABLE TO MEMBERS OF RECIPROCAL YACHT CLUBS. YOUR CLUB MUST HAVE RECIPROCAL PRIVILEGES AND YOU MUST FLY YOUR BURGEE.

CAUTION! This chartlet not intended for use in navigation.

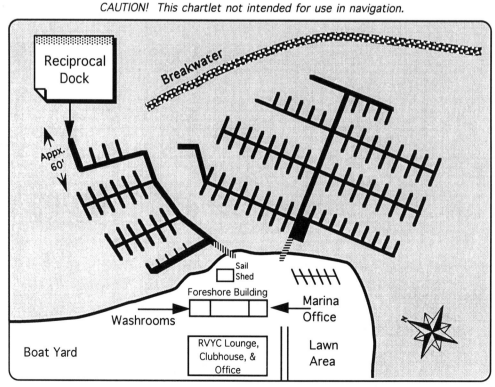

INDEX

INDEX

INDEX